A PHILOSOPHICAL ENQUIRY INTO THE ORIGIN OF OUR IDEAS OF THE SUBLIME AND BEAUTIFUL

EDMUND BURKE

A Philosophical Enquiry into the Origin of our Ideas of the Sublime and Beautiful

EDITED WITH AN INTRODUCTION AND NOTES BY

JAMES T. BOULTON

UNIVERSITY OF NOTRE DAME PRESS
NOTRE DAME LONDON

First paperback edition 1968

University of Notre Dame Press
Notre Dame, Indiana 46556

Second printing 1980
Third printing 1983
Fourth printing 1986

Printed by special arrangement with Humanities Press, Inc.

First published 1958 by
Routledge & Kegan Paul Ltd.

Library of Congress Catalog Card Number: 68–27583
Manufactured in the United States of America

CONTENTS

TO

MARGARET

ANDREW AND HELEN

EDITOR'S PREFACE

BURKE'S eminence as a political thinker has been long acknowledged: his claims as an aesthetician have rarely been seriously, never thoroughly considered. On the other hand, while his theory is no longer acceptable, no reputable historian of the aesthetics, the literary criticism, or the taste of the eighteenth century fails to give a mention—frequently a detailed analysis—to Burke's *Philosophical Enquiry into . . . the Sublime and Beautiful*. And yet no critical edition of this work has been published in the two hundred years since its first appearance. Without exaggerating the wisdom of the *Enquiry*, one must rank it among the most important documents of its century. Besides painters, architects, and a host of minor writers, such major figures as Johnson, Blake (despite his overt scorn for Burke's ideas), Wordsworth, Hardy, Diderot, Lessing, and Kant felt its influence. It is hoped, therefore, that this bicentenary edition will enable a just historical estimate to be made of a work in which, as Johnson remarked of him later, Burke's "stream of mind is perpetual".

The principal tasks facing an editor were to establish a definitive text, to show and account for Burke's extensive textual changes in the second edition, and to supply the necessary annotation. In addition, I have related the whole work to the historical development of ideas and shown some directions in which, in England and Europe, it appears to have been influential.

To whatever degree of adequacy and completeness has been achieved many have contributed; what faults remain are my sole responsibility. To Professor V. de S. Pinto and my colleagues in the Department of English in the University of Nottingham my thanks are due for their unfailing assistance; in particular I am indebted to Mr. G. R. Hibbard who read the manuscript, made valuable suggestions, and saved me from many errors. Mr. W. R. Chalmers and Dr. D. Brett-Evans kindly solved various problems connected with classical and German literature respectively; Mr. D. Jefferson, of the University of Leeds, generously put at my disposal his own work on the *Enquiry*; Professor T. W. Copeland, of the University of Chicago, answered many enquiries about the Burke manuscripts, as did Professor W. B. Todd, of Harvard University, about the printed texts; and to Professor I. Ehrenpreis, of Indiana University, who advised and assisted unstintingly, I am indebted in a score of ways. I am also grateful to Mr. H. Erskine-Hill for help in correcting the proofs. Finally, without the willing co-operation of the Librarians and staffs of the Bodleian Library and the Nottingham University Library, the task would have been impossible.

University of Nottingham J. T. B.

ACKNOWLEDGMENTS

I acknowledge permission from Mr. C. E. C. Hussey, Messrs. Putnam & Co. Ltd. (London), and Messrs. G. P. Putnam's Sons (New York), to quote from *The Picturesque* (1927); and from the Provost and Senior Fellows of Trinity College, Dublin, to quote from *The Early Life, Correspondence and Writings of the Rt. Hon. Edmund Burke* (Cambridge, 1923), by A. P. I. Samuels.

"I am satisfied I have done but little by these observations considered in themselves; and I never should have taken the pains to digest them, much less should I have ever ventured to publish them, if I was not convinced that nothing tends more to the corruption of science than to suffer it to stagnate. These waters must be troubled before they can exert their virtues. A man who works beyond the surface of things, though he may be wrong himself, yet he clears the way for others, and may chance to make even his errors subservient to the cause of truth. . . . I only desire one favour; that no part of this discourse may be judged of by itself and independently of the rest; for I am sensible I have not disposed my materials to abide the test of a captious controversy, but of a sober and even forgiving examination; that they are not armed at all points for battle; but dressed to visit those who are willing to give a peaceful entrance to truth."

Burke, *Enquiry*, p. 54.

EDITOR'S INTRODUCTION

I. COMPOSITION AND PUBLICATION

"IT is four years now since this enquiry was finished": so runs the Preface (not reprinted in later editions) to Edmund Burke's *Sublime and Beautiful* when it first appeared on 21 April 1757. Burke's assertion is untrue—he refers, for instance, in the work itself to Spence's *Account of the Life, Character, and Poems of Mr. Blacklock*, not published until 13 November 1754[1] —but, more important, it hides from view the length of time that the *Enquiry* had taken to evolve. A more helpful comment is recorded in Edmond Malone's journal for 28 July 1789. Malone had pressed Burke "to revise and enlarge his admirable book on the *Sublime and Beautiful*, which the experience, reading, and observation of thirty years could not but enable him to improve considerably."[2] While resisting this pressure Burke informed Malone that "the subject . . . had been long rolling in his thoughts before he wrote his book, he having been used from the time he was in college to speculate on the topics which form the subjects of it. He was six or seven years employed on it." This more accurate indication of the period of composition directs our principal attention to the years 1747–1753 or 1754, but clearly suggests that to begin no earlier than 1747 would be to falsify the picture.

Burke had entered Trinity College, Dublin, on 14 April 1744, a lad of fifteen. With an adolescent mixture of flippancy and high seriousness he already revealed a curiosity in subjects soon to have a more vital interest for him. In a letter to the son of

[1] See D. Wecter, "The Missing Years in Edmund Burke's Biography", *P.M.L.A.* (1938), LIII, 1120–1. I am generally indebted in this section to Wecter and to A. P. I. Samuels, *The Early Life . . . of Burke* (Cambridge, 1923).

[2] Sir James Prior, *Life of Edmond Malone* (1860), p. 154.

his Quaker schoolmaster and a lifelong friend, Richard Shackleton, Burke is writing about "beauty" as early as 14 June 1744: "for beauty consists in variety and uniformity and is not that abundantly shown in the motion and form of the heavenly bodies."[3] The notion was a commonplace—particularly after Hutcheson's *Inquiry into the Original of our Ideas of Beauty and Virtue*, 1725—but the interest in what Burke was later to call "Gradual Variation" is there.[4] The letter goes on to show his fascination for "infinite and boundless space", his wonder at the sight of the heavens covered with "innumerable luminaries at such an immense distance from us", and the awe which marks the reference to the "word of the Creator sufficient to create universe from nothing". All these reactions to grandeur were common enough at the time, but each was later to be connected systematically with the sublime.[5] Or again, in another letter to Shackleton, on 5 July 1744, Burke displays a considerable knowledge of chivalric romances: the reference to Don Bellianis in the "Essay on Taste" (introduced in the second edition of the *Enquiry*, 1759) had, therefore, roots at least fourteen years deep.[6] Indeed, the more one reads the letters of this early Dublin period—giving evidence, for example, of Burke's deeply religious nature, his capacity for sympathy, or his acquaintance with a "forsaken lover" who committed suicide—the more one is sure that when he wrote in the first Preface to the *Enquiry* that the confusion in aesthetic ideas could be remedied only by "a diligent examination of our passions in our own breasts", he was simply describing his own practice.

The greatest influence on the writing of the *Enquiry* was exerted by Burke's experiences at Trinity College. The reading of Longinus as a compulsory text in his "Sophister years", the animated discussions of literature, philosophy, and the classics in the "Club", the keen interest in drama among students and Dubliners alike, and above all the opportunity given to an observant youth to analyse human nature—all these factors were to make an incalculable contribution. It is likely, too,

[3] Samuels, *op. cit.*, p. 40.

[4] *Enquiry*, pp. 114–16.

[5] *Ibid.*, pp. 73–4, 78, 68–70.

[6] *Ibid.*, pp. 20–21. See Samuels, *op. cit.*, 45–9.

that passing allusions in the *Enquiry* were drawn from the experiences of a Dublin undergraduate. Lecky describes the celebrations on the anniversary of the discovery of the 1641 rebellion: "the Lord Lieutenant went in full state to Christ's Church, where a sermon on the rebellion was preached. At noon the great guns of the Castle were fired. The Church bells were rung, and the day concluded with bonfires and illuminations."[7] Burke's incidental references to a lighted torch making a circle of fire, to fireworks, and to "the successive firing of cannon . . . [which] always made me start a little",[8] may well have been suggested by such celebrations. Or, take the last reference together with Burke's observation that "the shouting of multitudes" causes "the best established tempers" to join in "the common cry, and common resolution of the croud"[9] and we may have an allusion to his experiences during a student attack on the Black Dog prison which provoked the constable of the Castle of Newgate gaol to fire his cannon.[10] The riot, on 21 May 1747, occurred during the period when the first draft of the *Enquiry* was probably being written. Whatever may be the truth, these (and other) references confirm a general truth about Burke's treatise: it was thoroughly grounded on a careful examination of his own (and sometimes of his friends') reactions to personal experience. "I have more than once observed . . . From hence I conclude"; "This I knew only by conjecture . . . but I have since experienced it"; "I have heard some ladies remark":[11] these are the stylistic symptoms of the general empirical approach to aesthetics.

A youth of varied experience, retentive memory, and an acute observer of men and manners: such was Burke when, in 1747, he drafted the work which appeared ten years later as the *Sublime and Beautiful*. He was also a youth with some literary experience. According to a letter of 15 May 1746 he had done "the latter part of the Second Georgic, *O fortunatus, &c*, into English";[12] two months later he is "deep in metaphysics and

[7] *A History of Ireland in the 18th Century* (1892), I, 322.

[8] *Enquiry*, pp. 138, 78, 140.

[9] *Ibid.*, p. 82.

[10] See Samuels, *op. cit.*, pp. 142–5.

[11] *Enquiry*, pp. 131, 148, 146.

[12] Samuels, *op. cit.*, p. 92. The translation appeared in *Poems on Several Occasions*, Dublin, 1747.

poetry";[13] in the same month, 25 July, he assures his correspondent, Shackleton, that he has read *Macbeth* again and is more in love with the passage, "Methought I heard a voice cry . . . Macbeth shall sleep no more"—"Observe with what horror it's attended";[14] he is found writing more verses in February 1747;[15] and on 21 March he tells Shackleton that he has passed from the "*furor mathematicus*", through the "*furor logicus*" and the "*furor historicus*" to the "*furor poeticus*".[16] Even allowing for youthful bravado and exaggeration such remarks at least indicate a lively mind and some degree of literary intelligence.

The first possible mention of the *Enquiry* occurs in a letter to Shackleton on 21 February 1747, a month after Burke had told him: "I could not get e'er a second-hand Longinus, but rather than you should want it I bought a new one."[17] In February Burke speaks of his friend's poem, *Phaeton*, and then continues: "As for my own scheme, it is going on, *bonis omnibus*, but slowly as yet. I seldom write half an hour in ten days." If here (as Samuels conjectures)[18] we have a reference to the *Enquiry*, and if he is also justified in thinking that, on 28 May, Burke again alludes to it in a joint letter with William Dennis, the writing had been speeded up after the first mention. In May Burke writes: "I have myself almost finished a piece an odd one, but you shall not see it until it comes out, if ever."[19] Later in this letter—in the portion written by Dennis—there is a statement almost certainly referring to the nearly completed work:

> Ned thought it preposterous to be threshing his brains for you, when he is writing for the public. Pray laugh heartily now lest you should split when you see the subject he has chosen and the manner he has treated it: but I will not anticipate your pleasure by acquainting you any more.

Both Dennis and Burke himself, it should be noted, adopt a

[13] 12 July 1746. *Correspondence of Burke* (ed. Fitzwilliam and Bourke, 1844), I, 18.

[14] Samuels, *op. cit.*, pp. 100–1.

[15] *Ibid.*, p. 111.

[16] *Ibid.*, pp. 128–9.

[17] *Ibid.*, p. 109.

[18] *Ibid.*, p. 115.

[19] *Ibid.*, p. 141. It appears that Shackleton did not indeed see the work until he received a complimentary copy on 10 Aug. 1757 (Samuels, p. 213).

similar attitude: they are both aware of the novelty of Burke's scheme and critical method. Their attitude anticipates the reactions of the reviewers in 1757.[20]

The increased speed of composition mentioned above may be accounted for by the foundation on 21 April 1747 in Trinity College of the "Club", the forerunner of the famous College Historical Society. Its object is described in the "Laws": "A weekly club instituted for the improvement of its members in the more refin'd elegant and usefull parts of Litterature."[21] The Club functioned chiefly by debates and declamations, each member in turn occupying the chair. Now it seems fairly clear that, wherever possible, Burke allowed his own and his friends' minds to play on the problems facing him as he drafted the *Enquiry*. A debate on poetry was held, under his presidency, on 12 May;[22] on 15 May, Burke, as president, "proposes that Mr. Dennis speak in the Character of Cato against Roman Luxury, and Mr. Buck in that of Scipio to oppose him";[23] and according to the minutes for 26 May Burke was ordered "to make a Declamation on praise of painting". In the *Enquiry* poetry is consistently placed above painting, but before the Club Burke has to exercise his ingenuity to support the claims of painting. It is noticeable, however, that he defends painting on the ground of its fidelity in copying nature and its power to encourage virtue; in the *Enquiry* these claims are not contradicted, but poetry is preferred for its power to arouse emotion.[24] But most interesting of all is the record of the debate, also on May 26th, between Burke and Dennis as to "whether Philosophy be of use to Poetry". The minutes give this summary of Burke's speech:

That the provinces of Phill: & poetry are so different that they can never coincide, that Phil: to gain its end addresses to the understanding, poetry to the imagination wch by pleasing it finds a nearer WAY to the heart, that the coldness of Philosophy hurts the imagination & taking away as much of its power must consequently

[20] See *ibid.*, p. 212, for Dennis's own appreciative criticism of the *Enquiry* in March 1758.

[21] *Ibid.*, p. 227.

[22] For this and subsequent references to Club minutes see *ibid.*, p. 238 ff.

[23] Cf. *Enquiry*, pp. 46, 111.

[24] Cf. *ibid.*, pp. 60–64.

lessen its effect, & so prejudice it. That such is the consequence of putting a rider on Pegasus that will prune his wings & incapacitate him from rising from the ground.

There is no question here of maintaining an uncongenial position: Burke's attitude in debate was identical with his attitude to poetry in the *Enquiry*. Throughout that work he emphasizes that the appeal of poetry is to the "passions" and that the place of reason in our response to it has been overstressed; in his view "the great power of the sublime" is that "it anticipates our reasonings, and hurries us on by an irresistible force";[25] and when he distinguishes between "a clear expression, and a strong expression" he claims that: "The former regards the understanding; the latter belongs to the passions. The one describes a thing as it is; the other describes it as it is felt."[26] It would appear conclusive that the sharp distinction between imaginative and non-imaginative writing argued before the Club proved satisfactory enough for inclusion in the critical work being prepared. The conviction which lay behind it was still alive when the "Essay on Taste" was added twelve years later:

the judgment is for the greater part employed in throwing stumbling blocks in the way of the imagination, in dissipating the scenes of its enchantment, and in tying us down to the disagreeable yoke of our reason.[27]

The concern here is with the "judgment" and not the "understanding" but the anti-intellectual bias is just as strong.

Shortly before this debate was held, actually on 23 April 1747, Burke had enrolled as a student of the Middle Temple in London. He did not, however, begin to keep term there until 1750. One of his activities in the meantime is significant: the management of *The Reformer* which he launched on 28 January 1748. Edited and almost entirely written by Burke, the periodical was issued for thirteen consecutive Thursdays and was devoted wellnigh exclusively to the state of the contemporary, and particularly the Dublin, theatre. The Dublin of Burke's college days was renowned for its theatre: with Thomas

[25] *Op. cit.*, p. 57. [26] *Ibid.*, p. 175. [27] *Ibid.*, p. 25.

Sheridan as manager of the Smock-alley from 1745, Burke had the opportunity of seeing Garrick, Barry, Miss Bellamy, and other first-rate actors. Burke and his friends Dennis and Buck made the acquaintance of Sheridan for whom Burke may have written a play only to have it refused.[28] Another member of the Club and a close friend of Burke, Beaumont Brennan, was writing a comedy in 1747, had already published another play, *Fleckno's Ghost*, and was the author of the unpublished play, *The Law-Suit*, which Burke once considered getting published by subscription and which he mentions in his *Hints for an Essay on the Drama*. Burke could, then, freely indulge that love of the theatre which, as the frequent allusions in his later writings and speeches testify, never deserted him.

The Reformer is a vigorous publication.[29] As always Burke had opinions and expressed them forcibly. Management, actors, and audience all come in for their share of censure: the first for lamentable choice of plays, the second for making the playwrights' intentions of less account than their own vanity, and the last for being "Spectators" rather than participants—"their whole Delight is in their Eyes". But his principal concern is the plays themselves. "*Farquhar*, *Cibber*, *Centlivre*, *&c.*, and the fustian Tragedies of *Lee* and *Young*" are not for him; Congreve and Wycherley do not come out unscathed from the analysis of comedy; indeed Ben Jonson "of all the Comic Writers is the only one in whom unite all the Graces of *true Comedy* without the monstrous Blemishes that stain and disfigure the Merit of the others." In tragedy Shakespeare outshines all Burke's contemporaries. The criticism is not outstanding, but the experience of writing it was valuable. When Burke came to prepare his *Hints on the Drama* he was thoroughly equipped: journalist-critic, student of dramatic theory, the acquaintance of writers and actors, and possibly, too, himself a would-be dramatist.

Burke's years as a law-student need not detain us: they are relatively obscure and offer little of immediate relevance. Dixon Wecter has shown that they reveal an energetic young man not in very good health, rather bored with the law and

[28] Samuels, *op. cit.*, pp. 113–4.

[29] See *ibid.*, Appendix II.

inclined to literary pursuits, and the writer of several conventional prose and verse pieces. During these years—probably as early as 1750—he met Jane Nugent, his future wife, and, about 1752, made the acquaintance of Robert Dodsley, the publisher, who was to bring out the *Enquiry* a few years later.

Burke had not, however, been wasting his time. Once Dodsley agreed to publish for him the rapidity with which three works appeared proves the industry of the apparently carefree student. In May 1756 there came the *Vindication of Natural Society*, purporting to be a posthumous work by Bolingbroke; then followed, in two volumes, the *Account of the European Settlements in America*, originally by William Burke but extensively revised by his friend Edmund; and finally, a week later, on 21 April 1757, the anonymous *Enquiry*. This last was the book which established Burke's reputation as an author: for the copyright he received twenty guineas.[30] Even this meagre sum would be acceptable to the newly-married writer,[31] but if this was the only payment he received—and there is no evidence to the contrary—then the publication proved highly profitable to Dodsley: a new edition was called for, on an average, every third year for thirty years.[32]

We know little about the preparation of the manuscript for publication. One of the "friends, men of learning and candour"[33] to whom Burke submitted the manuscript for criticism was William Markham (then Headmaster of Westminster School and later Archbishop of York); Burke had been introduced to him about 1753.[34] It is also known that the copyist for

[30] R. Straus, *Robert Dodsley* (1910), p. 255. The authorship of the *Enquiry* seems soon to have become generally known. Both Hume and Shenstone knew of it in 1759 (see pp. xxvi n., xxix n.); the Paris edition of the work in 1765 bore Burke's name on the title-page; and, in 1766 in the Commons, Horace Walpole referred to Burke's having "been known to the public for a few years" by his *Enquiry* and other works (*Memoirs of the Reign of King George III*, ed. Marchant, 1845, II, 273).

[31] He was married on 12 March 1757. See Wecter, *op. cit.*, p. 1121.

[32] 5th edn., 1767; "New" edn. (the 10th), 1787. See Appendix.

[33] Preface to 1st edn., p. 2.

[34] Sir C. Markham, *Memoir of Archbishop Markham* (Oxford, 1906), pp. 12–13. The Markham papers now contain no Burke MSS. (Information from Rev. G. W. Markham.)

the *Enquiry* (and for the *Vindication*) was Joseph Émïn, an Armenian, whom Burke had befriended since about 1755.[35]

The work was examined at length in the *Literary*, *Critical*, and *Monthly* reviews: the article in the first was by Arthur Murphy, and in the last by Goldsmith, Burke's contemporary at Trinity College though it is unlikely that they were well acquainted. The general opinion, despite many critical reservations, was favourable. Each critic acknowledged the newness of many of Burke's assertions, and praised his perspicuity and provocative method of presentation, but none fully accepted his theory: neither did any one of them fully reject it. They had been compelled to re-examine accepted critical standards; Burke had succeeded in troubling the stagnant waters of criticism;[36] and the general reaction can be gauged by the final comments of Murphy, the most censorious of the reviewers:

Upon the whole, though we think the author of this piece mistaken in his fundamental principles, and also in his deductions from them; yet we must say, we have read his book with pleasure: He has certainly employed much thinking; there are many ingenious and elegant remarks, which tho' they do not enforce or prove his first position, yet considering them detached from his system, they are new and just: and we cannot dismiss this article without recommending a perusal of the book to all our readers, as we think they will be recompensed by a great deal of sentiment, perspicuous, elegant, and harmonious stile, in many passages both sublime and beautiful.[37]

Burke was diligent in reading the reviews. When the *Enquiry* went into a second edition (10 January 1759) he added the introductory "Essay on Taste" and at the same time claimed to have taken account of the reviewers' objections:

I have endeavoured to make this edition something more full and satisfactory than the first. I have sought with the utmost care, and read with equal attention, every thing which has appeared in publick against my opinions. . . . Though I have not found sufficient reason, or what appeared to me sufficient, for making any material change in my theory, I have found it necessary in many places to explain, illustrate and enforce it.[38]

35 Wecter, *op. cit.*, pp. 1119–20.

36 Cf. *Enquiry*, p. 54.

37 *Literary Magazine* (1757), II, 189.

38 *Enquiry*, p. 3.

The extensive revisions—ranging from additions of a few sentences to the introduction of a completely new section (on "Power")—prove that Burke in his turn had been compelled to examine his position. He also took the opportunity to remove some stylistic blemishes; there is, indeed, evidence that he took great care over this kind of textual revision. Attention to the textual notes will show that in the second edition Burke alters several clumsy and periphrastic statements which he had allowed in the first; he avoids verbal repetitions which irritate the reader of the earlier version; he substitutes a more appropriate word (as in the case of "inclining" rather than "declining towards sleep") to correct his own, or the printer's, error; he rectifies an original statement, possibly where the reviewers had revealed a mistake (as at pp. 145–6); he corrects a single word in a quotation (though he frequently allows such errors to stand). In fact, there is considerable proof of attention to detail—and this over and above the major changes undoubtedly prompted by the reviewers of the first edition. A full analysis of these changes would be too cumbersome here—it has in any case been undertaken by an American scholar, Professor H. A. Wichelns.[39] It has been preferred to give, in notes to the text, the principal statement of the reviewer whom Burke appears to be answering by means of a major addition; the reader may then decide for himself on the adequacy of Burke's replies.

"The additions represent Burke's side of a debate with the reviewers," is Professor Wichelns's conclusion. In general, one can agree with this view though it does not indicate the extent to which Burke ignores his critics' objections or fails to answer them. He ignores, for example, two criticisms of his conception of "Grief";[40] two others of his claim that we find pleasure in the distress of others;[41] another of his ideas on the sublime in relation to the cries of animals and the sense of smell;[42] and another of his conclusions drawn from the story of the boy couched for a cataract.[43] These are only a few of the objections

[39] "Burke's Essay on the Sublime and its Reviewers", *Journal of English and Germanic Philology* (1922), XXI, 645–61.

[40] *Critical Review* (1757), III, 361; *Literary Magazine*, II, 183.

[41] *Ibid.*, II, 184; *Critical Review*, III, 362.

[42] *Literary Magazine*, II, 186.

[43] *Ibid.*, II, 188.

which find no answer in the second edition. On other occasions —as, for instance, when all the reviewers protest against the invariable association of the sublime with pain and terror[44]— Burke can be accused of not coming to close grips with his critics but rather, in the additions he makes, of relying on dogmatic reiteration of his initial argument. It may, therefore, be concluded that while Burke wished to justify himself in the face of opposition, the revisions in the second edition do not represent a full answer to his critics, nor do they on every occasion successfully meet the objections raised.

Apparently no textual revision was carried out later than the second edition. It would be wrong to assume, however, that Burke lost interest after 1759 in the subject of the *Enquiry* or that he had no further opportunity for writing on it. Later in his political career his detractors frequently accused him of trying to reproduce the terror and obscurity of the sublime in the *Reflections on the Revolution in France* (1790),[45] but, here, his activities as editor of the *Annual Register* are more immediately relevant. Professor Copeland maintains that up to 1766 there is "no reason to doubt that Burke was writing the entire magazine singlehanded."[46] During that period book-reviews in which the principles set out in the *Enquiry* could be invoked become, therefore, of great interest. We find, for example, in 1760, in a review of Daniel Webb's *Beauties of Painting* a lengthy footnote (appended to Webb's brief definition of taste) which strenuously opposes the idea that taste and judgment are separate faculties of the mind. It begins in this manner:

Many writers have opposed judgment to taste, as if they were distinct faculties of the mind; but this must be a mistake: the source of taste is feeling, so is it of judgment, which is nothing more than

[44] *Ibid.*, II, 185; *Critical Review*, III, 363; *Monthly Review* (1757), XVI, 475. Cf. Addition to *Enquiry*, p. 58.

[45] E.g. [J. Courtenay], *A Poetical and Philosophical Essay on the French Revolution* (1793), l. 104. Also the title of a pamphlet (advertised *St. James's Chronicle*, 19 April 1791): *The Wonderful Flights of Edmund the Rhapsodist into the Sublime and Beautiful regions of Fancy, Fiction, Extravagance, and Absurdity, exposed and laughed at.*

[46] *Our Eminent Friend Edmund Burke* (Yale, 1949), p. 143.

the same sensibility, improved by the study of its proper objects, and brought to a just point of certainty and correctness.[47]

In the "Essay on Taste" Burke had written one year earlier:

Before I leave this subject I cannot help taking notice of an opinion which many persons entertain, as if the Taste were a separate faculty of the mind, and distinct from the judgment and imagination.[48]

The attitudes in the two passages are obviously identical; the additional ideas in the first can easily be paralleled elsewhere in the *Enquiry*.[49] Again, in a review of Macpherson's *Ossian* he speaks of the work as sublime and notes its characteristics as being those of strangeness, wildness, and lack of restraint.[50] Furthermore, since the policy of the *Register* was to review only such books as it was disposed to praise, it is justifiable to assume that, for instance, Shenstone's *Unconnected Thoughts on Gardening* received Burke's approval.[51] Consequently, when we find passages quoted from Shenstone preferring the sublime to the "merely beautiful", or the bold abruptness of line in "ruinated structures" to the "waving line with more easy transitions" which produces "mere beauty", or distinguishing between "sublimity or magnificence and beauty or variety", they suggest Burke as the reviewer. They also suggest that his aesthetic values remained unchanged. Perhaps, too, when Burke found Shenstone making the distinction just noted, preferring the violence of the sublime to the less tempestuous nature of the beautiful, and attributing "smoothness and easy transitions" to beauty and "abrupt and rectangular breaks" to the sublime, he could confidently claim his aesthetic as already influential.[52]

47 *Annual Register* (1760), III, 250.

48 *Enquiry*, p. 26.

49 *Op. cit.*, pp. 24–5, 26.

50 *Annual Register* (1761), IV, 276 ff. (But see this introduction, pp. cxii–cxiii.)

51 *Ibid.* (1764), VII, 214 ff.

52 Shenstone was, in fact, one of the earliest recorded enthusiasts for Burke's theory. See in his *Works, in Verse and Prose* (2nd edn., 1769), III, 298, a letter to Richard Graves, 3 Oct. 1759: "Of all books whatever, read Burke (second edit.) 'Of the Sublime and Beautiful'."

II. ON TASTE

As Addison found it desirable to preface his papers on "The Pleasures of the Imagination" by one on Taste, so Burke thought it essential to introduce an "Essay on Taste" in which he too could examine the nature of aesthetic response. No writer on aesthetics of the time could afford to neglect the subject: the word occurred, Addison remarks, "very often in conversation". This was an understatement.

There are not only in every Age, but almost every Year, *Words*, *Terms*, and *Expressions* which become the favourite Mode of Speech, and which make our Language have as many Changes as our Fashions. . . . Of all our favourite Words lately, none has been more in Vogue, nor so long held its Esteem, as that of TASTE. A *Poem* OF TASTE, wrote by a favourite Author, seemed first to bring it into Fashion. Another poet, finding the Success of that Piece, wrote one which he called *The Man of Taste*, and still brought the Word more into Use. . . . It has now introduced so much Politeness among us, that we have scarce a grave Matron at *Covent-Garden*, or a jolly Dame at *Stocks-Market*, but what is elegant enough to have a *Taste* for Things.

So comments *The Universal Spectator* in 1747.[1] Six years later *The World* (a periodical conducted by Edward Moore, Horace Walpole, and others) protests:

It is a great abuse of language, according to Mr Locke, to make use of words to which we have no fixed and determinate ideas. There is a still greater . . . which is the almost-continually using words to which we have no ideas at all. I shall only instance in the poor monosyllable TASTE. Who has not heard it pronounced by the loveliest mouths in the world, when it has evidently meant nothing.[2]

And yet Addison and Burke were not trying merely to correct linguistic abuses, to bring philosophy to dwell at tea-tables, or to prove themselves "connoisseurs" or "men of taste" (terms with increasing social kudos): to define "taste" was to define one's aesthetic presuppositions. The investigation led with Burke—and with Hume, Gerard, Alison, and others[3]—to psychological criticism: an enquiry into the working of the

[1] Henry Stonecastle, *op. cit.*, III, 46–7. Cf. *The Connoisseur* (1756), No. 120.

[2] *Op. cit.*, I, 67.

[3] See G. McKenzie, *Critical Responsiveness, A Study of the Psychological Current in later 18th century Criticism* (University of California Press, 1949).

human mind when faced with an aesthetic experience. Burke's approach throughout the *Enquiry* is psychological: an analysis of "taste" was, therefore, an essential introduction.

The "Essay" has another significance for us. The conclusion that Burke reaches—that taste operates by fixed principles in all men—illustrates the eighteenth-century inclination to discover immutable laws governing human life and activities. In the Newtonian tradition Burke looks for—and finds—immutable laws governing taste. Burke believed with Hume that

> in the production and conduct of the passions, there is a certain regular mechanism, which is susceptible of as accurate a disquisition as the laws of motion, optics, hydrostatics, or any other part of natural philosophy.[4]

Consequently Burke was sure that a standard of taste could be determined; in his view, too, aesthetic values could be determined with equal certainty and precision—in terms of the physical qualities of objects. The *Enquiry*—and it should be clear now that the "Essay on Taste" is an organic part of it—is indeed a prize example of Newtonian experimental methods applied to aesthetics. Burke's awareness of the tradition in which he wrote is, in fact, implicit in the Preface (to the second edition) where he announces his intention of "looking into physical causes":

> whilst we investigate the springs and trace the courses of our passions, we may not only communicate to the taste a sort of philosophical solidity, but we may reflect back on the severer sciences some of the graces and elegancies of taste, without which the greatest proficiency in those sciences will always have the appearance of something illiberal.[5]

Why therefore, did not Burke prefix the "Essay on Taste" to the first edition of the *Enquiry*? Here Hume may be important. Despite their close agreement, suggested above, it may

[4] Hume, *Essays Moral, Political and Literary* (ed. Green and Grose, 1907), II, 166.

[5] *Enquiry*, p. 6. See also Burke's reference to Newton's inductive method, p. 150.

have been to oppose Hume's views on taste that Burke's "Essay" was written. Hume's *Dissertation on Taste* came out only two months before the *Enquiry* first appeared, obviously too close to permit an immediate answer. When the second edition of his book was called for, Burke took his opportunity.[6]

It must be emphasized at once that Burke and Hume are agreed on fundamentals: on the importance to taste of knowledge, practised judgment, sensibility, and on the dangers to it of prejudice, hasty opinion, and the like. Both regard with suspicion a liking for Bunyan; both are concerned with the same problem: whether or not a standard of taste can be determined. Yet despite this measure of agreement, Hume is sceptical, Burke convinced of the possibility of fixing such a standard; the first emphasizes the factors making for variety, the second those making for uniformity of taste among all men.

Hume proposes initially—as does Burke—that men are fundamentally alike in their sensory organs; he believes, too, that rules of art are based on experience and on observation of what is common among men. A standard of taste would therefore appear possible. But, in the first place, human feelings are not always consistent with what appear to be the common principles which govern them; and, secondly,

> Many and frequent are the defects in the internal organs, which prevent or weaken the influence of those general principles, on which depends our sentiment of beauty or deformity. Though some objects, by the structure of the mind, be naturally calculated to give pleasure, it is not to be expected, that in every individual the pleasure will be equally felt. Particular incidents and situations occur, which either throw a false light on the objects, or hinder the true from conveying to the imagination the proper sentiment and perception.[7]

Hume eventually concludes that the laws of taste cannot be ascertained on a scientific basis and that, though some standard can be defined, it will not be arrived at by philosophical means.

[6] For Hume's opinion of the *Enquiry* see his letter to Adam Smith, 12 April 1759, where he speaks of "Burke an Irish gentleman, who wrote lately a very pretty Treatise on the Sublime." (*New Letters*, ed. Klibansky and Mossner, Oxford, 1954, p. 51.)

[7] *Essays Moral, Political and Literary*, I, 272.

It can be deduced only from the joint verdict of those rare critics through the ages whom time has proved right. What has pleased long and has pleased the best judges provides the standard by which taste is measured.

While Burke starts from data largely the same as Hume's, he maintains that "the standard both of reason and Taste is the same in all human creatures."[8] Unless he can get assent to his claim that, at a certain level at least, objects of beauty make the same appeal to all men, his attempt to trace laws for the operation of taste is vain:

> if Taste has no fixed principles, if the imagination is not affected according to some invariable and certain laws, our labour is like to be employed to very little purpose; as it must be judged an useless, if not an absurd undertaking, to lay down rules for caprice, and to set up for a legislator of whims and fancies.[9]

Having argued his case (with obvious relevance to the frankly sensationist theory put forward in the *Enquiry*) Burke asserts:

> as the senses are the great originals of all our ideas, and consequently of all our pleasures, if they are not uncertain and arbitrary, the whole ground-work of Taste is common to all, and therefore there is a sufficient foundation for a conclusive reasoning on these matters.[10]

"The true standard of the arts is in every man's power",[11] he had asserted in the first edition of the *Enquiry*; after adding the "Essay" in the second, he could properly take for granted the argument which lay behind the assertion. It is, then, reasonable to suppose that the "Essay on Taste" was intended as a reply to Hume, and, moreover, that it became a vindication of the methods and assumptions in the *Enquiry*, and an introduction to the sensationist theory.

Whatever was Burke's original intention in writing the "Essay", let it be admitted at once that he did not make a major contribution to the contemporary discussion on taste: apart from a few distinctive features, his attitude was generally shared. Burke, with Cooper, Hume, Gerard, and the French Cyclopaedists (Voltaire, D'Alembert, and Montesquieu) were

[8] *Enquiry*, p. 11. [9] *Ibid.*, p. 12. [10] *Ibid.*, p. 23.
[11] *Ibid.*, p. 54.

all concerned with certain common problems: what taste is, whether it exists as a faculty in all men, why it is stronger in some than in others, whether there is a standard of taste, and so forth. It becomes necessary, therefore, to examine the views of these writers to determine Burke's position more precisely.

Cooper requires the briefest mention. Characterized chiefly by emotive and vague generalizations, his writing contains no systematic theory. For him,

> A *good* Taste is that instantaneous Glow of Pleasure which thrills thro' our whole Frame, and seizes upon the Applause of the Heart, before the intellectual Power, Reason, can descend from the Throne of the Mind to ratify its Approbation.[12]

It may be this conception to which Burke refers with scorn in his remark that many people think of taste as "a species of instinct by which we are struck naturally, and at the first glance, without any previous reasoning with the excellencies, or the defects of a composition."[13] Or, at this point, Burke may have had Voltaire in mind with his definition of taste as "a quick discernment, a sudden perception, which, like the sensation of the palate, anticipates reflexion."[14] Though Burke himself draws analogies with "the sensation of the palate", a simple comparison of this kind would not deceive him.

Alexander Gerard is a far more important writer than Cooper. In the preface to his *Essay on Taste* Gerard acknowledges a debt to Hutcheson's theory of "internal senses"; since this theory is his basic assumption—and is repudiated by Burke—something must be said about it. Hutcheson defines his theory thus:

> For there are many other sorts of Objects, which please or displease us as necessarily, as material Objects do when they operate upon our Organs of Sense. There is scarcely any Object which our Minds are employ'd about, which is not thus constituted the necessary occasion of some Pleasure or Pain: Thus we find ourselves pleas'd with a regular Form, a piece of Architecture, or Painting, a Composition of Notes, a Theorem, an Action, an Affection, a Character; and we

[12] *Letters concerning Taste* (1755), p. 3. [13] *Enquiry*, p. 26.

[14] *Essay on Taste*, in A. Gerard, *An Essay on Taste* (1759), p. 213.

are conscious that this Pleasure necessarily arises from the Contemplation of the Idea, which is then present to our Minds with all its Circumstances, altho some of these Ideas have nothing of what we commonly call sensible Perception in them; and in those which have, the Pleasure arises from some Uniformity, Order, Arrangement, Imitation; and not from the simple Ideas of Colour, or Sound, or mode of Extension separately consider'd.

These Determinations to be pleas'd with any Forms or Ideas which occur to our Observation, the Author chuses to call SENSES; distinguishing them from the Powers which commonly go by that Name, by calling our Power of perceiving the Beauty of Regularity, Order, Harmony, an INTERNAL SENSE.[15]

Hutcheson's argument (clearly influenced by Shaftesbury) is based on a belief in the existence of "general laws" ordained by the "Author of Nature"; he holds that God works methodically, evidenced by the regularity and uniformity apparent in the universe; God's creations are, by His wisdom, designed to achieve desirable ends—consequently it is natural for man to take a delight in objects which are regular and uniform. It is equally natural for him to respond through the internal sense: "a passive Power of receiving Ideas of Beauty from all Objects in which there is Uniformity amidst Variety." While this theory could lead to some insight into aesthetic responses—as it did with Gerard, for example—there were obvious dangers in it. Hutcheson wished to distinguish aesthetic and other perceptions from the organic senses; to do so he was too ready to create a special faculty to deal with every separate phase of experience. He had no time for philosophers who, through a "strange love of simplicity in the structure of Human Nature", wanted to limit the number of senses. Even the number of organic senses, he believed, could be increased beyond five; he also argued that innumerable non-organic perceptions (such as number, proportion, duration) should be taken into account. The result—and this was the main danger—was that human nature, and hence the aesthetic response, lost its complexity: it became a conglomeration of autonomous faculties each reacting to a particular facet of experience. "To multiply principles for

[15] *Inquiry into the Original of Our Ideas of Beauty and Virtue* (1725), pp. v–vi.

every different appearance, is useless, and unphilosophical too in a high degree", is Burke's comment.[16]

Gerard's *Essay*, published in 1757, would be read by Burke with great interest, though, as the above comment suggests, with some scepticism. "The powers of imagination" are assumed by Gerard (following Hutcheson) to consist of certain "*internal* or *reflex* senses"—those of novelty, sublimity, beauty, imitation, harmony, ridicule, and virtue. Taste, then, for this writer,

> is not one simple power, but an aggregate of many, which, by the resemblance of their energies, and the analogy of their subjects, and causes, readily associate, and are combined.[17]

For "correct" taste, however, all the internal senses must be exercised equally. From this premise he argues that no ancient, with the possible exception of Quintilian, had perfect taste: Longinus was unbalanced by excessive sensibility, Dionysius by refinement, and Aristotle by judgment.[18] Proportion, as well as complexity, of response was essential. The comment on the ancients suggests that other things are also necessary. Taste is improved by that delicate sensibility which makes a man more easily moved, and by judgment, the critical faculty whose task in art is "to ascertain truth, to unmask falsehood, however artfully disguised".[19] Gerard recognizes that in some men the internal senses will be more acute, in others, judgment; the former will "*feel* what pleases or displeases", the latter will *know* "what ought to gratify or disgust". Thus, Longinus was defective in judgment while Aristotle lacked delicate sensibility. But the man of true taste is one who, with the judgment of a critic and the sensibility of an artist, responds in due proportion with the whole range of his senses.

Like Hutcheson, Gerard made the error of multiplying senses and faculties. Yet, however tentatively, he had recognized that an organized sensibility was necessary to the complex reaction known as aesthetic response. This was an important step forward though it involved the error described.

Burke avoided this trap; he avoided, too, the errors connected

[16] *Enquiry*, p. 27. [17] *Op. cit.*, p. 148. [18] *Ibid.*, p. 157.
[19] *Ibid.*, pp. 86, 95.

with the associationist theory. Writers as early as Hobbes[20] and Locke[21] had recognized the importance of associationism, but the principal exponent of the theory was, of course, Hartley in his *Observations on Man* (1749). Among aesthetic theorists, while Hutcheson gave only slight emphasis to it,[22] the theory became of increasing importance from Gerard onwards, through Kames, Alison, and Payne Knight to Jeffrey, particularly for the insights it provided into the way in which emotional effect depends on association.[23] There is little need to trace its history since Burke rejected the theory almost completely, but it should, and may, most conveniently be illustrated from his nearest contemporary, Gerard. He writes:

the beauty of colours is, in most instances, resolvable into *association*; those being approved, which either by a natural resemblance, or by custom, or opinion, introduce and are connected with agreeable ideas of any sort; and those being disapproved, which have any way become related to disagreeable ones. The verdure of the fields is delightful, not only by being inoffensive to the eye, but chiefly by its suggesting the pleasant idea of fertility. Heath in bloom would form a carpet agreeable enough to sight, if we could separate from its appearance the idea of the barrenness of the mountains and wilds it covers.[24]

There is a degree of truth in Gerard's argument, but his error is obvious: he has overlooked the fact that to some fertility is not a "pleasant" idea and to others wildness is "agreeable". What, indeed, he overlooks is the subjective element in his argument: he generalizes a personal liking for certain ideas into an assertion that the colours associated in his mind with these ideas are beautiful. (The habit of elevating personal predilections into general truths was widespread among eighteenth-century aestheticians.) Gerard's mistake—in common with all devotees of the associationist theory—was to identify concomitants of beauty with beauty itself. Burke, for his part, cursorily acknowledges the validity of associationism, but emphatically denies that it explains all aesthetic response:

20 *Leviathan* (1651), I, iii.

21 *Essay* (1690), II, xxxiii.

22 See *Inquiry*, p. 68.

23 See McKenzie, *op. cit.*, ch. v.

24 *Op. cit.*, p. 43.

But as it must be allowed that many things affect us after a certain manner, not by any natural powers they have for that purpose, but by association; so it would be absurd on the other hand, to say that all things affect us by association only.[25]

The "natural properties of things" remain for him the source of aesthetic experience.

Sense experience is, for Burke, the obvious starting-point; provided they are organically sound, all men are alike in their perceptions of external objects. Despite the complications caused by "acquired" as distinct from "natural relish", he firmly maintains that "the pleasure of all the senses . . . is the same in all, high and low, learned and unlearned".[26] Such is Burke's first premise, for, although he divides the faculties concerned with taste into the senses, the imagination, and the judgment, sense experience is the groundwork of all. The imagination works by regrouping images received from the senses; it is pleased or displeased "from the same principle on which the sense is pleased or displeased with the realities".[27] (The faulty assumption that "the realities" remain unchanged when they are transmuted into art, is obvious.) It is by the imagination, too, that the passions are aroused: these again do not operate "in an arbitrary or casual manner, but upon certain, natural and uniform principles".[28] Consequently, in Burke's view, there is a large area of human experience in which universal laws may be said to operate. It is in the sphere of the judgment that the main causes of diversity are found; here the imagination is not confined to sense-data but is involved with "the manners, the characters, the actions, and designs of men, their relations, their virtues and vices". But even here the same uniformity of opinion is possible as is found in real life. Arguing in this manner, Burke arrives at his most extended definition:

Taste, in its most general acceptation, is not a simple idea, but is partly made up of a perception of the primary pleasures of sense, of the secondary pleasures of the imagination, and of the conclusions of the reasoning faculty, concerning the various relations of these, and concerning the human passions, manners and actions.[29]

25 *Enquiry*, pp. 130–31. 26 *Ibid.*, p. 16. 27 *Ibid.*, p. 17. 28 *Ibid.*, p. 22.
29 *Ibid.*, p. 23.

Burke, of course, followed in a great tradition in holding his sensationist philosophy: the dependence of the mind, for its ideas, on the senses was fundamental to the work of Locke, Berkeley, and Hume. Addison used this principle as the starting-point for an analysis of aesthetic experience. To him sight is the principal source of material for the imagination:

We cannot indeed have a single Image in the Fancy that did not make its first Entrance through the Sight; but we have the Power of retaining, altering and compounding those Images, which we have once received, into all the Varieties of Picture and Vision that are most agreeable to the Imagination.[30]

From this premise it was argued that aesthetic values are appreciated through the senses. Thus the senses became accepted as the faculties involved in the enjoyment of beauty; beauty was thought to depend on physical properties in objects —properties, therefore, apprehended through sensation.

While the fundamentals of Burke's position were not indeed new in 1757, he was the first writer on aesthetics in English to take up the uncompromising sensationist viewpoint. It is likely, however, that he came under the influence of the Abbé du Bos (though his only mention of this critic in the *Enquiry* is to disagree with him) whose work, *Réflexions Critiques sur la Poësie et sur la Peinture*, appeared in 1719 and was translated into English by Thomas Nugent in 1748. Du Bos holds no brief for "the way of discussion and analysis" when the question is, "Does the work please, or does it not?" Reason, he maintains, ought not to interfere except "to account for the decision of our senses".

Do we ever reason, in order to know whether a ragoo be good or bad; and has it ever entered into any body's head, after having settled the geometrical principles of taste, and defined the qualities of each ingredient that enters into the composition of those messes, to examine into the proportion observed in their mixture, in order to decide whether the ragoo be good or bad? No, this is never practised. We have a sense given us by nature to distinguish whether the cook acted according to the rules of his art. People taste the ragoo, and tho' unacquainted with those rules, they are able to tell,

[30] *Spectator* No. 411.

whether it be good or no. The same may be said in some respect of the productions of the mind, and of pictures made to please and move us.

We have a sense, which judges of the merit of works, that consist in the imitation of objects of a moving nature. This is the very sense, which would have judged of the object, that the painter, poet, or musician has imitated. 'Tis the eye, when we are to judge of the coloring of a picture. 'Tis the ear, when we are to decide, whether the accents of a recitative be moving, whether they agree with the words, and whether the music be melodious.[31]

Burke largely agrees. For him sense experience is primary and the function of the judgment (which comes last in his listing of the three faculties involved in taste) is to evaluate the "various relations" between the original in nature and the responses it evokes there, and its appearance and effect in art. Thus, in the *Enquiry*, Burke assumes, for example, that beauty is immediately perceived and that it depends on sensible properties: his task is to discover their identity.

The fallacies of the sensationist position are clear enough. The sensationist ignores, among other things, the difference between life and art, and the whole question of aesthetic "significance"; he must omit the subjective element which decides this significance, the fact that it is in our personal "ideas" of objects which we call beautiful that the beauty lies and that, in turn, these ideas depend on personal interests, predilections, emotions, and so on. He confuses, indeed, sense-data, the crude material of the aesthetic experience, with aesthetic perception which has its own distinctive values. Sensationism with all its fallacies obviously committed Burke to a number of ludicrous and extreme statements, yet, in spite of its absurdities, it lends itself to pseudo-scientific treatment which, in turn, produces the lucidity and peculiar strength of argument so characteristic of the *Enquiry*. "When we go but one step beyond the immediately sensible qualities of things, we go out of our depth":[32] Burke was never in any danger of drowning.

Finally, after the attempt has been made to distinguish Burke's views on taste from those of his contemporaries, it must

[31] *Op. cit.* (1748), II, 238–9.

[32] *Enquiry*, pp. 129–30.

briefly be noted that there were many similarities between them, despite different philosophical assumptions. There was, indeed, a large group of commonplaces on the subject of taste on which all writers of the time drew. Almost without exception they insist on "sensibility" as a prerequisite to good taste: Burke points to the obvious when he remarks that good taste largely depends

> upon sensibility; because if the mind has no bent to the pleasures of the imagination, it will never apply itself sufficiently to works of that species to acquire a competent knowledge in them.[33]

No writer would disagree. Like Burke, Gerard considers insensibility as making for weakness of taste;[34] like him again, he observes that sensibility becomes less acute with age, but more alive to degrees of beauty and refinements of experience.[35] The French critics, by and large, echo the same sentiments.[36] But sensibility alone was not enough. Every writer recognized that the judgment was involved, though some imagined that taste and judgment were separate faculties.[37] As we have seen, Burke strenuously repudiated this view.[38] Again, both in Burke and Gerard we are reminded of T. S. Eliot's dictum, "comparison and analysis are the chief tools of the critic", which suggests that sensibility, judgment, and knowledge are all equally essential.[39] The eighteenth-century writers realized the importance of each of these qualities and both allow that judgment and knowledge can be cultivated whereas sensibility is organic. Furthermore, this broad area of agreed opinion, together with the use of a common terminology, led almost inevitably to great similarity of expression, a feature which it would be tedious to illustrate at large.

In view of the evidence given, it would be foolish to claim that Burke made a major contribution to the discussion on

[33] *Ibid.*, p. 24.

[34] *Ibid.*, pp. 23–4; Gerard, *Essay on Taste*, p. 105.

[35] *Enquiry*, pp. 24–6; Gerard, *op. cit.*, p. 105.

[36] See in Gerard, *op. cit.*: Voltaire, p. 209; D'Alembert, p. 227; Montesquieu, pp. 281–2.

[37] E.g. *ibid.*: D'Alembert, p. 225; Montesquieu, p. 252.

[38] See pp. xxv–xxvi.

[39] *Enquiry*, pp. 21–3, 26; Gerard, *op. cit.*, p. 110.

taste. He reiterates the commonplaces of his time; he indulges, like his contemporaries, in dubious generalizations supported by highly selective evidence; and he gives scarcely any hint of the important developments to come later in the century. But he is distinctive, chiefly by his bold sensationism and by his style. The "Essay" is a vigorous and lively piece of writing, the work of a young man seeking to justify the principles assumed in the longer work to which this was introductory. What is lacking in profundity of argument and mature reflection is recompensed by a more than usual freshness of expression and vividness of illustration.

III. THE SUBLIME AND BEAUTIFUL

(i) *Introductory*

Burke is occupied in the first Part of the *Enquiry* with a statement of principles that proves to be an analysis of the psychological factors which cause men to respond to the sublime and beautiful.

> I believed that an attempt to range and methodize some of our most leading passions, would be a good preparative to such an enquiry as we are going to make in the ensuing discourse.[1]

The division of the "leading passions" into those of "self-preservation" and "society" perhaps recalls the discussion of "self-love" and "benevolence" in Butler, Hutcheson, and others, and reminds us of the attempt on the part of eighteenth-century philosophers and poets to reconcile a legitimate self-interest with a regard for the general good. But Burke's use of the categories is otherwise. For him they are directly connected with the central problem: the distinction between the sublime and beautiful.

From the outset it is clear that this division will be rigid: Burke will have nothing to do with imprecision of thought and therefore of language. He is convinced that pleasure "of a positive and independent nature" is different in kind from the pleasure which results from a diminution of pain, and since the difference between "pleasure" (the first kind) and "delight"

[1] *Enquiry*, p. 52.

(the second) is crucial, Burke tries to establish it precisely. On the one hand he claims that delight results from the idea of self-preservation, provided that the pain and danger inevitably associated with the latter do not "press too nearly" but involve us only through the effect of curiosity, sympathy, or imitation. He then goes on to maintain that whatever arouses this delight (in effect the Romantic "delightful horror") is sublime. On the other hand, the second division of the passions—those relating to society—is founded on love of woman (society of sex) or of men and the animate world (general society); love is a positive pleasure,

> and its object is beauty; which is a name I shall apply to all such qualities in things as induce in us a sense of affection and tenderness, or some other passion the most nearly resembling these.[2]

The distinction, then, between the passions of self-preservation and society is central. It leads directly to the distinction between the sublime and beautiful, at once marking the latter as producing a much less violent response than the former—the sublime is "productive of the strongest emotion which the mind is capable of feeling".[3] Burke is consistently interested in strong emotional responses and clearly prefers, on grounds of intensity, the sublime to the beautiful. And what is for him a concomitant, there is that constant interest in the irrational response to art and life, the kind of response which is "natural" (a word later used freely in his attack on Richard Price in the *Reflections*) and not at all under the control of the analytic reason. He strongly objects to attributing the cause of feelings "to certain conclusions of the reasoning faculty"; he claims that the delight arising from scenes of distress (real or fictitious) is "antecedent to any reasoning"; and, again, he points out that the pleasure of imitation acts "without any intervention of the reasoning faculty".[4] We are, in fact, dealing with a bold and, to some extent, an original mind, the principal exponent of the sublime as at once an irrational and a violent aesthetic experience.

Nevertheless, Burke was indebted to earlier and contemporary writers for many of his ideas. The pleasure–pain principle

[2] *Ibid.*, p. 51. [3] *Ibid.*, p. 39. [4] *Ibid.*, pp. 45, 46, 49.

had been a common point of discussion for Shaftesbury, Locke, and Hume, among others. Burke, however, directly contradicts Locke's claim that the diminution of pain causes positive pleasure and *vice versa*.[5] He argues that the feeling which results from the diminution of the one does not sufficiently resemble the other "to have it considered as of the same nature". Moreover, where Locke asserts that there are only two states of being—pain and pleasure—Burke introduces a third, the state of indifference. (He may have had in mind here a passage from Plato's *Philebus*.[6])

In Burke's comments on the emotion of sex Hutcheson seems to have played a part. Both writers view the task of propagating the species as a laborious responsibility accompanied by (in Burke's words) "a very high pleasure", but Burke does not follow Hutcheson in tending to elevate the "moral" at the expense of the "sensible pleasures".[7] Also on the question of sex Burke appears to be influenced by Hume to whom, perhaps, he is generally indebted in this first part of the *Enquiry*. Hume had analysed sex into three components—delight in beauty, bodily appetite, and kindness or goodwill—any one of which "affections", he claimed, might operate first, to be reinforced subsequently by the others. Burke discovers only two elements—physical passion and love for beauty—

> Men are carried to the sex in general, as it is the sex, and by the common law of nature; but they are attached to particulars by personal *beauty*.[8]

but beauty, he goes on to say, is a "social quality" which inspires "sentiments of tenderness and affection". Indeed, his analysis proves to be a close parallel to Hume's.

The section on "Sympathy" also suggests Hume's influence. This writer reduced nearly all moral response to sympathy and though Burke does not reproduce his careful analysis of it, the very importance he attaches to it—"It is by this principle chiefly that poetry, painting, and other affecting arts, transfuse their passions from one breast to another"[9]—may indicate a close contact between the two minds. On the other hand, it

[5] *Essay*, II, xx, 16. Cf. *Enquiry*, pp. 32-5.

[6] *Philebus*, 43.

[7] *Enquiry*, pp. 41-2. Cf. Hutcheson, *Inquiry*, VI, v.

[8] *Enquiry*, p. 42.

[9] *Ibid.*, p. 44.

may be that Burke was simply at one with his age in showing an increasing interest—both moral and aesthetic—in the importance of sympathy. A growing reliance on feeling as a means of insight, allied to the current belief that the best poet was the one with the widest experience, led to the development of sympathetic imagination as an aesthetic idea: it led ultimately to Keats's "negative capability". Adam Smith who, two years after Burke's *Enquiry*, crystallized many existing assumptions in his *Theory of Moral Sentiments*, speaks of imagination as the source of sympathetic emotion. In a passage such as the following, in which he is speaking of the case in which "our brother is on the rack", Smith echoes Burke, though giving greater prominence to the term "imagination":

> By the imagination we place ourselves in his situation, we conceive ourselves enduring all the same torments, we enter as it were into his body and become in some measure him, and thence form some idea of his sensations, and even feel something which, though weaker in degree, is not altogether unlike them.[10]

Or again, Burke gives marked emphasis to the delight we experience in sympathizing with the distresses of others:

> there is no spectacle we so eagerly pursue, as that of some uncommon and grievous calamity . . . The delight we have in such things, hinders us from shunning scenes of misery; and the pain we feel, prompts us to relieve ourselves in relieving those who suffer.[11]

Smith reproduces this idea exactly:

> As the person who is principally interested in any event is pleased with our sympathy, and hurt by the want of it, so we, too, seem to be pleased when we are able to sympathize with him, and to be hurt when we are unable to do so. We run not only to congratulate the successful, but to condole with the afflicted; and the pleasure which we find in conversing with a man whom we can entirely sympathize with in all his passions, seems to do more than compensate the painfulness of that sorrow with which the view of his situation affects us.[12]

Some writers extended the notion of sympathy to the bodily sphere, arguing that vivid sympathy with a person or thing

[10] *Op. cit.* (1759), pp. 2–3. Cf. *Enquiry*, p. 44.

[11] *Enquiry*, p. 46.

[12] *Op. cit.*, pp. 19–20.

leads to physical adaptation to the particular situation. Joseph Priestley, twenty years after the *Enquiry*, quotes the instance of people playing bowls writhing their bodies "into every possible attitude, according to the course they would have their bowl to take."[13] Burke argues for a similar version of sympathetic identification in his illustration of Campanella who, working the process in reverse, composed his face and gestures to resemble another person and was thereby able "to enter into the dispositions and thoughts of people, as effectually as if he had been changed into the very men."[14]

In addition to the instances already mentioned of Hume's possible influence, Burke is probably inspired by him in believing that human nature could be atomized on a scientific basis. The *Treatise on Human Nature* is an impressive attempt to systematize the phenomena of the passions on a few general principles such as "sympathy" and "association". Burke tries to get the same effect of unity in his account of the passions. He is not, however, a subservient disciple. Beyond the differences already noted, he places much less emphasis on association which is the foundation of Hume's system, and he pursues sensationism much further.

While there can be little doubt, then, that Burke is indebted in Part I either to specific writers or to the general climate of ideas, one's overall impression of vigorous originality still remains. The reviews of the *Enquiry* sufficiently indicate how he challenged established psychological and aesthetic beliefs; the critics were provoked, for example, by the pleasure–delight distinction and by the stress Burke places on the delight we experience from witnessing the distresses of others. But of more immediate importance is the original way in which he handled his ideas with one object in view: to provide a convincing basis for the subsequent treatment of the sublime and beautiful.[15]

[13] *Lectures on Oratory and Criticism* (1777), p. 127. Quoted by W. J. Bate, *From Classic to Romantic, Premises of Taste in 18th century England* (Harvard, 1946), pp. 138–9, to whom I am generally indebted.

[14] *Enquiry*, p. 133.

[15] How consistently he works from this section to those following may be illustrated by his confident conclusion to Part II, and by his incidental definition of beauty on p. 91.

And as the reviewers discovered, even when we feel Burke is wrong, we are usually moved to argue and not merely to sneer. This is the general reaction to the work as a whole. Where his contemporaries were content timidly to accept the lead given by their predecessors, Burke boldly scrutinizes accepted views and puts forward his own case without equivocation. As a result he is perhaps more often at fault than they; he takes up an extreme position exposed to attack; but he is alone in being fearlessly provocative and mentally stimulating.

(ii) *The Sublime*

For Burke to write on the sublime and scarcely to mention the name of Longinus is some indication of the degree to which a writer in the mid-eighteenth century assumed in his readers an acquaintance with the work of the Greek critic.[1]

> In it are treasured up the laws and precepts of fine writing, and a fine taste. *Here* are the rules, which polish the writer's invention, and refine the critic's judgment. *Here* is an object proposed at once for our admiration and imitation.[2]

This extravagant comment from the translator of the Greek treatise, W. Smith, points to a widespread (though not a universal) attitude to Longinus which Burke could expect to influence the reception of his own contribution to one of the most popular literary debates of his time.

The direct influence of Longinus on English criticism was no more than a hundred years old when Burke came to write his *Enquiry*, the significant influence probably little more than eighty.[3] The first English translation (by John Hall) appeared in 1652, but it was not until 1698 (after Boileau's French version in 1674) that an English translator used the term "sublime" in the title of Longinus's work. Boileau undoubtedly played a major part in establishing the popularity of *Peri*

[1] Longinus is mentioned twice: in the Preface to the 1st edn. and on p. 51.

[2] Longinus, *On the Sublime* (3rd edn., 1752), p. 180.

[3] Dryden makes considerable use of Longinus in *The Author's Apology*, etc., 1677, where he is mentioned by name; Dryden also seems to have been influenced by him in *Of Heroic Plays*, 1672.

Hupsous, both in England and France,[4] and although the word "sublime" had been used in England much earlier[5] it was only after Boileau's translation that the word assumed distinctive and increased literary significance.

What did Longinus himself mean by the word? This at least must be decided before Burke's immediate predecessors can be considered, because they were not all satisfied with Longinus's explanation. John Baillie made this comment in 1747:

the Bulk of the Performance relates more to the *Perfection* of Writing in *general*, than to any particular *Kind* or *Species*. . . . Besides, *Longinus* has entirely passed over the Inquiry of what the *Sublime* is, as a thing perfectly well known, and is principally intent upon giving *Rules* to arrive at the elevated *Turn* and *Manner*.[6]

While there is some truth in Baillie's contention, it is possible to arrive at some idea "of what the *Sublime* is" for Longinus. He stresses at all times, not merely the technique of persuasion—though it should be remembered that he was writing a work of rhetoric—but the spiritual and emotional qualities and effects of literature. "Sublimity is the note which rings from a great mind",[7] and "the soul is raised by true sublimity, it gains a proud step upwards, it is filled with joy and exultation, as though itself had produced what it hears."[8] Longinus thoroughly examines the technical means for producing sublime effects, but it is to these two qualities that he constantly returns. The appeal they made to the eighteenth century is everywhere evident in the text and notes of Smith's influential translation; he adds, for example, a remark by Condé as a note to his version of the second quotation above: "Voilà le Sublime! voilà son véritable caractère." It is not surprising, then, that contemporary writers regularly turned to the Bible and to Milton for their examples of sublimity.

Longinus is consistent, too, in emphasizing the emotional

[4] See A. F. B. Clark, *Boileau and the French Classical Critics in England, 1660–1830* (Paris, 1925).

[5] Meaning "the highest and stateliest maner, and loftiest deliverance of anything that may be": Day, *The English Secretorie* (1586) (*N.E.D.*).

[6] *An Essay on the Sublime*, p. 2.

[7] *On the Sublime* (transl. A. O. Prickard, Oxford, 1946), IX.

[8] *Ibid.*, VII.

intensity which is a mark of the sublime. "Sublimity lies in intensity", he says,[9] and in his list of the sources of the sublime the first two are, "the faculty of grasping great conceptions", and "passion, strong and impetuous"[10] (which Smith renders as "the power of raising the passions to a violent and even enthusiastic degree"). Moreover, the effect on the reader is intense: "it is not to persuasion but to ecstasy that passages of extraordinary genius carry the hearer"; and the effect is immediate.[11] And it remains true that Longinus's emphasis is on intensity despite his assertion (which gave such offence to John Dennis) that "there is sublimity without passion",[12] for he subsequently lays down as an indispensable element the organization, into a unity, of the "most vital" elements in an experience, these elements to be selected in a mood of intense emotion.[13]

These, then, are the main features of the Longinian sublime, and it remains to show briefly how they were interpreted and elaborated by eighteenth-century theorists. Boileau, as has been suggested, exerted a powerful influence both on the general conception of the sublime and on the vocabulary used in writings about it. The simplified account of Longinus given in the Preface to his translation ensured that the emotive aspect of the sublime and such terms as "extraordinary", "surprising", and "marvellous" were found at every turn in later English writers:

Il faut savoir que par le sublime Longin n'entend pas ce que les orateurs appellent le style sublime, mais cet extraordinaire et ce merveilleux qui frappe dans le discours, et qui fait qu'un ouvrage enlève, ravit, transporte. Le style sublime veut toujours de grands mots; mais le sublime se peut trouver dans une seule pensée, dans une seule figure, dans un seul tour de paroles. Une chose peut être dans le style sublime et n'être pourtant pas sublime, c'est-à-dire n'avoir rien d'extraordinaire ni de surprenant. Par example: *Le souverain arbitre de la nature, d'une seule parole forma la lumière*: voila qui est dans le style sublime; cela n'est pas néanmoins sublime, parce qu'il n'y a rien là de fort merveilleux, et qu'on ne pût aisément trouver. Mais *Dieu dit*: *Que la lumière se fasse*; *et la lumière se fit*: ce

[9] *On the Sublime*, XII.
[10] *Ibid.*, VIII. [11] *Ibid.*, I. [12] *Ibid.*, VIII. [13] *Ibid.*, X.

tour extraordinaire d'expression, qui marque si bien l'obéissance de la créature aux ordres du créateur, est véritablement sublime et a quelque chose de divin. Il faut donc entendre par sublime, dans Longin, l'extraordinaire, le surprenant, et, comme je l'ai traduit, le merveilleux dans le discours.

Only one English writer needs to be quoted to illustrate the influence of such a passage:

The Sublime therefore must be Marvellous, and Surprizing. It must strike vehemently upon the Mind, and Fill, and Captivate it Irresistably.[14]

After Boileau, therefore, "sublime" was a recognized critical term. By the time of Burke's *Enquiry*, however, it had undergone important changes: in one respect it was extended, in another contracted. Whereas in the early stages the sublime is essentially a style of writing, with Burke it becomes a mode of aesthetic experience found in literature and far beyond it. On the other hand, the sublime acquires a more rigid definition as a quality in objects which excites such an experience. Another change alters the approach to the whole subject of sublimity. In the time of Boileau "sublime" is a term primarily for literary critics; later, sublimity is a subject for psychological study by philosophers interested in the relation between human emotions and sublime objects. To some extent Longinus had suggested the psychological approach by emphasizing the reaction to the sublime in "the soul" of the reader. He had also, in some degree, encouraged the belief that the analysis of objects—particularly those of great size—would explain the "natural" cause of sublimity:

So it is that, as by some physical law, we admire, not surely the little streams, transparent though they be, and useful too, but Nile, or Tiber, or Rhine, and far more than all, Ocean.[15]

The reference to the ocean echoes throughout the eighteenth-century debate on the sublime.[16]

Professor Monk names John Dennis as being the first to

[14] Jonathan Richardson, *An Essay on the whole Art of Criticism as it relates to Painting* (1719), p. 35.

[15] *On the Sublime*, XXXV.

[16] Cf. Addison, *Spectator* No. 412; Burke, *Enquiry*, pp. 57-8.

investigate both the nature of the sublime object and its effect on the mind of the reader.[17] Dennis is singularly important for his emphasis on passion as the cardinal feature of poetry: "Poetry unless it is transporting is abominable."[18] He goes beyond both Longinus and Boileau in this respect, and, it should be noted, he considered the former to have had "no clear and distinct Idea" of the sublime.[19] In his *Grounds of Criticism in Poetry* Dennis regards the end of poetry as moral instruction, but decides that in order to achieve this end the poet "excites Passion". There are, in his view, two types of passion, "Vulgar" and "Enthusiastic", and the latter is of six kinds: "Admiration, Terror, Horror, Joy, Sadness, Desire".[20] Only the first two in this list are thoroughly treated as the work remained unfinished.

Writing of admiration Dennis echoes the passage in which Longinus says the soul is "filled with joy and exultation" when contemplating the sublime. For Dennis, when man is moved by admiration he experiences a feeling of heightened spiritual stature, particularly when reflecting on his Maker. Terror had never before received such critical attention as Dennis gives to it: among the passions, "if it is rightly manag'd, none is more capable of giving a great Spirit to Poetry."[21] This is important as foreshadowing Burke's attitude; the connection he goes on to show between terror and power is even more so:

> Things then that are powerful, and likely to hurt, are the causes of Common Terror, and the more they are powerful and likely to hurt, the more they become the causes of Terror, which Terror, the greater it is, the more it is join'd with wonder, and the nearer it comes to astonishment.[22]

The objects of religious ideas, because they are the most powerful, provide the sources of the greatest enthusiastic terror.[23] And further hints of what is to come in Burke's theory

[17] S. H. Monk, *The Sublime: A Study of Critical Theories in 18th Century England* (M.L.A., New York, 1935), p. 45. No writer on the sublime can fail to be indebted to Professor Monk's work: much of what is said here must inevitably encroach on the ground he has covered.

[18] *The Grounds of Criticism in Poetry* (1704), p. 9.

[19] *Ibid.*, p. 81. [20] *Ibid.*, p. 16. [21] *Ibid.*, p. 68. [22] *Ibid.*, pp. 69–70.

[23] Cf. *Enquiry*, pp. 67–70.

are found in Dennis's interest in the power of God, coupled with the obscurity which surrounds the limits of His power and therefore His capacity to inflict pain. Indeed, Dennis is a significant forerunner of Burke in the general stress he lays on violent emotion.

Yet it would be wrong to overestimate his importance in the development of the theory of the sublime. His subject is "the place of the emotions in poetry"; his use of "sublime" as a critical term is not frequent, and it is noticeable that the word does not appear until he begins to make specific reference to Longinus. In fact, the term has not yet become indispensable in a discussion of the subject with which Dennis is concerned.

The same point must be made when we turn to Addison. In the *Spectator* papers 411–421 he divides the "Pleasures of the Imagination" into those arising from the "*Great*, *Uncommon*, or *Beautiful*" (perhaps based on Longinus's reference to "the extraordinary, the great, the beautiful").[24] By treating the Great and the Beautiful as separate qualities he undoubtedly helps to establish the distinction which Burke fully develops between the sublime and the beautiful, but two qualifications must be made: firstly, Addison does not use the term "sublime" in this connection, in fact the term is very infrequently used throughout these papers; and secondly, the distinction is obviously not firmly established in his own mind. He argues, for instance, that under certain circumstances the Great and the Beautiful may combine, "as in a troubled Ocean, a Heaven adorned with Stars and Meteors, or a spacious Landskip cut out into Rivers, Woods, Rocks, and Meadows."[25] Or again, in the final paper on *Paradise Lost* Addison writes as if he considered sublimity a concomitant of beauty: "I have endeavoured to shew how some Passages are beautifull by being Sublime, others by being Soft, others by being Natural."[26] Indeed, from an examination of Addison's use of "sublime" under various conditions, it is apparent that he attaches no very precise ideas to it. Furthermore, he is apart from Dennis and, still more, from Burke, in thinking it possible for the sublime to exist "not mixt and work'd up with Passion", and for the reader's mind to be filled

[24] *On the Sublime*, XXXV. [25] *Spectator*, No. 412. [26] *Ibid.*, No. 369.

"without producing in it any thing like Tumult or Agitation".[27]

Addison does, however, provide some analysis of the psychological effects of Greatness:

Our Imagination loves to be filled with an Object, or to grasp at any thing that is too big for its Capacity. We are flung into a pleasing Astonishment at such unbounded Views, and feel a delightful Stilness and Amazement in the Soul at the Apprehension of them. The Mind of Man naturally hates every thing that looks like a Restraint upon it, and is apt to fancy it self under a sort of Confinement, when the Sight is pent up in a narrow Compass, and shortned on every side by the Neighbourhood of Walls or Mountains. On the contrary, a spacious Horizon is an Image of Liberty, where the Eye has Room to range abroad, to expatiate at large on the Immensity of its Views, and to lose itself amidst the Variety of Objects that offer themselves to its Observation.[28]

Longinus, it is clear, has prompted the analysis, but Addison has made some attempt at originality. When he comes to "Final Causes" he claims that the delight afforded by "Greatness" was divinely ordained to lead to contemplation of the nature and power of God.[29] While this view slightly anticipates Baillie in his *Essay on the Sublime*,[30] it is quite apart from Burke's sensationist explanation in the *Enquiry*.

Like Addison, Hume uses the word "greatness" rather than "sublimity",[31] but he is important here for his contribution to the psychological treatment of the subject. For example, he explains (paraphrasing Longinus) "why a great distance increases our esteem and admiration for an object"; he shows, in the course of his explanation, that he sees no essential opposition between beauty and greatness; and he then goes on to account for the feelings he has described:

'Tis a quality very observable in human nature, that any opposition which does not entirely discourage and intimidate us, has rather a contrary effect, and inspires us with a more than ordinary grandeur and magnanimity. In collecting our force to overcome the opposition, we invigorate the soul, and give it an elevation with which otherwise it would never have been acquainted. Compliance, by

[27] *Spectator*, No. 339. [28] *Ibid.*, No. 412. [29] *Ibid.*, No. 413.
[30] *Op. cit.*, p. 6.
[31] *Treatise of Human Nature* (ed. Green and Grose, 1898), II, 209 ff.

rendering our strength useless, makes us insensible of it; but opposition awakens and employs it.

This is also true in the inverse. Opposition not only enlarges the soul; but the soul, when full of courage and magnanimity, in a manner seeks opposition.

> Spumantemque dari pecora inter inertia votis
> Optat aprum, aut fulvum descendere monte leonem.

Whatever supports and fills the passions is agreeable to us; as on the contrary, what weakens and enfeebles them is uneasy.

This psychological analysis, interesting enough in itself, is far more searching than anything Addison was capable of, but more important is the evidence for the shift of interest from the sublime object to the experience of the beholder. It should also be noticed that the conception of "opposition" as a source of sublimity foreshadows Burke's section on "Difficulty".[32]

In the same year that Hume published his *Treatise*, 1739, there appeared Smith's translation of Longinus's *On the Sublime*. Smith did much to popularize Longinus, and by his comments and illustrations from native (as well as other) literature, he was influential in preparing the way for Burke in one important respect: the aesthetic of terror. Smith comments, for instance, on Longinus's quotation from Hesiod that it is "nasty" and "offends the stomach"; he approves of describing the terrible but not the nauseous and disagreeable, claiming that there is "a serious turn, an inborn sedateness in the mind, which renders images of terror grateful and engaging."[33] "Agreeable sensations", Smith insists, are sometimes produced by objects of terror such as "the silent night, the distant howling wilderness, the melancholy grot, the dark wood, and hanging precipice." Again, in section X on the rules for infusing great thoughts into literature, Smith illustrates Longinus's meaning from *Lear* and refers to the "judicious horror" with which Shakespeare paints the mental disorders of Lear and Edgar. Such illustrations are not foreign to the spirit of the Greek writer, but their importance lies both in their being chosen from native authors and in the respectability which the name

32 *Enquiry*, p. 77.
33 *On the Sublime* (transl. W. Smith), IX.

of Longinus would give to the sublime of terror which Burke was to make the basis of his aesthetic theory.

So far we have been concerned with scattered hints rather than with coherent theories of the sublime. "The first important theory that bears any resemblance to aesthetic" was John Baillie's *Essay on the Sublime*, 1747.[34] It is a slight and unpretentious work to which no critic before Gerard, in 1759, refers, but which none the less shows significant advances. In the first place, Baillie discusses sublimity as an aesthetic quality in objects of all kinds, not only in literature. Furthermore, he uses "sublime" throughout; the term is no longer reserved for questions of style but has become, equally with "beauty", a general and accepted expression for use in aesthetics.

True to his age, Baillie regards the function of the critic as being to define "the *Limits* of each *Kind* of *Writing*, and to prescribe their proper *Distinctions*", and it is on these grounds that he finds Longinus's work defective.[35] He begins by stating his terms of reference and at once they are important to a study of Burke's *Enquiry*:

as the *Sublime* in *Writing* is no more than a Description of the *Sublime* in *Nature*, and as it were painting to the *Imagination* what *Nature* herself offers to the *Senses*, I shall begin with an Inquiry into the *Sublime* of *Natural Objects*, which I shall afterwards apply to *Writing*.[36]

Here is the sensationist approach, the interest not in sublimity as a quality present in an object, but in the kind of sensory experience stimulated by the sublime object. After describing sublimity as something which "extends [man's] very Being", elevates the soul, and "disposes the Mind to this *Enlargement* of itself",[37] Baillie proceeds to limit the concept to sensation:

whatever the *Essence* of the *Soul* may be, it is the *Reflections* arising from *Sensations* only which makes her acquainted with Herself, and know her *Faculties*. Vast Objects occasion vast Sensations, and vast Sensations give the Mind a higher Idea of her own Powers.[38]

[34] S. H. Monk, *op. cit.*, p. 77. (Akenside's *Pleasures of Imagination*, 1744, is not treated because it adds nothing of importance to Addison's comments on Greatness.)

[35] See p. xlv. [36] *Op. cit.*, p. 3. [37] *Ibid.*, p. 4. [38] *Ibid.*, p. 7.

It is precisely this kind of psychological method, linked more thoroughly to physiology, that Burke was to employ ten years later.

The first quality Baillie believes productive of sublimity is vastness: on this topic he largely paraphrases Longinus.[39] In his treatment of the second quality, uniformity (which differs from Shaftesbury's "Uniformity amid Variety"), Baillie once more points forward to Burke:

when the Object is uniform, by seeing *Part*, the least Glimpse gives a full and compleat Idea of the *Whole*, and thus at once may be distinctly conveyed the vastest *Sensation*. On the contrary, where this *Uniformity* is wanting, the Mind must run from Object to Object, and never get a full and compleat Prospect. Thus instead of having one large and *grand Idea*, a thousand *little ones* are shuffled in. . . . Where an Object is *vast*, and at the same Time *uniform*, there is to the Imagination no Limits of its Vastness, and the Mind runs out into *Infinity*, continually *creating* as it were from the *Pattern*.[40]

Almost certainly this interesting idea prompted Burke's treatment of the "artificial infinite" which springs from "succession and *uniformity* of parts".[41] Burke does not, however, agree that "Difficulty" reduces sublimity but, rather, claims it as "a source of greatness"; Baillie asserts that infinity must be easily perceived for the full effect of the sublime to be experienced. There is, moreover, a further divergence of opinion. Infinity (and, one may suppose, the artificial infinite) for Burke produces "delightful horror", always, for him, the true test of the sublime; for Baillie the vast and uniform arouse in the mind "a solemn Sedateness . . . for altho' the *Pathetic* may be often join'd with it, yet of itself the *Sublime* rather *composes*, than *agitates* the Mind."[42] This denial of violent emotion as part of the sublime experience places Baillie apart from Burke and, before him, Dennis. Baillie's "*Admiration*, a Passion always attending the *Sublime*"[43] is something of a totally different order from Burke's "astonishment", "that state of the soul, in which all its motions are suspended, with some degree of horror".[44]

[39] *Op cit.*, p. 5. Cf. Longinus, *On the Sublime*, XXXV. [40] *Ibid.*, p. 9.
[41] *Enquiry*, pp. 74–6. [42] *Op. cit.*, pp. 10–11. [43] *Ibid.*, p. 12.
[44] *Enquiry*, p. 57.

When Baillie comes to analyse the "Sublime of the Passions" he does not, like Burke, examine the emotional response in the beholder of sublime objects; he treats, rather, those "Affections" which are called great when observed in another person and cause exaltation in the observer. He avoids, then, an analysis of the direct impact of sublimity and comments on it at one remove. When he discusses "Power" he argues that sublimity depends on the degree to which the power approaches infinity. Thus the most quoted passage in investigations of the sublime, "God said, Let there be Light, and there was Light", suggests the unlimited power of the Creator.[45] Baillie does not, however, like Burke, connect the idea of power with those of terror and pain. Indeed, he does not believe that fear is compatible with sublimity "when it exists *simple* and unmixed": "The *Sublime* dilates and elevates the Soul, *Fear* sinks and contracts it."[46] And later, referring to a storm at sea, he asserts:

Here the *complex* Sensation is generally esteemed the *sublime*; but . . . the *Vastness* only of the Objects produces it, by no means the *Agitation* of the Passions, which, if nicely consider'd, has rather *Fear* than the *Sublime* for its Cause.[47]

To Burke, on the contrary, that the ocean is "an object of no small terror" makes it a source of the sublime.

Finally, Baillie claims that "the *Eyes* and *Ears* are the only *Inlets* to the Sublime. *Taste*, *Smell*, nor *Touch* convey nothing that is Great and Exalted."[48] By so doing he does indeed enlarge the scope of the sublime beyond the Addisonian single sense of sight, but this in its turn is to be sharply challenged by Burke who extends his analysis to all the senses. Despite the resulting absurdities, Burke at least tries to produce an aesthetic theory which accounts for the whole range of human responses.

The last evidence of indebtedness on Burke's part comes from Du Bos' *Réflexions Critiques*. In the early chapters of that work the author makes some suggestions about the relationship

[45] Lowth comments on the frequency with which this passage is quoted (*Lectures on the Sacred Poetry of the Hebrews*, transl. G. Gregory (1787), I, 350). Burke is one of the few writers who ignore it.

[46] *Essay on the Sublime*, p. 32.

[47] *Ibid.*, p. 40.

[48] *Ibid.*, p. 41.

between emotion and art which may have influenced Burke. Du Bos argues that man dreads mental inaction and that the soul needs exercise as much as the body:

The soul hath its wants no less than the body; and one of the greatest wants of man is to have his mind incessantly occupied. The heaviness which quickly attends the inactivity of the mind, is a situation so very disagreeable to man, that he frequently chuses to expose himself to the most painful exercises, rather than be troubled with it.[49]

For this reason man is led to pursue emotional experiences although he knows that the consequences will be "nights and days of pain and calamity". Gladiatorial combats and bull-fights are quoted by Du Bos as examples of the sources of such painful, but delightful, emotions: "the attractive of the emotion felt on those occasions, carries a greater weight with it than all the reflections and advice of experience."[50] The difference between reality and art, argues Du Bos, is that while art induces a passion similar to that excited by the object in real life, the art-experience is less violent and less lasting.[51] Such arguments recall Burke's *Enquiry*. During his discussion of pain as a source of delight, Burke claims that the "more delicate organs" require exercise just as much as do the "coarser organs" of the body.[52] Again, while considering the effects of tragedy, he asserts that the news of an execution would empty a theatre witnessing "the most sublime and affecting tragedy we have", because, "be its power of what kind it will, it never approaches to what it represents."[53] Burke is equally close to Du Bos in the conclusion he draws from the discussion of tragedy: "We delight in seeing things, which so far from doing, our heartiest wishes would be to see redressed." Du Bos had made almost the same point: "the pleasing charm of emotion cancels the first principles of humanity in the most polite and most tender-hearted nations; and obliterates, in people of the greatest christianity, the most evident maxims of their religion."[54]

There is, then, abundant evidence of Burke's reliance on inherited ideas, but his claim to originality remains unimpaired.

[49] *Op. cit.*, I, 5. [50] *Ibid.*, I, 10. [51] *Ibid.*, I, 22–3.
[52] *Enquiry*, p. 135. [53] *Ibid.*, p. 47. [54] *Op. cit.*, I, 18–9.

Greatness of dimension, it is true, had been regarded as a source of sublimity from Longinus onwards; Addison, Hume, and others had tried to explain it psychologically; but none before Burke had attempted a physiological explanation. The association of the sublime with terror had been found in Dennis and, slightly, in Smith's comments on Longinus; Baillie may have prompted the idea of the artificial infinite; and some debt to Du Bos is clear. But whatever Burke took over from earlier writers was invariably developed in his own vigorous and original way; it was, too, used only in so far as it proved an organic part of his basic theory—that "whatever is fitted in any sort to excite the ideas of pain, and danger, . . . is a source of the *sublime*." This theory had no precedent.

It is chiefly because of this innovation that, viewed historically, Burke's *Enquiry* "is certainly one of the most important aesthetic documents that eighteenth-century England produced."[55] The link between sublimity and terror had been suggested before; it was used, consciously perhaps, in Thomson's *Seasons*;[56] but Burke was the first to convert it into a system. Inevitably the desire to systematize led to absurdities. Burke, we are told by Payne Knight,[57] subsequently recognized and laughed at the absurdities, but in the later 1740's they sprang from firm conviction. For example, the sight of the swollen river Liffey inspired the following passage in a letter to Richard Shackleton, 25 January 1746: "It gives me pleasure to see nature in those great, but terrible scenes. It fills the mind with grand ideas, and turns the soul in upon herself."[58] Such emotions were not peculiar to Burke; they were almost fashionable, particularly when the eighteenth-century traveller came upon some awe-inspiring mountain scenery. When Dennis, as early as 1688, felt "a delightful Horrour, a terrible Joy" in the face of such scenery,[59] he was struggling to express a

[55] S. H. Monk, *op. cit.*, pp. 86–7.

[56] Cf. A. D. McKillop, *The Background of Thomson's Seasons* (University of Minnesota Press, 1942), pp. 70, 129; J. Butt, *The Augustan Age* (1950), pp. 78–83.

[57] *Analytical Inquiry into the Principles of Taste* (2nd edn., 1805), I, ii, 5.

[58] *Correspondence*, I, 11.

[59] *Miscellanies in Verse and Prose* (1693), pp. 133–4.

complex response for which the age had not yet provided a term. It was largely due to Burke's popular treatise that the second half of the eighteenth century was provided with the word "sublime" consciously to express the type of emotion Dennis had experienced. The growing taste for ruins and melancholy terror,[60] for graveyard poetry, for wild and desolate scenery, and indeed for many of those interests normally dubbed "pre-Romantic", combined to give Burke's *Enquiry* a (possibly inflated) significance as realizing and systematizing a change in aesthetic values. To claim Burke as a "Romantic" would be manifestly absurd—he is rooted too firmly in his empirical age—but the *Enquiry* (probably by seeming to lend them a philosophical respectability) undoubtedly gave to attitudes already prevalent and terms which had been used without systematic reference, a popularity that forwarded the movement known as "Romantic".

The same point may be made about Burke's remarks on infinity, vastness, power, magnificence, and obscurity. By emphasizing these qualities as sources of the sublime, he is in open revolt against neo-classic principles. Each had, it is true, been separately treated at an earlier date: vastness and, to some degree, infinity by Longinus; power by Baillie, magnificence by Boileau, and obscurity by Hartley.[61] But never before had they been brought together in a coherent and unified theory, and elaborated with such disregard for established aesthetic presuppositions. The way in which Burke develops the idea of power beyond Baillie has been shown; Boileau for his part had countenanced "un beau désordre" merely on technical grounds, as a device to imitate Pindar, whereas Burke looks on disorder as increasing grandeur by suggesting infinity; and regarding obscurity, he goes far beyond Hartley. Instead of Hartley's tentative reference to "a moderate degree of obscurity",[62] we get Burke's unequivocal assertions:

[60] Cf. Burke's letter to Matthew Smith, "London, 1750": "I have not the least doubt, that the finest poem in the English language, I mean Milton's Il Penseroso, was composed in the long resounding isle of a mouldering cloister or ivy'd abbey." (Samuels, *Early Life*, p. 221.)

[61] Thomson had combined some of these elements in his natural descriptions in *The Seasons* (e.g. *Autumn*, *l.* 1138 ff.).

[62] *Observations on Man* (5th edn., 1810), I, 443.

It is one thing to make an idea clear, and another to make it *affecting* to the imagination.

It is our ignorance of things that causes all our admiration, and chiefly excites our passions. Knowledge and acquaintance make the most striking causes affect but little.

A clear idea is therefore another name for a little idea.[63]

Nothing could be more definite; nothing could so powerfully attack the existing love of clarity. Burke is unfortunately hampered by the restricted power he attributes to the imagination which, for him, can only re-group sense-impressions but cannot produce anything new. Consequently, in his analysis of Milton's portrait of Satan, he speaks of obscurity because he lacks the insight into, and the terminology with which to assess, the working of the poetic imagination.[64] Nevertheless, Burke does, by implication, direct attention to the limitations of poetry which endeavours to be determinate by supplying a series of perceptions of detail; he is aware, even if only faintly, of the evocative power of suggestiveness and of the value of giving to the reader's imagination an important re-creative function in poetry. He would be vigorously opposed to the critics (such as Kames, Campbell, Knight and Alison) who later assented to the view expressed by Joseph Warton: "The use, the force and the excellence of language, certainly consists in raising *clear*, *complete*, and *circumstantial* images, and in turning *readers* into *spectators*."[65] Rather does Burke, however dimly, look forward to the Coleridgean view that genius is not shown by

elaborating a picture: we have had many specimens of this sort of work in modern poems, where all is so dutchified, if I may use the word, by the most minute touches, that the reader naturally asks why words, and not painting are used. . . . The power of poetry is, by a single word, perhaps, to instil energy into the mind, which compels the imagination to produce the picture.[66]

63 *Enquiry*, pp. 60, 61, 63.

64 *Ibid.*, pp. 61-2.

65 *Essay on the Genius and Writings of Pope* (4th edn., 1782), II, 165. Cited by G. McKenzie, *Critical Responsiveness*, p. 243.

66 *Shakespearean Criticism* (ed. Raysor, 1930), II, 174.

It would be easy, as Knight found,[67] to ridicule the absurdities into which Burke was led by his desire for thoroughness, but it should at least be recognized that when Burke treats the sublime physiologically he is trying to account for the aesthetic experience in its entirety.[68] More balanced than Knight's witticisms is Dugald Stewart's observation on the distortion of facts to suit the systems of theorists:

> The speculations of Mr. Burke himself are far from being invulnerable in this point of view; although he may justly claim the merit of having taken a more comprehensive survey of his subject, and of having combined, in his induction, a far more valuable collection of particular illustrations, than any of his predecessors.[69]

Stewart is here calling attention to Burke's superiority as a writer which distinguishes him from all the theorists of his time whose work has been mentioned. Burke is not only capable of forceful, terse writing, in contrast to the rather pedestrian style of his contemporaries; he is also capable of conveying something of the aesthetic experience he is trying to analyse. This quality is probably best exemplified by his choice and use of illustrations. Influenced no doubt by the existing interest in Biblical sublimity (especially in the Book of Job), and in Milton's "sublime genius", Burke nevertheless selects and presents his quotations cogently to support his argument and to convey their full impact to the reader. The possibility that the "noble panegyric on the high priest Simon the son of Onias"[70] was still a potent influence when he came to write his apostrophe to Marie Antoinette in 1790, suggests the vivid literary experience which such a quotation represented in 1757. Burke's theory of the sublime stands, indeed, not only as a daring adventure in philosophy, but also as a powerful expression of a certain mode of feeling. It provided for the eighteenth century its most spirited exploration of a range of emotional stimuli which, in

[67] *Analytical Inquiry*, III, i, 69, *et passim.*

[68] The present writer agrees with Professor Monk that Burke does not follow any contemporary physiologist with sufficient consistency to merit a lengthy analysis. (See Monk, *op. cit.*, p. 97 n.)

[69] *Philosophical Essays* (Edinburgh, 3rd edn., 1818), p. 378.

[70] *Enquiry*, p. 79.

the previous two centuries, had been largely the province of tragedy.

(iii) *The Beautiful*

"Beauty is, for the greater part, some quality in bodies, acting mechanically upon the human mind by the intervention of the senses."[1] In these words, with uncompromising boldness, Burke makes his central definition. It is, of course, demonstrably false, but in 1757 it was refreshingly novel. Yet its significance in the history of aesthetics does not rest in its novelty—it is no more than a thorough-going application to aesthetics of the empirical philosophy so popular at the time—but in the challenge it offered to established theories. Before he arrives at this definition Burke has not only laid the foundations for it with care; he has also cleared away much that was accepted without question by his contemporaries. Despite his own errors, therefore, by scrutinizing existing notions and offering alternatives Burke compelled his age to re-think the position that traditional attitudes had led it to adopt.

He first considers three theories widely held in mid-century: those theories which connect beauty with proportion, with fitness (or utility), and with goodness or perfection. Each of these had existed since the time of Plato but none, so far, had been subjected to a searching examination in the early eighteenth century.

Burke recognizes that in attacking the theory that beauty consists "in certain proportions of parts" he is taking issue with a belief "as hath been so generally . . . affirmed". The belief had, indeed, originated with Pythagoras's discovery that musical intervals depended on certain mathematical ratios of lengths of string held at the same tension, which ratios were later held to be applicable to the other arts. The principle was adopted, for example, by the early Renaissance architect, Leone Battista Alberti, who argued that, since Nature acts consistently in all her operations, "the same numbers, by means of which the agreement of Sounds affects our ears with delight, are the very same which please our eyes and our mind."[2]

[1] *Enquiry*, p. 112.

[2] *De Re Aedificatoria*, IX, v (trans. J. Leoni, 1726, vol. II, fol. 86v.)

Another version of the proportionist theory originated with the Greeks in Plato's *Philebus* where Socrates affirms the presence of natural and absolute beauty in regular lines and figures.[3] The result was that there emerged among Greek sculptors and painters a belief in proportion and symmetry, which led in turn to the search for the perfectly proportioned human form.[4]

The revival of classical theories of beauty at the Renaissance provoked further attempts to determine human proportions. Burke refers to the lack of agreement among the theorists about the proportions of the body decided in terms of the height of the head.[5] He may be referring to a writer such as Albrecht Dürer who, in his *Four Books of Human Proportion*, gave examples of different graded types, ranging from seven to ten heads.[6] On the other hand Leonardo da Vinci suggested eight heads as a normal height,[7] whereas Vasari claimed that nine was the common estimate among artists.[8] Other ratios between parts of the body were established, some as absurd as those ridiculed by Burke:

> The measures which are *unisone* and equall betweene themselves are these. First the space betweene the chin & the throat-pit, is asmuch as the diameter of the necke. The circumference of the necke, is asmuch as frō the throat-pit to the Navile. The diameter of the wast answereth to the distãce betweene the knobbe of the throate and the top of the head, and this is the length of the foote.[9]

It was inevitable that proportion would also be emphasized in treatises on architecture. What Burke objected to was "forced analogy" between "the proportions of building" and

[3] *Op. cit.*, 51 B. For this and other references see E. F. Carritt's excellent book of selections, *Philosophies of Beauty* (Oxford, 1931).

[4] Pliny lists as exponents of symmetry, Myron, Lysippus, Parrhasius, and Euphranor (*Historia Naturalis*, XXXIV, 57–8, 65; XXXV, 67, 128).

[5] *Enquiry*, pp. 97–8.

[6] See W. M. Conway, *Literary Remains of Albrecht Dürer* (Cambridge, 1889), pp. 232–9. (Cf. Donne, *Satire IV*, 204–6, and Pope's imitation.)

[7] J. P. Richter, *Literary Works of Leonardo da Vinci* (1883), I, 172.

[8] *Vasari on Technique* (trans. L. S. Maclehose, 1907), p. 146.

[9] G. P. Lomazzo, *A Tracte containing the Artes of curious Paintinge etc.* (trans. R. Haydocke, Oxford, 1598), p. 34. (A copy of Lomazzo, *Trattato dell'Arte della Pittura*, Milan, 1585, was included in the sale (item no. 358) of Burke's library.)

"those of the human body".[10] This analogy, originating with the authoritative architect for the Renaissance, Vitruvius, had been widely accepted. Michaelangelo, for example, asserted:

> It is also certain, that the members of architecture have a reference to those of the human body, and he who does not understand the human figure, and particularly anatomy, can know nothing of the subject.[11]

Another Renaissance theorist, Lomazzo, contended that "*Shippes, Barkes, Gallies* etc. were after the resemblance of the *Arke*, taken from the proportion of mans body".[12]

The proportionist theory, then, became so widely held that it was taken for granted, even down to the eighteenth century. Addison unquestioningly assumes that "Symmetry and Proportion of Parts" is a constituent of beauty;[13] Joseph Spence is equally orthodox in maintaining that the general cause of beauty in human beings "is a Proportion, or an Union and Harmony, in all Parts of the Body";[14] and indeed Hogarth is perhaps the only writer who qualifies his acceptance of the general view. With him, "fitness" is the first criterion and "*fit proportion*" is a major constituent of beauty, but he does argue that "whatever may have been pretended by some authors, no exact mathematical measurements by lines can be given for the true proportion of a human body."[15] Hogarth is not, however, so rigorous and thorough in his questioning of the general theory as is Burke.

The association of proportion with fitness or utility is clearly in tune with eighteenth-century materialistic philosophy, but the belief in the validity of the association was as traditional as the theory outlined above. A passage in Xenophon's *Memorabilia* shows Socrates arguing that a dung-basket may be beautiful and a golden shield ugly, "if the one be beautifully fitted to its purpose and the other ill".[16] Little advance has

10 *Enquiry*, p. 100.

11 R. Duppa, *Life of Michel Angelo Buonarroti* (1806), pp. 212–3.

12 *Op. cit.*, p. 109.

13 *Spectator* No. 412.

14 [Sir H. Beaumont] *Crito: Or, A Dialogue on Beauty* (1752), p. 12.

15 *The Analysis of Beauty* (1753), p. 75.

16 *Op. cit.*, III, viii, 4–7.

been made beyond this view by the time of Shaftesbury who declares in his *Characteristicks*:

the same Shapes and Proportions which make Beauty, afford Advantage, by adapting to Activity and Use. Even in the imitative or *designing* Arts . . . the *Truth* or *Beauty* of every Figure or Statue is measur'd from the Perfection of Nature, in her just adapting of every Limb and Proportion to the Activity, Strength, Dexterity, Life and Vigour of the particular Species or Animal *design'd*.[17]

Fitness, as has been suggested, is central to Hogarth's theory of beauty; indeed, if an object lacks this quality it cannot, for Hogarth, be beautiful.[18] Gerard is equally convinced. In his view proportion consists "in a general aptitude of the structure to the end proposed. . . . Its influence on beauty is therefore derived from *fitness*."[19] The presence of this kind of proportion, together with uniformity and variety, suggests the wisdom of the creator of the object, and the sense of a controlling mind is, for Gerard, one of the pleasures excited by beauty.

The third theory which Burke attacks—that which connects beauty with moral perfection—is also found from Plato onwards. Socrates, in the *Republic*, argues that "good style and harmony and grace and rhythm spring naturally from goodness of nature—not the good-nature we politely speak of when we really mean weakness—but from a truly good and beautiful character of mind."[20] Aquinas is also convinced that "a certain wholeness or perfection" is an essential element of beauty, and, while they are distinguishable, "beauty and goodness are inseparable".[21] In the eighteenth century Shaftesbury perpetuates the same arguments:

what is BEAUTIFUL is *Harmonious* and *Proportionable*; what is Harmonious and Proportionable, is TRUE; and what is at once both *Beautiful* and *True*, is, of consequence, *Agreeable* and GOOD.[22]

Platonic influence is marked here, as it is in Hutcheson's *Inquiry*[23] and in the pamphlet by Spence previously quoted.[24]

17 *Op. cit.* (6th edn., 1737), III, 180.

18 *Analysis of Beauty*, pp. 13–16.

19 *Essay on Taste*, p. 36.

20 *Op. cit.*, 400 D.

21 *Summa*, xxxiv, 8; I, v, 4.

22 *Characteristicks*, III, 182–3.

23 *Op. cit.*, Part II, *passim*.

24 *Crito*, p. 58.

To demolish theories with such distinguished ancestries was a formidable task. Burke set about it with his customary wit, intelligence and independence of mind. With reference to the claim that the proportions of architecture are based on those of the human body, he observes that "in the first place, men are very rarely seen in this strained posture [with arms raised and extended at full length]; it is not natural to them; neither is it at all becoming."[25] Later he ridicules the idea that beauty depends on "the fitness of the parts for their several purposes" by pointing out that, on this principle,

> the wedge-like snout of a swine, with its tough cartilage at the end, the little sunk eyes, and the whole make of the head, so well adapted to its offices of digging, and rooting, would be extremely beautiful.[26]

Burke adds, as further illustrations, the pelican with its large pouch, the hedgehog and its "prickly hide", the porcupine with its "missile quills", and the monkey with its adaptable limbs. He thus subtly avoids the virtues of the theories in question while throwing into relief the absurdities which they allowed. But there is more to his counter-attack than ridicule. Burke strenuously attempts to isolate the aesthetic from the non-aesthetic. He insists that the satisfaction afforded by beauty is something totally different from the pleasure arising from proportion, fitness or custom which are fundamentally non-aesthetic qualities. They make their appeal to the understanding; they depend for their effect, to a certain extent, on experience and knowledge; and the impact they make is one which produces "approbation, the acquiescence of the understanding, but not love, nor any passion of that species."[27] Beauty, Burke claims, makes an immediate impact on the emotions; the satisfaction it gives is vital and intense, and is not to be identified with mere "approbation":

> It is not by the force of long attention and enquiry that we find any object to be beautiful; beauty demands no assistance from our reasoning; even the will is unconcerned; the appearance of beauty as effectually causes some degree of love in us, as the application of ice or fire produces the ideas of heat or cold.[28]

[25] *Enquiry*, p. 100. [26] *Ibid.*, p. 105. [27] *Ibid.*, p. 108. [28] *Ibid.*, p. 92.

The aesthetic experience, then, is distinctive and not to be confused with the effect of non-aesthetic values.

When he deals with the relation between beauty and perfection, Burke's object is the same:

> I know, it is in every body's mouth, that we ought to love perfection. This is to me a sufficient proof, that it is not the proper object of love. Who ever said, we *ought* to love a fine woman, or even any of these beautiful animals, which please us? Here to be affected, there is no need of the concurrence of our will.[29]

Here again he is trying to determine the distinctive nature of the aesthetic experience.

Similarly his objection to the view that "deformity" is the opposite to beauty is based on the fervent belief that beauty is "a *positive* and powerful quality".[30] Deformity, he argues, is the absence of "the *compleat, common form*" that custom has led us to expect in any species, but to insist that the absence of deformity infers the presence of beauty makes the latter merely negative. Burke would claim that the snout of a swine is not deformed—utility and custom cause us to associate such an appearance with that species—but ugly. He opposes ugliness to beauty and remarks (in contradiction of the Socratic view quoted earlier) that "a thing may be very ugly with any proportions, and with a perfect fitness to any uses".[31]

In the opening sections of his discussion of beauty, therefore, Burke consistently tries to isolate the aesthetic experience, to reveal its distinctive character, and to insist that it should not be identified with qualities which, while they may be concomitants of beauty, are not beauty itself. This is one of the most valuable aspects of his work. Unfortunately it is obscured by the crude confusion of the aesthetic and non-aesthetic in his own analysis of beauty. Having rightly and cogently shown that beauty is not a matter of intellectual and moral approbation, he wrongly attributes it wholly to qualities of objects which act mechanically through the senses.

[29] *Enquiry*, p. 110.

[30] *Ibid.*, p. 103. Deformity is opposed to beauty by Shaftesbury (*Characteristicks*, I, 207; II, 28).

[31] *Ibid.*, p. 119. Cf. p. lxii.

At this point, Burke's own theory—as distinct from his critical evaluation of traditional attitudes to beauty—calls for examination. But his personal contribution to the eighteenth-century debate on the subject can be clearly seen only by setting it beside the views of his immediate predecessors.

Addison's remarks on beauty are not significant enough to warrant much attention: the division of the "Pleasures of the Imagination" is not followed by an attempt to analyse beauty systematically. "Several Modifications of Matter", he says, strike the mind as beautiful or deformed, but we are given no information as to what they are or how they operate.[32] He does, however, suggest that the effect of beauty is immediate—"without any previous Consideration"—which brings him close to one part of Burke's theory already noticed. Addison goes on to speak of sexual beauty, affirming that each species has its own type of attractiveness, but his theory that animals possess a sense of beauty did not find favour with Burke.[33] He then refers to the non-sexual, concluding that it "consists either in the Gaiety or Variety of Colours, in the Symmetry and Proportion of Parts, in the Arrangement and Disposition of Bodies, or in a just Mixture and Concurrence of all together."[34] There could scarcely be a description which contains more contemporary commonplaces or has less of the forthright certainty which characterizes Burke's statements.

Shaftesbury's views on fitness, proportion, and moral perfection have already been mentioned. That he was a popular and influential writer cannot be disputed. James Arbuckle gives one view (albeit disapproving) of his popularity:

I have seen the Lord *Shaftesbury's* Works on a Shopkeeper's Counter, and hear him every day quoted by Persons, whose Business it neither is to understand him, nor have they the proper Means of doing it; and who when they have got a little *smattering* of him, for the most part employ it to very ill purposes.[35]

Arbuckle, it seems, is drawing attention to the fervency and

[32] *Spectator* No. 412. Cf. James Arbuckle, *A Collection of Letters and Essays on Several Subjects* (1729), I, 40–1.

[33] *Enquiry*, p. 42.

[34] *Spectator* No. 412.

[35] *Op. cit.*, II, 227. For a contemporary comment on Shaftesbury's imprecision, see Blair, *Lectures on Rhetoric and Belles Lettres* (1839), pp. 121–3.

the imprecision which characterize Shaftesbury's writings: it is exactly these qualities which make difficult any accurate appraisal of his influence. However, two points must be made. First, though Shaftesbury consistently stresses the moral nature of beauty, he admits that "in certain *Figures* a natural Beauty" is recognized by the eye "as soon as the Object is presented to it".[36] He affirms here the immediacy with which we perceive the beautiful and, like Burke, frees the aesthetic judgment from a dependence on the reason. In the second place, while Shaftesbury does not himself distinguish between the sublime and the beautiful, his philosophy provides the foundation for the distinction:

> The logical conclusion of philosophical optimism was that not only the great and awe-inspiring, but even the terrible and ugly aspects of nature must have an aesthetic appeal. The whole of nature is a revelation of God's goodness and bounty, and everything must be, if not beautiful, at least aesthetically valuable.[37]

Hutcheson follows logically after Shaftesbury among English thinkers, but a brief reference ought to be made to the work of the Swiss philosopher, Crousaz, if only because his theory is typical of those to which Burke is resolutely opposed. In the *Traité du Beau* (1715) Crousaz (like Hutcheson) centres his theory of beauty on the principle of "Uniformity and Variety"; he insists that proportion and fitness are essential qualities; and he puts moral beauty into the same category as aesthetic beauty. Furthermore, Crousaz argues that beauty is a quality more for intellectual than sensory appreciation. With the spirit of this last, and with the detail of the former arguments, Burke is completely at variance.

Hutcheson's *Inquiry*—which follows Shaftesbury and Crousaz in its central principles—merits more attention: it was the most systematic examination of beauty in the eighteenth century before Burke. At the outset, Hutcheson introduces the concept of "Internal Senses" which he defines as "these Determinations to be pleas'd with any Forms or Ideas which occur to our Observation".[38] He thus adopts as axiomatic Shaftesbury's

[36] *Characteristicks* II, 414.
[37] R. L. Brett, *The Third Earl of Shaftesbury* (1951), p. 161.
[38] *Op. cit.*, p. vi.

suggestion that man cannot avoid being delighted by some objects of sense, and displeased by others; the will, in other words, is not involved in the perception of beauty. He is here close to Burke, as he is also in his attempt to isolate the essential pleasure afforded by beauty. While he claims that the sense of beauty is a separate faculty, he does insist that it has its own distinct pleasure apart from "the knowledge of principles, proportions, causes, or of the usefulness of the object". Hutcheson, in fact, tries to distinguish the aesthetic from the non-aesthetic, and in so doing anticipates Burke's arguments against the fitness theory.[39]

Hutcheson then divides beauty into absolute and comparative: the first is found in the object itself, the second in works of art where the imitative power of the artist is a principal source of pleasure.[40] Absolute beauty, he claims, springs from "*Uniformity amidst Variety*", an idea which he finds capable of mathematical elaboration:

The Figures that excite in us the Ideas of Beauty, seem to be those in which there is *Uniformity amidst Variety*. . . . But what we call Beautiful in Objects, to speak in the Mathematical Style, seems to be in a compound Ratio of Uniformity and Variety; so that where the Uniformity of Bodys is equal, the Beauty is as the Variety; and where the Variety is equal, the Beauty is as the Uniformity.[41]

From this premise he can argue that "the Beauty of an equilateral Triangle is less than that of the Square; which is less than that of a Pentagon; and this again is surpass'd by the Hexagon." The idea is applied to the heavenly bodies, animals (in whose beauty he believes, contrary to Burke, that proportion plays a part), gardening, and architecture, and Hutcheson then goes on to consider comparative beauty. This, he maintains, "is founded on a *Conformity*, or a kind of *Unity* between the Original and the Copy".[42] Like Burke he claims that a good imitation of an unpleasing object may be beautiful, though that of a pleasing object will be more so. Like Burke,

[39] *Enquiry*, pp. 104–7.

[40] For a similar classification see Kames, *Elements of Criticism* (Edinburgh, 7th edn., 1788), I, 197.

[41] *Inquiry*, pp. 15–16.

[42] *Ibid.*, p. 35.

indeed, Hutcheson repeats many commonplaces on the subject of imitation.[43]

Burke's attitude to "deformity" is anticipated by Hutcheson who defines it as "only *the absence of Beauty*, or *deficiency in the Beauty expected in any Species*".[44] More important, however, is his anticipation of Burke's views on association. We are reminded of Burke's "Essay on Taste" by Hutcheson's argument that there is a fundamental conformity in men's conception of beauty, and of the *Enquiry* itself when he asserts that association of ideas is not the cause of beauty, though it may enrich, or even warp, our perception of beauty.[45] Hutcheson admits that it may be the effect of education, custom, or prejudice which prevents our recognizing certain types of beauty, but, for all that, "there is a *natural* Power of *Perception*, or *Sense of Beauty* in Objects, antecedent to all *Custom*, *Education*, or *Example*."[46] That Burke concurred in these views may be seen from the distinction he draws between "the natural and the acquired relish" in his introductory "Essay".[47]

On many important matters Hutcheson and Burke are poles apart. Burke, for example, does not give his allegiance to the principle of "Uniformity amidst Variety"; he does not connect beauty with moral perfection; nor would he see any beauty in the geometrical figures so pleasing to Hutcheson. But there are similarities in their approach to the subject. Both writers feel that it is an evasion of the central issue to rely on associationist theories in a discussion of beauty. Further, each in his own way tries to avoid non-aesthetic considerations and to keep strictly to the aesthetic.

Hutcheson and Shaftesbury were answered by Berkeley in his *Alciphron, or the Minute Philosopher* (1732),[48] but this work is of little significance here. It is interesting because it shows as very much alive the theories of proportion and fitness which Alciphron is forced to accept in the course of the dialogue. Burke was not, indeed, beating his wings in the void.

A slight work which requires a passing reference is Joseph Spence's *Crito: Or, A Dialogue on Beauty*.[49] Spence confines his

[43] Cf. *Enquiry*, pp. 49–50. [44] *Inquiry*, p. 66. [45] *Ibid.*, pp. 68–70, 76–7. [46] *Ibid.*, p. 79. [47] *Enquiry*, pp. 14–15. [48] *Works* (Oxford, 1901), Vol. II. [49] Spence wrote under the name of Sir Harry Beaumont.

attention to "personal, or human Beauty", treating it under four heads: "Color, Form, Expression, and Grace". With many of his remarks Burke would not agree: Spence regards the general cause of beauty as "a Proportion, or an Union and Harmony, in all Parts of the Body";[50] he considers "an Idea of Usefulness" important;[51] and he is convinced that the beauty of virtue is supreme.[52] To speak of indebtedness on Burke's part might, then, appear rash, but there are minor similarities between his sections on "The Physiognomy", "The Eye", and "Grace",[53] and Spence's comments on Expression and Grace.[54] Moreover, *Crito* was published in London in 1752 when Burke was engaged there with the writing of his *Enquiry*.

Another problem concerning Burke's debts to earlier writers is raised by the last work to be treated, Hogarth's *Analysis of Beauty*. Despite Burke's error (noted at the outset) in asserting that the *Enquiry* was finished in 1753, it may well be that the main body of the writing was completed by that date, and his main principles were established long before.[55] There was, then, scarcely time for Hogarth's work, appearing in 1753, to be directly influential. Burke's tone in a passage added to the second edition of the *Enquiry* probably gives us the answer:

> It gives me no small pleasure to find that I can strengthen my theory in this point [of gradual variation], by the opinion of the very ingenious Mr. Hogarth.[56]

It seems likely that Burke did not discover the *Analysis of Beauty* until either his own work was complete in manuscript and awaiting a publisher, or the first edition was actually set up in type; he was then heartened to find some of his own theories confirmed by the experienced artist. But whatever the truth may be about "indebtedness", Hogarth's book anticipates some of his ideas.

It has already been observed that while, unlike Burke, Hogarth sees fitness as centrally important, he anticipates him

[50] *Op. cit.*, p. 12. [51] *Ibid.*, p. 47. [52] *Ibid.*, p. 58.

[53] *Enquiry*, pp. 118–119. [54] *Op. cit.*, p. 19 ff.

[55] Cf. Burke's comment (*Enquiry*, p. 168): "Since I wrote these papers I found. . . ."

[56] *Enquiry*, p. 115.

in rejecting the notion that mathematical proportion is a cause of beauty.[57] Their main point of agreement, however, may be shown most clearly by setting side by side passages from both writers. Burke, introducing his section on "Gradual Variation", makes this comment:

But as perfectly beautiful bodies are not composed of angular parts, so their parts never continue long in the same right line. They vary their direction every moment, and they change under the eye by a deviation continually carrying on, but for whose beginning or end you will find it difficult to ascertain a point.[58]

Hogarth argues that an active mind enjoys the pursuit of an elusive object, and that this kind of enjoyment may be part of the pleasure given by beauty:

The eye hath this sort of enjoyment in winding walks, and serpentine rivers, and all sorts of objects, whose forms, as we shall see hereafter, are composed principally of what, I call, the *waving* and *serpentine* lines.

Intricacy in form, therefore, I shall define to be that peculiarity in the lines, which compose it, that *leads the eye a wanton kind of chase*, and from the pleasure that it gives the mind, intitles it to the name of beautiful.[59]

Both writers are clearly maintaining that a constituent of beauty is the kind of stimulating variety which neither completely baffles the mind, nor degenerates into repetitive symmetry. Hogarth centres his argument on what he calls the "line of beauty". This, a waving line with two contrasted curves, allows us to account "*lineally*" for the ugliness of objects without the line and for "the different degrees of beauty belonging to those objects that possess it".[60] Undoubtedly, in his comments on female beauty, Burke is close to the principle invoked by Hogarth:

Observe that part of a beautiful woman where she is perhaps the most beautiful, about the neck and breasts; the smoothness; the softness; the easy and insensible swell; the variety of the surface, which is never for the smallest space the same; the deceitful maze,

57 See p. lxii. 58 *Enquiry*, pp. 114–15. 59 *Analysis of Beauty*, p. 25.
60 *Ibid.*, p. 50.

through which the unsteady eye slides giddily, without knowing where to fix, or whither it is carried.[61]

The two writers part company when Burke protests against Hogarth's tendency to systematize his theory too rigidly: "there is no particular line which is always found in the most completely beautiful; and which is therefore beautiful in preference to all other lines."[62] There are, however, a few other minor points of contact between them. Both writers agree that difficulty is mentally stimulating and pleasurable;[63] Hogarth considers "smoothness" important in human beauty, where Burke claims that it is an essential quality in beauty of all kinds;[64] and, finally, both men assert that distinctness, clarity, variety, and intricacy are qualities of the colouring associated with beautiful objects.[65]

Despite such points of agreement, this brief survey of Burke's predecessors in the eighteenth-century debate on beauty reveals but few instances of possible indebtedness on his part: it shows more clearly how markedly he departs from orthodoxy. He is alone in his uncompromising sensationism; his description of the qualities of beautiful objects in Part III of the *Enquiry*, and his analysis of the causes of aesthetic experiences, in Part IV, are wholly in terms of the senses. Consequently Burke avoids "that vague and mysterious phraseology concerning Beauty in general, in which so many of [his] predecessors delighted",[66] but he is also led into numerous fallacies and absurdities.

He examines, one by one, the qualities of beautiful objects, beginning with those which are "taken in by the eye". This emphasis on sight puts him in the tradition of Aristotle (who claims sight as the most important organ of knowledge), Locke (who considers it "the most comprehensive of all our senses"),[67] and Addison (whose description of the importance of sight closely echoes Locke's).[68] The visible qualities of beauty are

[61] *Enquiry*, p. 115.
[62] *Ibid.*, pp. 115–16.
[63] *Ibid.*, p. 77; *Analysis*, p. 24.
[64] *Enquiry*, p. 114; *Analysis*, pp. 59–60.
[65] *Enquiry*, p. 117; *Analysis*, p. 117.
[66] D. Stewart, *Philosophical Essays*, pp. 280–1.
[67] *Essay*, II, ix, 9.
[68] *Spectator* No. 411.

those of smoothness,[69] smallness, subtle variation, delicacy (which includes fragility and weakness), mild colours, and, in human beauty, gentleness of face, languor, and graceful posture. Burke then asserts that the other senses respond to beauty in a similar way: the touch to softness, smoothness, and gradual variation, the hearing to sounds which are "clear, even, smooth, and weak", and so forth.

Burke's object in this examination (which avoids absurdity more effectively than the later analysis of causes) is threefold: the first, obviously, is to determine what are the sensible qualities in objects we call beautiful; the second is to establish that these qualities "on which beauty depends . . . operate by nature, and are less liable to be altered by caprice, or confounded by a diversity of tastes, than any others";[70] and the third object is to show that the senses all conform "in the article of their pleasures"—

> There is a chain in all our sensations; they are all but different sorts of feeling, calculated to be affected by various sorts of objects, but all to be affected after the same manner.[71]

The first object requires no further comment; the second relies on the validity of Burke's arguments in the "Essay on Taste" and Part I of the *Enquiry*; but the third breaks new ground. It is of major significance in the history of aesthetics since it prompts the first thorough-going treatment of what is now termed "synaesthesia", the process by which a perception by one sense causes the other senses to react sympathetically, resulting in a complex but harmonious experience on the part of all. While Burke was the first to incorporate a treatment of this experience in a systematic aesthetic theory,[72] interest in it was common. Newton claimed to have co-ordinated the primary colours with the notes of the octave; Locke (among others) told of the blind man who compared the colour scarlet to the sound of a trumpet;

[69] Although Burke claims (p. 114) that no previous writer had included smoothness as a quality of beautiful objects, Socrates makes the suggestive remark that "Beauty is certainly a soft, smooth, slippery thing, . . . which easily slips in and permeates our souls" (Plato, *Lysis*, 216).

[70] *Enquiry*, p. 117.

[71] *Ibid.*, p. 120.

[72] This claim is made in spite of Addison's recognition that the "ideas" of two senses "recommend each other" (*Spectator* No. 412).

and Père Louis Castel exhibited in London in 1757 (and in France twenty-two years earlier) his "colour organ" by which the deaf might "see the music of the ears", the blind hear "the music of the eyes", and normal people might "enjoy music and colours better by enjoying them both at the same time".[73] The interest in synaesthesia led, then, to some absurdities, but it also induced an increased awareness of the complexity of the aesthetic experience. This awareness, in turn, allowed of more immediacy in poetic expression, a daring imaginative fusion of sensuous experiences. Akenside had already written—

So while we taste the fragrance of the rose,
Glows not her blush the fairer—

and Thomson, "taste the smell of dairy", but it was only with Keats and his "embalmed darkness", "delicious moan", and "velvet summersong", and the like, that the new awareness was most audaciously exploited.

This keen interest in sensory activity is further illustrated by a post-Newtonian obsession with light and colour among eighteenth-century poets, and "also a growing interest in light and color in connection with the 'Sublime' and 'Beautiful' which came to a climax in Burke's *Enquiry*".[74] The association of intense light with the sublime is first found there, and when Burke links mild colours with beauty he is systematizing what Thomson had done in practice and Akenside had hinted at in his *Pleasures of Imagination.* Thomson beautifies Spring with mild colours and delicate tints; Akenside is consistent in linking colour with beauty; but it is not until the *Enquiry* that colour plays an integral part in a full-scale theory of beauty. It cannot be argued that Burke's section on "Beauty in Colour" depends directly on earlier poets and theorists; nor would it be justified to label Burke an eclectic; for, while agreeing with the tenor of

[73] See Erika von Erhardt-Siebold, "Harmony of the Senses in English, German, and French Romanticism", *P.M.L.A.* (1932), XLVII, 578. I am also indebted here to W. J. Bate, *From Classic to Romantic*, and M. H. Nicolson, *Newton Demands the Muse* (Princeton, 1946).

[74] M. H. Nicolson, *Newton Demands the Muse*, p. 4. Professor Nicolson's book gives a masterly account of this "obsession".

earlier writings, this one section is primarily dependent on, and wholly consistent with, the principles guiding his general analysis of beauty.

Burke's chief weakness in working out his sensationist theory is due to the sharp distinction he draws between the sublime and the beautiful. By reserving to sublimity all that is impressive and awe-inspiring, he robs beauty of any power to be intensely moving, and leaves it a weak and sentimentalized conception. Beauty becomes, in fact, mere prettiness. Later critics did not hesitate to point out that "the idea of *female beauty* was evidently uppermost in Mr. Burke's mind when he wrote his book."[75] Payne Knight observes that a temporary fashion among women, "of false delicacy and affected timidity prevailed at the time the treatise in question was published", and may have influenced Burke's conception of beauty.[76] If this is valid Burke stands condemned for failing to recognize transient superficialities. A further suggestion is that he may have been swayed by the type of beauty he saw in Jane Nugent, afterwards his wife. In a prose "character" by Burke she is said to have eyes with "a mild light", features which are not "animated", a "Delicacy that does not Exclude firmness, . . . the softness that does not imply weakness", and a voice (like Cordelia's) whose tone is "low" and "soft".[77] Whatever the truth may be, Payne Knight argues correctly that the qualities Burke attributes to beauty are insipid, and that we are not disposed to love a beautiful object by the pity it arouses.[78]

Knight also points to a contributory weakness in Burke's theorizing: his tendency to deduce general principles from particular truths. For example, he regards weakness as part of female beauty and therefore assumes that delicacy is an element in beauty.[79] Or again, from the use of diminutives

[75] D. Stewart, *Philosophical Essays*, p. 297 n. See also an ironic description of Burke's "Taste for Women" in [F. Plumer], *Letter from a Gentleman to his Nephew at Oxford* (1772), p. 15.

[76] *Analytical Inquiry*, III, i, 34. Cf. *Spectator* No. 492 for comments on fashionable women who lisp, trip, weep, and are frighted.

[77] D. Wecter, "The Missing Years in Edmund Burke's Biography", *P.M.L.A.*, LIII, 1114.

[78] *Op. cit.*, I, v, 22; III, i, 32.

[79] *Ibid.*, III, i, 34.

Burke deduces the general law that beautiful objects are small, but Knight observes that where no affectionate relationship exists between two people (as in the case of terms like "lordling" or "witling") no such generalization is valid.[80]

There is little point in emphasizing the absurdities into which Burke is led when, in Part IV, he explains the cause of beauty. Again, from the somewhat ludicrous description of the man under the influence of love, he establishes the general law "that beauty acts by relaxing the solids of the whole system . . . and a relaxation somewhat below the natural tone [is] the cause of all positive pleasure."[81] Thus, claiming that smoothness is relaxing, he accounts for the "beautiful of taste" by arguing that sweetness of liquids results from their smoothness and softness, and from the globular shape of the sugar particles which cause pleasurable sensations and relaxation in "the nervous papillae of that nice organ the tongue".[82] This explanation may, as Stewart remarks,

> be valued chiefly as an illustration of the absurdities in which men of the most exalted genius are sure to involve themselves, the moment they lose sight, in their inquiries concerning the Human Mind, of the sober rules of experimental science.[83]

While, therefore, Burke's theory of beauty is, intrinsically, of slight importance, historically it is of great interest. He compelled his age to reconsider attitudes and aesthetic values which had been unquestioningly accepted; even though the age refused to follow his sensationist lead, at least subsequent theorists could not readily assume an unbroken tradition of orthodoxy. If nothing more, Burke succeeded in stirring the waters of criticism which had tended to stagnate.

(iv) *On Words*

"The account of words and images given in the concluding section of 'On the Sublime' is to a modern reader the most interesting part of Burke's inquiry."[1] If the modern reader is looking for intrinsic, as distinct from historical, value, this

80 *Op. cit.*, II, ii, 107. 81 *Enquiry*, pp. 149–50. 82 *Ibid.*, p. 153.
83 *Philosophical Essays*, p. 294.
1 G. McKenzie, *Critical Responsiveness*, p. 246.

comment may well be true; yet, apart from one or two exceptions,[2] critics fail to give adequate attention to the final, brief section of Burke's work.

In this section (Part V) which is organic to the whole treatise, Burke considers the power of language to evoke beauty and sublimity, and the manner of its operation.[3] Looking back to his bold remark, "a clear idea is another name for a little idea", to the section on obscurity, and, implicitly, to that on infinity, he contends that the emotive power of language is not proportionate to its image-raising capacity; further, he argues that, whereas "a clear expression" appeals to the understanding by its description of the object as it really is, "a strong expression" appeals to the emotions by its description of the object "as it is felt". This last, he would claim, is applicable to the language of poetry. (He also extends the application of this truth to rhetoric: the traditional link between poetry and rhetoric is evident throughout the *Enquiry*.)

Burke's principal contention is, if not entirely original,[4] phrased and argued in an audacious and revolutionary manner. He represents a reaction against the distrust of language among post-Baconian writers in the previous century, against their desire to evolve a language in which words would simply be marks of things and in which emotional and historical associations would be non-existent.[5] How markedly Burke departs from the contemporary view that the power of poetry depends on specific imagery is best seen by a comparison with two representative statements. Arthur Murphy, in his review of the *Enquiry*, makes this comment:

He who is most picturesque and clearest in his imagery, is ever

[2] E.g. McKenzie, *op. cit.*; D. Wecter, "Burke's Theory concerning Words, Images, and Emotion", *P.M.L.A.* (1940), LV, 167–81.

[3] It should be noted how ready Burke is at all times to draw on linguistic usage to support other arguments, e.g. pp. 58, 113, 154.

[4] Addison makes a suggestion along similar lines, but does not elaborate or express it forcibly. See *Spectator* No. 416. See also Wecter, *op. cit.*, pp. 174–7, for Burke's limited debt to Berkeley's *Treatise concerning the Principles of Human Knowledge* (1710).

[5] See R. Jones, "Science and Language in England of the Mid-Seventeenth Century", *J.E.G.P.* (1932), XXXI, 315–31.

stiled the best poet, because from such a one we see things clearer, and of course we feel more intensely.[6]

The demand for accurate and specific detail is taken further by the later writer, Joseph Warton:

The use, the force and the excellence of language, certainly consists in raising *clear*, *complete*, and *circumstantial* images, and in turning *readers* into *spectators*.[7]

Burke, on the contrary, asserts:

there are words, and certain dispositions of words, which being peculiarly devoted to passionate subjects, and always used by those who are under the influence of any passion . . . touch and move us more than those which far more clearly and distinctly express the subject matter. We yield to sympathy, what we refuse to description.[8]

More, then, than those of his contemporaries, Burke's theory looks forward tentatively to Wordsworth and Coleridge with their insistence that language, and poetic imagery, must be modified by intense and relevant emotion before poetry can be great. It may be related at a further remove (only, admittedly, as a prophetic view) to Day Lewis's quarrel, in *The Poetic Image*, with T. E. Hulme's claim that the aim of poetry is "accurate, precise and definite description". "Precision is not everything", says Day Lewis;[9] "the truth is", says Burke,

all verbal description, merely as naked description, though never so exact, conveys so poor and insufficient an idea of the thing described, that it could scarcely have the smallest effect, if the speaker did not call in to his aid those modes of speech that mark a strong and lively feeling in himself. Then, by the contagion of our passions, we catch a fire already kindled in another, which probably might never have been struck out by the object described.[10]

[6] *Literary Magazine* (1757), II, 188.

[7] *Essay on the Genius and Writings of Pope* (4th edn., 1782), II, 165. Cf. *ibid.*, I, 48: "A minute and particular enumeration of circumstances judiciously selected, is what chiefly discriminates poetry from history, and renders the former, for that reason, a more close and faithful representation of nature than the latter." (Cited McKenzie, *op. cit.*, pp. 243–4.)

[8] *Enquiry*, p. 175. [9] *Op. cit.* (1947), p. 24. [10] *Enquiry*, pp. 175–6.

Burke begins his examination of words and images by classifying the former into three types: "aggregate" (a complex term such as "man" or "horse", the natural fusion of several simple ideas); "simple abstract" (one simple idea, such as "red" or "round", used in forming an "aggregate"); and "compounded abstract" (an arbitrary union of the other two types to form concepts like "virtue" or "persuasion"). It is a classification which seems to have been based on Locke's division of words into modes, substances, and relations.[11] From this beginning, Burke argues that in the hurry of conversation we neither can nor need to analyse the complexes of thought which words represent, and that therefore we respond to words without any specific images being called up in the mind. When he tries to account for the effect of words, though he does not use the term "association", he relies on an associationist explanation. Habit, he claims, causes automatic responses prompted, not by the image first associated with any particular word, but by the emotion which accompanied our first encounter with it and which the sound continues to evoke. As evidence Burke cites a prose passage, apparently from a geographical text-book, which is calculated to produce the desired effect—that of leaving the reader unaffected. He also quotes the examples of Blacklock and Saunderson who, though blind, responded to the names of colours. Considering his claim proved, Burke then passes to poetry and asserts that its effect too is independent of sensible images being aroused.

The position thus (however strangely) attained, Burke proceeds to make some perceptive observations. He omits, of course, many vital factors. He forgets, for example, that the argument about the effect of language in hurried conversation does not necessarily apply to the reading of poetry. Again, linked with this error, he fails to recognize that the poet compels us to reassess stereotyped responses to language by using fresh, vivid, and startling images. His failings are, indeed, only too obvious. Nevertheless, some remarks are prophetic. Burke's contention, for instance, that a poetic description does not require that a series of emotive phrases be linked together after the fashion of a representation in painting (or, one assumes, in

[11] *Essay*, II, xii ff. See Wecter, *op. cit.*, *P.M.L.A.*, LV, 169–72

prose) points forward to Browning[12] and to the practice of modern poets. Again, when he attributes the effect of poetic language to original combinations of ideas, to the power of sympathetic emotion and of suggestion, Burke shows himself aware that such language functions simultaneously on more than one level: it can convey descriptive information; at the same time it suggests the emotional relationship which exists between the writer and the object.[13] For Burke the second feature is crucial. Poetry and rhetoric, he claims,

> do not succeed in exact description so well as painting does; their business is to affect rather by sympathy than imitation; to display rather the effect of things on the mind of the speaker, or of others, than to present a clear idea of the things themselves. This is their most extensive province, and that in which they succeed the best.[14]

In this insistence on the prime importance of emotional relationship and not on descriptive detail for its own sake, we have a critical principle which anticipates tentatively the (certainly more profound) remark by Coleridge on imagery:

> images, however beautiful . . . do not of themselves characterize the poet. They become proofs of original genius only as far as they are modified by a predominant passion; or by associated thoughts or images awakened by that passion.[15]

Almost invariably throughout the *Enquiry* Burke is principally concerned with the responses of the human mind to

[12] Cf. Letter to Ruskin, 10 Dec. 1855: "I *know* that I don't make out my conception by my language; all poetry being a putting the infinite within the finite. You would have me paint it all plain out, which can't be; but by various artifices I try to make shift with touches and bits of outlines which *succeed* if they bear the conception from me to you. You ought, I think, to keep pace with the thought tripping from ledge to ledge of my 'glaciers', as you call them; not stand poking your alpenstock into the holes, and demonstrating that no foot could have stood there;—suppose it sprang over there? In *prose* you may criticize so . . . but in asking more of *ultimates* you must accept less *mediates*." (W. Collingwood, *Life of Ruskin*, 1900, p. 164.)

[13] *Enquiry*, pp. 173–4.

[14] *Ibid.*, p. 172.

[15] *Biographia Literaria*, ed. J. Shawcross (Oxford, 1907), II, 16. Cf. also Hazlitt, "On Poetry in General": "[The imaginative language of poetry] is not the less true to nature, because it is false in point of fact; but so much the more true and natural, if it conveys the impression which the object under the influence of passion makes on the mind." (*Works*, ed. P. P. Howe, 1930, V, 4.)

emotive objects and experiences. This is true of his account of the sublime and beautiful: it is equally true of the section on words. He does not require that poetry should excite "clear" ideas so as to make no demands on the reader; he realizes that such ideas may, as Day Lewis remarks, be so accurate as to be "*dead* accurate".[16] What Burke looks for is that the reader should "catch a fire already kindled in another, which probably might never have been struck out by the object described." It is perhaps not surprising, then, that the demand he makes of poetry should fairly describe the achievement of one of his own celebrated prose passages: the apostrophe to the Queen in the *Reflections*. While it might be argued unkindly that some of his remarks on bombast in the *Enquiry* should be applied to parts of the apostrophe, it remains true that his comments on Homer's description of Helen are applicable (with a change of name only) to his own evocation of Marie Antoinette:

> Here is not one word said of the particulars of her beauty; no thing which can in the least help us to any precise idea of her person; but yet we are much more touched by this manner of mentioning her than by these long and laboured descriptions of Helen, whether handed down by tradition, or formed by fancy, which are to be met with in some authors.[17]

The section on words provides, therefore, an organic and stimulating conclusion to Burke's *Enquiry*. It forms, certainly, part of a general examination of language and its uses being made during the century, but it makes suggestions—of potential if not immediate value—which transcend the restrictions imposed by tradition on the majority of critics.

IV. INFLUENCE

(i) *England*

Johnson: " We have an example of true criticism in Burke's 'Essay on the Sublime and Beautiful'."[1]

16 *The Poetic Image*, p. 24.

17 *Enquiry*, p. 172. For a description of Marie Antoinette which, more than Burke's, relies on physical details, see J. Weber, *Mémoires* (1822), I, 25–6. (Cited by E. L. Higgins, *The French Revolution as told by Contemporaries* (1939) p. 12.)

1 J. Boswell, *Life of Johnson* (ed. Hill and Powell, 1934), II, 90.

Uvedale Price: "I am certainly convinced of the general truth and accuracy of Mr. Burke's system, for it is the foundation of my own."[2]

Payne Knight: ". . . except [Uvedale Price] I have never met with any man of learning, by whom the philosophy of the *Inquiry into the Sublime and Beautiful* was not as much despised and ridiculed, as the brilliancy and animation of its style were applauded, and admired."[3]

Blake: "Burke's Treatise on the Sublime & Beautiful is founded on the Opinions of Newton & Locke; on this Treatise Reynolds has grounded many of his assertions in all his Discourses. I read Burke's Treatise when very Young . . . I felt the same Contempt & Abhorrence then that I do now. They [Bacon, Locke, Burke, and Reynolds] mock Inspiration & Vision."[4]

Burke's *Enquiry* was not, it seems, received with equanimity: either approbation or marked disapproval were aroused, not mere indifference. All these comments emphasize that Burke presented a challenge both to his contemporaries and to his successors: as late as 1810 Dugald Stewart considered it essential to examine the *Enquiry* in order "to remove the chief stumbling-blocks, which a theory, recommended by so illustrious a name, has thrown in my way."[5] While the lustre attaching to Burke's name in the early nineteenth century did not stem from the *Enquiry*, nevertheless this work could not simply be ignored over fifty years after its first appearance. Still later, Thomas Hardy found in it a source of imaginative stimulus and G. H. Lewes, in *The Principles of Success in Literature* (1898), was prompted to take issue with Burke's theories of obscurity and indistinctness of imagery.[6] Finally, on the Continent, with Lessing and Kant, Burke's challenge was readily acknowledged and accepted.

Yet, it must be said at once, that among those of his contemporaries and successors who carried on the debate on beauty and sublimity and allied topics, Burke's theories caused scarcely a tremor. He was as isolated in his originality and boldness as

[2] *Essays on the Picturesque* (1810), I, 92–3.
[3] *Analytical Inquiry*, III, i, 59.
[4] *Works* (Nonesuch, 1948), p. 809.
[5] *Philosophical Essays*, p. 286.
[6] *Op. cit.* (n.d.), pp. 68–74.

he was by his extreme sensationism. Those writers who followed were as orthodox in their elaboration of traditional theories as they were unexceptionable in the expression of their views. Moreover, their tendency to eclecticism gives them the appearance of moderation in contrast to the extreme, if original, positions into which Burke was led by his faith in one daringly simple principle.

Gerard and Kames may be termed "contemporaries" of Burke: Gerard's *Essay on Taste* appeared too late to influence the *Enquiry*; Kames's *Elements of Criticism*, though not published until 1761, was partly written and possibly wholly planned before Burke's work could have exerted any influence.[7] Among Burke's successors may be included such writers as Blair, Beattie, Alison, Payne Knight, and Stewart. An exhaustive study of the works of these men would—besides being tedious—be of little value since they take such little notice of the basic principles of the *Enquiry*. Some points must, however, be made to stress Burke's isolation from those who may loosely be called English philosophical writers.

Sensationism is not favoured by any one of them: for all of them, in varying degrees, association is the important factor in aesthetic experiences. Gerard gives prominence to this principle as the major element in the perception of beauty;[8] Kames, while he adopts the phrase, "train of ideas", in preference to "association of ideas", falls back on Hume's principle of association to explain the connection of ideas;[9] Beattie acknowledges Gerard as his master and follows the well-trodden associationist path; and Alison is undoubtedly the extreme associationist among Burke's successors. He arrives at the bold conclusion that, because we have certain associations with the principal qualities of matter, "when the Material Qualities cease to be significant of the Associated Qualities, they cease also to produce the Emotions of Sublimity or Beauty."[10] Payne Knight, for his part, reacts strongly against Alison's theory, but is driven to admit that the single sensation can hardly ever be considered in isolation because it is always (particularly when

[7] See *op. cit.*, I, 313 n.

[8] *Essay on Taste*, p. 49 ff.

[9] *Elements of Criticism*, I, 17 ff.

[10] *Essays on the Nature and Principles of Taste* (Edinburgh, 1790), p. 410.

the individual's experience increases with age) mixed with "associated ideas".[11] Rejecting Burke's sensationism (Payne Knight most vociferously), all these writers concur in their acceptance of associationism. They do, indeed, cumulatively and progressively deepen our understanding of aesthetic perception, but, inevitably, they rely on their predecessors more slavishly than was ever possible for Burke.

His theory of beauty had almost as little influence on later philosophical writers as his sensationism. Possibly as a reply to Burke, Reynolds maintains, in *Idler* No. 82, that the beauty which a painter should reproduce is found in the norm of each species; he should copy the "fixed or determinate form" which nature realizes in each species, and not the deformities and minute irregularities which occur in reality.[12] Reynolds, in fact, sees beauty where Burke finds mediocrity. Kames is equally orthodox. Beauty for him is either intrinsic or relative: when he discusses the former he relies on the established ideas of uniformity and variety, symmetry and proportion; relative beauty, he claims, depends on a recognition of the utility or associated significance of an object.[13] The outstanding plagiarist of the group, Hugh Blair, relies on orthodox theories but is sceptical of the existence of a single principle which will account for all types of beauty.[14] All the traditional commonplaces of association, regularity, variety, fitness, and the rest are used by Blair, but he makes no attempt to formulate a unified theory. Instead, he regards "beauty" as a comprehensive term given to several distinct qualities. The same disinclination to emphasize the formal elements of beauty is found among associationists like Payne Knight and Stewart. Symmetry, fitness, proportion, and other accepted principles recur time and again, but they lose their central importance under the levelling influence of association. Stewart, for example, claims (like Blair) that "beauty" applies to many different qualities rather than one in particular, and he charges Burke with confining his attention to elements of intrinsic beauty and ignoring relative

[11] E.g. *Analytical Inquiry*, II, ii, 44.

[12] Cf. *ibid.*, I, v, 23. (Knight's reference to *Idler* No. 8 is erroneous.)

[13] *Elements of Criticism*, I, 197 ff.

[14] *Lectures on Rhetoric and Belles Lettres* (1839), p. 52.

beauty altogether.[15] (Stewart's adoption of Kames's division of beauty into intrinsic and relative illustrates yet again the eclectic tendencies of these writers.)

This marked eclecticism prompts, of course, the borrowing of some points from Burke's *Enquiry*. Beattie and Blair provide unmistakable evidence. Beattie clearly recognized the importance of the *Enquiry* and, on one occasion, acknowledges his debt to it. He argues that poetic descriptions should not relate facts merely to give information, "but to awaken the passions, and captivate the imagination". He adds that minute descriptions are not effective, especially if lengthy, and then goes on:

> It has been justly remarked by the best critics, that, in the descriptions of great objects, a certain degree of obscurity, not in the language, but in the picture or notion presented to the mind, has sometimes a happy effect in producing admiration, terror, and other emotions connected with the sublime.[16]

Burke is acknowledged, in a note, as one of "the best critics". It is almost certain that Beattie is indebted to him on other occasions, but no further acknowledgments are made. The *Enquiry* seems to lie behind the following passage, for example:

> *Sweetness* of tone, and beauty of shape and colour, produce a placid acquiescence of mind, accompanied with some degree of joy, which plays in a gentle smile upon the countenance of the hearer and beholder. *Equable* sounds, like smooth and level surfaces, are in general more pleasing than such as are rough, uneven, or interrupted; yet, as the flowing curve, so essential to elegance of figure, and so conspicuous in the outlines of beautiful animals, is delightful to the eye; so notes *gradually swelling*, and *gradually decaying*, have an agreeable effect on the ear, and on the mind; the former tending to rouse the faculties, and the latter to compose them; the one promoting gentle exercise, and the other rest.[17]

The stress here on smoothness of sound, the comparison between aural and tactile smoothness—in fact, the principle of synaesthesia—the suggestion that roughness interrupts the pleasure

[15] *Philosophical Essays*, pp. 308–9.

[16] *Essays: on Poetry and Music, as they affect the mind* (Edinburgh, 1778), p. 100.

[17] *Ibid.*, p. 151.

associated with beauty, and the emphasis on gradual variation, all point to Burke as the source of the ideas.[18] In his *Dissertations Moral and Critical* Beattie arouses further suspicions of unacknowledged debts. He begins his "Illustrations on Sublimity" with the complaint that Longinus does not distinguish between beauty and sublimity: "The distinction, however, ought to be made."[19] From here he argues that the distinguishing mark of the sublime is "whatever awakens in us . . . pleasurable astonishment", and he illustrates his remark by Milton's Satan.[20] Beattie next considers the pleasurable effect of horror; he is certain that such pleasure is aroused—"Why do people run to see battles, executions, and shipwrecks?"—and accounts for it on the grounds of curiosity and a type of "terrifick pleasure".[21] He discusses the effect of darkness and silence,[22] of sublime music which produces "pleasing horror", and of poetry which, "without any great pomp of images or of words, infuses horror by a happy choice of circumstances".[23] Every one of these ideas was to be found in the *Enquiry*. Later, Beattie quotes the same biblical description of the horse as does Burke,[24] and is clearly indebted to him for the idea of poetical suggestiveness.[25] Finally, when insisting that some indefiniteness in poetic imagery is often desirable, Beattie writes thus:

> Of Helen's person [Homer] gives no minute account: but, when he tells us, that her loveliness was such as to extort the admiration of the *oldest* Trojan senators, . . . he gives a higher idea of the power of her charms, than could have been conveyed by any description of her eyes, mouth, shape, and other distinguishing beauties.[26]

Not only does this follow Burke in content and intention, it almost reproduces his phrasing.

There can be little doubt, therefore, but that Beattie was heavily indebted to Burke. His example (supported, as it will

[18] Cf. *Enquiry*, pp. 114–16, 121–3, 151.
[19] *Op. cit.* (Dublin, 1783), II, 359.
[20] *Ibid.*, II, 368.
[21] *Ibid.*, II, 372. Cf. *Enquiry*, pp. 47–8.
[22] *Ibid.*, II, 372–3. Cf. *Enquiry*, pp. 71, 143–4.
[23] *Ibid.*, II, 383. Cf. *Enquiry*, pp. 82, 173–5.
[24] *Ibid.*, II, 389. Cf. *Enquiry*, pp. 65–6.
[25] *Ibid.*, II, 405. Cf. *Enquiry*, pp. 174–6.
[26] *Ibid.*, II, 406 n. Cf. *Enquiry*, pp. 171–2.

be, by Blair's) suggests that while theorists who followed Burke did not accept his central, sensationist principle, they were ready enough to pillage his work for new ideas.

The relationship between Burke and Blair has already received some attention from T. R. Henn in *Longinus and English Criticism* (1934). Blair, it is claimed there, "was to be followed blindly by Burke", and also, "it will be seen that Burke has taken over many of [Blair's] ideas and quotations almost word for word, although [Mr. Henn] can find no acknowledgment in that writer."[27] The reason for the failure to find acknowledgment is not hard to explain since the reverse is true: Blair borrowed extensively from Burke. A comparison of dates would have prevented the error: Blair's lectures were delivered from 1759 onwards[28] and published in 1783; Burke's *Enquiry* appeared in 1757. Moreover, Blair expressly states in his preface that he has used "the ideas and reflections of others" as well as his own—to do so seemed to him part of the duty of a "public professor"—and on four occasions he refers to Burke's treatise by name.[29]

Blair specifically discusses Burke's ideas of the sublime. He admits that he has adopted many of Burke's "sentiments" but considers that to account for the sublime "wholly in modes of danger, or of pain" is too sweeping.[30] Rather he prefers, apparently, to rely on Baillie who had emphasized the importance of "Power". Blair claims that

> mighty force or power, whether accompanied with terror or not, whether employed in protecting or in alarming us, has a better title, than any thing that has yet been mentioned, to be the fundamental quality of the sublime.

Nevertheless, Blair does not hesitate to repeat, without specific acknowledgment, several of the "ingenious and original thoughts" which, he says, we find in Burke. Burke had asserted that "the noise of vast cataracts, raging storms, thunder, or artillery, awakes a great and aweful sensation in the mind. . . .

[27] *Op. cit.*, pp. 109, 107.

[28] *Lectures on Rhetoric and Belles Lettres*, p. 2 n.

[29] *Ibid.*, pp. 11 n., 30 n., 35–6, 51 n.

[30] *Ibid.*, p. 36.

The shouting of multitudes has a similar effect";[31] Blair's version is that "the burst of thunder or of cannon, the roaring of winds, the shouting of multitudes, the sound of vast cataracts of water, are all incontestably grand objects."[32] As examples of power Blair, following Burke, quotes the lion and the horse "whose neck is clothed with thunder" [33] Burke lists "*Darkness, Solitude*, and *Silence*" as "*general* privations" which are great because terrible; Blair imitates him exactly, quoting the same Virgilian illustration and the translations of the passage by Dryden and Pitt.[34] He repeats Burke's ideas on obscurity, quoting his exact words—as those of "an ingenious author"—that "it is one thing to make an idea clear, and another to make it affecting to the imagination", and his illustration from *Job*.[35] Similarly, Blair takes over Burke's ideas on the part played in sublimity by infinity, irregularity, and greatness of dimension.[36] While, as already observed, Blair does not accept any single principle as the cause of beauty, he—like Burke—clearly regards the emotion aroused by beauty as being much less intense than that excited by sublimity. He speaks of "objects that are merely beautiful, gay, or elegant", as distinct from those which "raise ideas of that elevating, that awful and magnificent kind, which we call Sublime".[37] And a similar distinction obviously lies behind the following passage:

> What are the scenes of nature that elevate the mind in the highest degree, and produce the sublime sensation? Not the gay landscape, the flowery field, or the flourishing city; but the hoary mountain, and the solitary lake; the aged forest, and the torrent falling over the rock.[38]

Yet, despite this evidence of undeniable, though unacknowledged, borrowing, Burke's theory of beauty found no agreement among his contemporaries and no fundamental acceptance among his successors. The same is true of his theory of the sublime. Gerard and Kames tend to follow the lead given by

[31] *Enquiry*, p. 82.
[32] *Lectures*, p. 31.
[33] *Ibid.*, p. 31. Cf. *Enquiry*, pp. 65–6.
[34] *Enquiry*, p. 71. Cf. *Lectures*, pp. 31–2.
[35] *Lectures*, pp. 32–3. Cf. *Enquiry*, pp. 60, 63.
[36] *Ibid.*, pp. 30, 33. Cf. *Enquiry*, pp. 73–4, 76–7.
[37] *Ibid.*, p. 38.
[38] *Ibid.*, p. 31.

Baillie on the subject; they thus inherit and transmit a "milder" idea of the sublime than Burke's. Payne Knight (as noted already) makes trenchant criticisms of the *Enquiry*.[39] Like Stewart later, he objects to the meaning Burke attaches to the word "sublime":

the word *sublime*, both according to its use and etymology, must signify *high* or *exalted*; and, if an individual chooses that, in his writings, it should signify *terrible*, he only involves his meaning in a confusion of terms, which naturally leads to a confusion of ideas.[40]

Equally damaging is his denial of Burke's central idea: the connection between sublimity and terror. Fear, he says, "is the most humiliating and depressing of passions", and it is impossible for a fearful man "to join in any sentiments of exultation" with the object inspiring his fear.[41] For Knight, sublimity has its source in a great mental energy which excites a sympathetic energy in the mind of the reader or spectator. The conflict between these views and those of Uvedale Price brought Dugald Stewart into the fray. He insists on the traditional, literal meaning of "sublime" and on its essential connection with height. The imagination, Stewart claims, is impressed by height, partly because ascent is a principle contrary to the law of gravitation, and consequently involves an active exertion of the faculties.[42] Stewart consistently emphasizes this connection of the active powers (in contrast to passive obedience to physical laws) with sublimity. Thus the sublime effect of impressive natural scenes is due partly to the suggestion of "Creative Power" which is superior to physical laws.[43] Moreover, with physical height certain religious ideas have been associated, the objects of religious worship having always been considered as dwelling above. Consequently,

instead of considering, with Mr. Burke, Terror as the ruling principle of the *religious sublime*, it would be nearer the truth to say, that

[39] It is interesting to note that, despite the ridicule poured by Knight on Burke's sublime of terror, his diary of a tour of Sicily in 1777 betrays the clear influence of Burke's theory. See C. Hussey, *The Picturesque* (1927), pp. 124–6.

[40] *Analytical Inquiry*, III, i, 19.

[41] *Ibid.*, III, i, 46.

[42] *Philosophical Essays*, p. 381.

[43] *Ibid.*, p. 400.

the Terrible derives whatever character of Sublimity belongs to it from religious associations.[44]

Further evidence is not required to prove how little impact Burke's ideas made on the theorists. The English philosophical writers refused to admit his main theory; they were both sceptical and cautious; and the most that can be said is that, as in the case of Beattie and Blair, the *Enquiry* provided a source for new ideas which could be assimilated without either full acknowledgment or the full acceptance of Burke's fundamental principles.

It would, however, give an inadequate view of the impact of his book if the discussion were limited to writers on beauty and sublimity. Johnson, for instance, provides an interesting example of Burke's influence on a distinguished writer who was apart from the debate on these topics. A favourable reaction to the *Enquiry* would, of course, be expected from Johnson whose great and frequently expressed regard for Burke's capacities is recorded by Boswell—but the nature of his comment on Burke's work is significant. On 16 October 1769 he was speaking of "the right method" of criticism, with reference to Kames's *Elements*; he went on to say:

> We have an example of true criticism in Burke's "Essay on the Sublime and Beautiful"; and, if I recollect, there is also Du Bos; and Bouhours, who shews all beauty to depend on truth. There is no great merit in telling how many plays have ghosts in them, and how this ghost is better than that. You must shew how terrour is impressed on the human heart.[45]

In the same conversation Johnson had maintained that "real criticism" should be fundamentally concerned with "the workings of the human heart". This remark is particularly relevant because it highlights the reason for Johnson's praise of the *Enquiry*: he presumably agreed with Burke's analysis of the sublime and beautiful, but his attention would be engaged principally by Burke's psychological investigations. "I shall enquire what things they are that cause in us the affections of the sublime and beautiful," says Burke, and, in Part IV which

[44] *Philosophical Essays*, p. 402.

[45] J. Boswell, *Life of Johnson*, II, 90.

would especially interest Johnson, he hopes to produce "something not unuseful towards a distinct knowledge of our passions."[46] This, in the Doctor's view, was "real criticism".

Johnson's high regard for Burke's criticism was not expressed only in oral comments; he seems to have given the strongest possible evidence of approval by adopting Burke's distinction between the sublime and beautiful, and accepting as valid the qualities he attaches to each.[47] In the *Dictionary* (1755) Johnson makes no sharp distinction: "sublime" (in the third sense) is connected with style and its loftiness, and "grand" with lofty or noble conceptions; "beauty" is inadequately defined as "an assemblage of graces that pleases the eye," and under "elegance" we discover that beauty may also be "grand": "elegance" is "beauty without grandeur". The ideas connected with the key-terms are, then, by no means sharply distinguished. However, when Johnson writes *Rasselas* two years after the *Enquiry* Burke's theory appears to have made its mark:

> To a poet nothing can be useless. Whatever is beautiful, and whatever is dreadful, must be familiar to his imagination: he must be conversant with all that is awfully vast or elegantly little.[48]

Here experience falls into two sharply defined categories, with beauty and smallness on the one hand, and vastness with its awe-inspiring quality on the other. Moreover, in the *Lives of the Poets*, Johnson frequently distinguishes between sublimity (or grandeur) and beauty (or elegance): in *Paradise Lost*, where Milton's "characteristic quality . . . is sublimity", the poet "sometimes descends to the elegant, but his element is the great"; and in the same *Life* Johnson acknowledges "pleasure and terror" as "the genuine sources of poetry".[49] Elsewhere he opposes "the awfulness of grandeur" to "the splendour of elegance",[50] the "pleasing" to the "dreadful",[51] and he speaks

[46] *Enquiry*, pp. 54, 129.

[47] See Jean H. Hagstrum, *Samuel Johnson's Literary Criticism* (University of Minnesota Press, 1952), pp. 130–1, to whom I am indebted here.

[48] *Op. cit.* (10th edn., 1798), p. 67.

[49] *Lives of the Poets* (Everyman's edn.), I, 104, 107.

[50] *Ibid.* (Life of Addison), I, 351.

[51] *Ibid.* (Life of Thomson), II, 292.

of "these admirers of the sublime and the terrible".[52] While, then, Johnson cannot be claimed as a devotee of the *Enquiry*—*Rambler* No. 80 shows him aware of sublimity in 1750—it seems conclusive that his regard for the work was such that the theory it contained directed to some extent his classification of experience and the terminology he used to express it.

It seems, too, that the Johnson circle was well acquainted with Burke's treatise even though what evidence remains suggests that his theory was not always treated with the seriousness he intended. In *Thraliana* (for Nov. 1776–May 1777) Mrs. Thrale records a story told her by Dr. Parker, which she introduces by a pertinent comment:

Burke would have liked it—so well does it tally with his Notions of the Sublime.

A little Girl of ten Years old—a Shopkeeper's Daughter, was carried to see Wanstead House—the long Suite of Rooms were suddenly thrown open, the whole blaze of Splendour burst upon her Eye—She said nothing but cried copiously, such was the violence of its Effect upon her Mind.[53]

Burke's theory allowed, it appears, of a ludicrous application: given violent emotion, astonishment, terror, provoked by no matter what stimulus, his "sublime" could be invoked. (Forty years later, in *Nightmare Abbey*, Peacock felt sure enough of his reader's ability to appreciate a passing reference to invoke Burke's sublime in a similar, though more fully satirical, manner.[54]) It should be noted, however, that Mrs. Thrale could also apply Burke's principles aptly and with more seriousness:

I observed it was in Manners as in Architecture, the Gothick struck one most forcibly, the Grecian delighted one more sensibly.
Tis the Sublime & beautiful of Burke over again.[55]

The interesting feature about both references is the ease and casualness with which Mrs. Thrale introduces them into her

[52] *Lives of the Poets* (Life of Young), II, 347.

[53] *Op. cit.* (ed. K. C. Balderston, Oxford, 1942), I, 21.

[54] *Op. cit.* (ed. R. Garnett, 1891), p. 88. See also *Crotchet Castle* (ed. R. Garnett, 1893), p. 141: "the perception of the sublime was probably heightened by an intermingled sense of danger".

[55] *Thraliana*, I, 421.

journal: it is indicative of the thoroughness with which she had assimilated Burke's theory.

An eminent contemporary of Mrs. Thrale, the orientalist (Sir) William Jones, had also absorbed the theory and with unfailing high seriousness. Some evidence is found in two essays published in 1772: *On the Poetry of the Eastern Nations* and *On the Arts, commonly called Imitative*. In the first Jones asserts that oriental poetry does not please solely by its descriptions of beauty "since the gloomy and terrible objects, which produce the *sublime*, . . . are no where more common than in the *Desert* and *Stony Arabia's*."[56] In the second he ranges himself alongside Burke (though he does not mention him by name) in affirming that "*there is one uniform standard of taste*",[57] that poetry, music, and painting affect the passions through the working of sympathy and not by imitation, and that where these arts are "merely descriptive, [they] act by a kind of *substitution*".[58] The major proof, however, is contained in the far more important and scholarly work, *Poeseos Asiaticae Commentariorum*, 1774. This work, as a recent writer declares, "was given widespread attention and universal acclaim throughout western Europe".[59] In it Jones clearly adopts the definitions of the sublime and beautiful proposed by "vir disertissimus Edmundus Bourke",[60] and he refers to the *Enquiry* on several occasions. A single quotation will demonstrate his indebtedness:

Id est igitur Elatum, quod fit incertum, horridum, obscurum, periculosum, vastum, difficile, turbulentum; & quod eos qui legunt usque adeò percellat, ut admirentur, vereantur, tumultuentur, exhorrescant, doleant, stupeant. Sunt autem Elationis praecipui fontes, terror, magnificentia, potentia, & in eâ describendâ brevitas. Alii sunt quasi fonticuli, sed qui omnes terrori subjunguntur, ut solitudo, silentium, caligo; intermissio, eaque vel sonorum, ut luporum ululatus in sylvâ noctu auditus, vel lucis: ad summam quodcunque sensibus est maximè injucundum, id cùm describatur, Elatum reddit poesin.[61]

[56] Sir William Jones, *Works* (1799), IV, 530.

[57] *Ibid.*, IV, 561. Cf. *Enquiry*, p. 11.

[58] *Ibid.*, IV, 559. Cf. *Enquiry*, pp. 172, 173.

[59] Garland H. Cannon, "Sir William Jones and Edmund Burke", *Modern Philology* (1957), LIV, iii, 166.

[60] *Works*, II, 482.

[61] *Ibid.*, II, 479.

Though on this occasion Jones does not specify his source virtually the whole passage is merely a Latin version of parts of the *Enquiry*; even the slightly melodramatic (at first sight almost Senecan) flavour of the nocturnal cries of the wolves derives from one of Burke's Virgilian quotations.[62] But the significant point is that Jones unhesitatingly adopts Burke's ideas as a sound basis for examining specific details of oriental poetry: these ideas provide certain criteria which he can apply to a strange literature; they are criteria which he does not feel compelled to prove and which he assumes will be familiar to European readers. (By 1774 translations of the *Enquiry* into French (1765) and German (1773) had been published.) In all, then, Burke exerted considerable influence on this celebrated writer; the reputation of his own work would undoubtedly profit by it. Indeed many reviewers of *Poeseos Asiaticae Commentariorum*, Mr. Cannon informs us, pointed out that its author "had taken his definition of beauty from Burke's *Philosophical Enquiry*. . . . The acclaim for Jones's new book naturally brought new attention to Burke and his book."[63]

Going beyond the philosophical critics first discussed, and writers, like Johnson and Jones, concerned with literary theory, the task of assessing Burke's influence becomes a complex undertaking. So much of his theory of the sublime—in its general application—would be found simply to systematize and explain the taste for Gothicism, graveyard poetry, wild and uncultivated nature, the paintings of Salvator Rosa and Ruysdael, and so forth. The vogue of feeling on which Burke depended had long been growing: the emotional fervour of Shaftesbury's style, Hume's interest in "the sentiments of humanity", and the novel of sensibility are but a few obvious signs. Consequently, it becomes difficult, from the mass of aggregating factors, to detect the features of Burke's influen[illegible]ith precision.

Indeed, before we can go further, some attention must be given to the growing importance of the "picturesque" which eventually provided a third category in addition to Burke's sublime and beautiful. The definition of Burke's influence on

[62] *Enquiry*, p. 84.

[63] *Op. cit.*, p. 166.

writings in which all three terms are used thus becomes complicated; the complication is increased by the direct influence of the *Enquiry* on the theorists of the picturesque themselves. The first full-scale statement of the theory appeared in 1792—Gilpin's *Three Essays on Picturesque Beauty*—but it was merely a systematization of the ideas which had directed Gilpin in his earlier *Observations on the River Wye* (1782) and on the *Mountains, and Lakes of Cumberland, and Westmoreland* (1786). The *Essays* prove—what is clear from the *Observations*—that, while he dissents from some of Burke's views, Gilpin accepts Burke as in some measure authoritative. For example, in the second of the *Observations* mentioned above (made in 1772), Gilpin disputes Burke's claim that when the effects of both sublimity and beauty mix in the same object "the effect is in a good measure destroyed in both", but he accepts without question the qualities which Burke attaches to each type of experience.[64] The same kind of qualified acceptance is a mark of Gilpin's *Essays*, but it is significant that, in 1792, he can refer to the *Enquiry* without feeling that he must remind his readers of its existence or justify his use of it as an authority. In fact, his idea of "roughness" as the key distinction between beauty and the picturesque is introduced as a rejoinder to Burke's claim that "smoothness" is "the *most considerable* source of beauty".[65]

Burke is even more vitally present in Uvedale Price's *Essay on the Picturesque* (1794): Price's admiration for Burke is so great that he appears loth to differ from him. He makes no attempt to dispute Burke's analysis of the sublime and beautiful, claiming only that there is a "distinct class" of objects which "may properly be called the picturesque";[66] he frequently echoes Burke's phrases and rhythms; he acknowledges Burke's system as the basis of his own;[67] and later he adopts a tone almost of veneration:

[64] *Op. cit.* (2nd edn., 1788), II, 53–4. Cf. II, 15–17.

[65] *Three Essays* (2nd edn., 1794), pp. 5–6.

[66] *Essays on the Picturesque* (1810), I, 43. Cf. I, 50: "the two opposite qualities of roughness, and of sudden variation, joined to that of irregularity, are the most efficient causes of the picturesque."

[67] *Ibid.*, I, 93.

The causes and effects of the sublime and of the beautiful have been investigated by a great master, whose footsteps I have followed in a road, which his penetrating and comprehensive genius had so nobly opened: I have ventured indeed to explore a new track, and to discriminate the causes and the effects of the picturesque from those of the other two characters: still, however, I have in some degree proceeded under his auspices; for it is a track I never should have discovered, had not he first cleared and adorned the principal avenues.[68]

Now, it is a commonplace that, by mid-century, vast numbers of people were not only interested in mountain scenery and anxious to enjoy the emotional experiences associated with it, but were also prepared to undertake tours of the Lake District and other mountainous areas. It was to be expected that on such travellers and on writers who catered for them in "Guides to the Lakes", Burke would exercise a profound influence. But the increasing popularity of the picturesque between, say, Gray's *Journal in the Lakes* (1769) and Wordsworth's *Guide* (1810) clearly makes difficult the task of determining the exact quality of that influence. It should be remembered that, on the one hand, Gilpin's second essay is entitled *On Picturesque Travel*, and that, on the other, Price assumes in the reader of his *Essay on the Picturesque* an intimate knowledge of Burke's *Enquiry*.[69] However, despite this disturbing conglomeration of "influences", certain claims for Burke may be hazarded.

Gray's reliance on the "theoretical" manner of looking at natural scenery is slight. His *Journal* is, indeed, a modest, personal account marked by what Wordsworth called "distinctness and unaffected simplicity".[70] He makes the Burkean distinction between the "sweetness" of "pastoral beauty" and the more awe-inspiring scenery "in a sublimer style";[71] he also experiences pleasing horror on a visit to Gordale;[72] but it would be extravagant to make further claims for Burke's influence.

The case is otherwise with Richard West. The effect of the

[68] *Essays on the Picturesque*, II, 197.
[69] *Ibid.*, III, 183 ff.
[70] *Guide through the District of the Lakes* (ed. W. M. Merchant, 1951), p. 104.
[71] *Works* (ed. Gosse, 1902), I, 260.
[72] *Ibid.*, I, 276–7.

Enquiry on him is best illustrated by first looking at Dr. John Brown's *Letter* (describing the Lake and Vale of Keswick) which was most likely written before the publication of Burke's treatise. In the *Letter* are found many of the attitudes and terms which Burke was to systematize: Brown speaks of "beauty" and "grandeur", of "horrible grandeur", of "rude and terrible magnificence", and of the perfection of Keswick as consisting of "*beauty*, *horror*, and *immensity* united".[73] He is, indeed, in the Addisonian line, using "grandeur" where later writers use "sublime"; he sees no sharp distinction between beauty and grandeur; and he uses these terms unselfconsciously and for their emotional connotation rather than for any theoretical significance. A comparison between this usage and Arthur Young's (whose Tours were undertaken for scientific and practical reasons) reveals the change both in terminology and in reliance on aesthetic theory:

> Picture the mountains rearing their majestic heads with native sublimity; the vast rocks boldly projecting their terrible craggy points; and in the path of beauty, the variegated inclosures of the most charming verdure, hanging to the eye in every picturesque form that can grace landscape, with the most exquisite touches of *la belle nature*.[74]

Young does not, like Brown, commit himself to a phrase such as "beautifully dreadful";[75] he draws a sharp line between sublimity and beauty; the former is linked with height, vastness, irregularity, and terror, the latter with variety, charm, and a general suggestion of grace and softness. One suspects that Young had assimilated Burke's theory and was using its principles unconsciously. With West the suspicion is that the use was more conscious.

In West's descriptions of the Lake country sublimity is regularly opposed to beauty: Levens Park, for example, is beautiful in its "variety of contrast", its winding, calm stream, and, in fact, because "all is variety with pleasing transition";[76] in Borrowdale, on the other hand, the scenes are "sublimely

[73] *Op. cit.*, printed in R. West, *A Guide to the Lakes* (4th edn., 1789), pp. 193, 194.

[74] R. West, *Guide*, p. 70.

[75] J. Brown, *Letter*, in R. West, *Guide*, p. 195.

[76] *Guide*, p. 181.

terrible", they are composed of "magnificent objects so stupendously great", and the emotions they excite are "wonder and surprise", "reverential awe and admiration".[77] And not only does West consistently rely on Burke's theory for classifying his emotional responses, he is also well aware of the principles—pleasure and pain—which are the foundation for Burke's sublime and beautiful. Speaking of Derwentwater, Windermere, and Ullswater, West remarks:

> The stiles are all different, and therefore the sensations they excite will also be different; and the idea that gives pleasure or pain in the highest degree, will be the rule of comparative judgment.[78]

Again, when he wishes to make his views precise, West relies on Burke's terminology while expressly shifting the emphasis normal in the *Enquiry*:

> It will be allowed, that the views on this lake [Coniston] are beautiful and picturesque, yet they please more than surprise. The hills that immediately inclose the lake, are ornamental but humble. The mountains at the head of the lake are great, noble, and sublime, without anything that is horrid or terrible.[79]

From the time of the second edition (published in the year of West's death, 1779) other "miscellaneous pieces . . . respecting the lakes" were included in West's *Guide*. Several of them betray Burke's influence. A description by Mr. Adam Walker of the mountains and caves of West Yorkshire (taken from a letter in the *General Evening Post*, 25 September 1779) contains remarks like the following: "To a mind capable of being impressed with the grand and sublime of nature, this is a scene that inspires a pleasure chastised by astonishment."[80] Or, in another letter describing "A Tour to the Caves in the West-Riding of Yorkshire", we find the Burkean distinction between sublimity and beauty, together with the inference that the former is the more emotionally disturbing: "While some are pleased with the gay and beautiful, others are only to be roused and affected by the grand and terrible."[81] This writer consistently associates terror with the sublime.[82]

[77] *Guide*, p. 96.
[78] *Ibid.*, p. 72.
[79] *Ibid.*, pp. 52–3.
[80] *Ibid.*, p. 233.
[81] *Ibid.*, p. 237.
[82] *Ibid.*, pp. 255, 258, 278, 279.

This type of influence, it might be argued, was inevitable: mountains had been traditionally associated, because of their height, with the sublime; add to this the fashionable Augustan horror, and, it might be claimed, Burke's influence was only marginal. In the first place, however, writers mentioned so far are clearly conscious of more than Burke's "terror"; they use, in addition, other features of his sublime, such as "astonishment", irregularity, and the pleasure–pain principle; and they distinguish sharply between sublimity and beauty, attributing to the latter such qualities as "gradual variation", "smoothness", and a less violent emotional impact. The second point to be made is that it was not only the minor writers who felt Burke's influence; the major writer of "Guides", while he was, on most counts, superior to fashionable taste, could not avoid the effect of the *Enquiry*. This writer was Wordsworth.

"It would appear that *The Guide to the Lakes* is a document illustrative more of *The Prelude* than of Burke's *Sublime and Beautiful*."[83] W. M. Merchant's summing-up is fair—but some qualifications must be urged. Wordsworth, it is true, wrote for "the spectator, who has learned to observe and feel, chiefly from Nature herself";[84] he was no longer, as in youth,

disliking here, and there
Liking, by rules of mimic art transferred
To things above all art;

he was not, in fact, concerned with what the theorists had instructed the traveller to look for. Nevertheless, his terminology, his method of analysing scenes, his choice of details which seem noteworthy, are directed in large measure by eighteenth-century aesthetic theory. Burke's distinction between the sublime and beautiful is, indeed, fundamental to Wordsworth's descriptive technique. Admittedly he does redefine the two principal terms:

Sublimity is the result of Nature's first great dealings with the superficies of the earth; but the general tendency of her subsequent operations is towards the production of beauty; by a multiplicity of symmetrical parts uniting in a consistent whole.[85]

[83] Wordsworth, *Guide*, p. 29. [84] *Ibid.*, p. 139. [85] *Ibid.*, p. 69.

This definition is made, as Merchant points out, "by reference to the activities of natural forces"; Wordsworth is indeed scornful of people who thought of sublimity merely in terms of magnitude;[86] but his use of the key terms does not in fact prove that he has managed to throw off Burke's influence. Qualities associated with beauty remain those of smoothness, calmness, variety, and the rest; those linked with the sublime are still such as power, magnificence, "tumultuous confusion", and intense emotion. Writing of "Winandermere", for instance, Wordsworth contrasts the "gentle and lovely scenes" with "the grand";[87] and in the same paragraph he notes that to move from the plains to the mountains is to make "an ascent of almost regular gradation, from elegance and richness, to their highest point of grandeur and sublimity." Again, in the following passage, he is clearly connecting with the sublime, magnitude, magnificent confusion and violence, and the sense of a vast power moving in and upon the waters:

Having dwelt so much upon the beauty of pure and still water, and pointed out the advantage which the Lakes of the North of England have in this particular over those of the Alps, it would be injustice not to advert to the sublimity that must often be given to Alpine scenes, by the agitations to which those vast bodies of diffused water are there subject. . . . If the commotions be at all proportionable to the expanse and depth of the waters, and the height of the surrounding mountains, then if I may judge from what is frequently seen here, the exhibition must be awful and astonishing.[88]

And as a final, and, it would seem, incontrovertible piece of evidence for Burke's influence, there is the passage on the merits of the larch as a tree for ornamental planting in the Lake District:

It is indeed true, that in countries where the larch is a native, and where, without interruption, it may sweep from valley to valley, and from hill to hill, a sublime image may be produced by such a forest, in the same manner as by one composed of any other single

[86] Wordsworth, *Guide*, p. 68. Cf. *Enquiry*, p. 57. "Whatever therefore is terrible, with regard to sight, is sublime too, whether this cause of terror, be endued with greatness of dimensions or not."

[87] *Ibid.*. p. 58.

[88] *Ibid.*, pp. 145–6.

tree, to the spreading of which no limits can be assigned. For sublimity will never be wanting, where the sense of innumerable multitude is lost in, and alternates with, that of intense unity; and to the ready perception of this effect, similarity and almost identity of individual form and monotony of colour contribute. But this feeling is confined to the native immeasurable forest; no artificial plantation can give it.[89]

This judgment is based almost entirely on principles inherited from the *Enquiry*: there Burke insists on the part played in sublimity by the infinite, by "the succession and *uniformity* of parts" which constitute the "artificial infinite", and by "magnificence" which he illustrates from the "appearance of infinity" produced by the stars through their numbers and apparent disorder. He adds, too, that "the appearance of care is highly contrary to our ideas of magnificence". There is little doubt about the origin of Wordsworth's ideas here. So that, while Wordsworth was no slavish disciple of any aesthetic theory, the pervasive influence of Burke's *Enquiry* on language and habits of observation cannot be discounted. To go even further, in the discipline of "beauty" and of "fear" of which Wordsworth makes so much in *The Prelude*, we may have a relic—given, of course, added significance by the poet's personal vision—of Burke's division of aesthetic experience into that which causes "love, or some passion similar to it", and that which "operates in a manner analogous to terror". The presentation of certain events in the poem also gives more than a hint that Wordsworth's method of self-analysis had been at least partly shaped by his reading of the *Enquiry*. Book I of *The Prelude*, for example, in which he begins to show how Nature filled his mind "with forms sublime or fair", turns principally on evidence of "the impressive discipline of fear". The descriptions of the robbing of the snares and the stealing of the boat convey the kind of terror which was aroused by a mysterious power, terrible—as Burke had said—because of its "uncertainty", and which he had illustrated by a quotation from *Job*: "*. . . fear came upon me and trembling . . . a spirit passed before my face* . . . but I could not discern the form thereof" (p. 63).

[89] Wordsworth, *Guide*, p. 123. Cf. *Enquiry*, pp. 73-6, 78.

Similarly, the experience on Snowdon in Book XIV could well be described as "sublime", and of the dream about the Bedouin Arab in Book V De Quincey remarked that it was "the very *ne plus ultra* of sublimity".[90]

The Romantics generally had, however, little time for Burke's theory. His sensationism, his limited conception of the imagination, and his too great readiness to categorize aesthetic experience, were unlikely to appeal, above all, to Blake. One remark in the marginalia to Reynolds's *Discourses* is representative of the sharp dismissal accorded to Burke's ideas: "Obscurity is Neither the Source of the Sublime nor of any Thing Else."[91] In such pungent brevities was Burke's system swept away. Above all, his utter reliance on sensationism was anathema to Blake: Burke appeared to "mock Inspiration & Vision" which were Blake's "Eternal Dwelling place".

To Coleridge, too, the *Enquiry* was "a poor thing".[92] Although he recognized Burke's "transcendent greatness" as a political philosopher, the early critical work found no favour. Yet, perhaps, even Coleridge unconsciously submitted to its influence. In 1795, writing graciously about Joseph Cottle's poetry, he maintains that Cottle found his inspiration in "A mead of mildest charm" below the "lofty-frowning brow" of "the Poetic mount".

Not there the cloud-climb'd rock, sublime and vast,
That like some giant king, o'er-glooms the hill;
Nor there the Pine-grove to the midnight blast
Makes solemn music! But th'unceasing rill
To the soft Wren or Lark's descending trill
Murmurs sweet undersong 'mid jasmin bowers.
In this same pleasant meadow, at your will
I ween you wander'd . . .[93]

The very mention of the word "sublime" seems to have suggested Burkean ideas of obscurity, gloom, dark groves, vastness, and solemn music; more than that, it seems inevitable that the awful grandeur of the sublime should prompt a description of

[90] *Op. cit.*, text of 1805 (ed. E. de Selincourt, 1933), p. 265.
[91] *Works*, p. 804.
[92] *Specimens of Table Talk* (New Edn., 1905), p. 48.
[93] *Poems* ("Oxford Standard Authors" edn., 1945), p. 103.

the contrasting softness, sweetness, charm, and delicate sounds associated with beauty. Direct "influence" here is admittedly slight, but the ultimate source of the complex of ideas appears evident.[94]

A more thorough-going influence on the arts of the second half of the eighteenth century, and even beyond that time, has been confidently claimed by Mr. Hussey: "In relating Terror, Obscurity, and the Infinite to aesthetic emotion [Burke] provided a basis for the art of the coming hundred years."[95] The same writer also states that Burke's

> description of the sensation aroused by beauty explains clearly the physical basis for the "waving" and "serpentine" forms predominant in the art of the mid-century, in the lines of Chippendale's furniture, "Capability" Brown's serpentine paths and lakes, and Hogarth's "line of beauty."[96]

At first sight, such claims seem extravagant. Yet, as has been shown already, the *Enquiry* gave currency to a new complex of ideas which proved more influential than the theory on which it was based: it was certainly influential enough to leave an indelible mark on the artistic practice of the age. Payne Knight, a witness for the prosecution, ridicules those of Burke's disciples who took his principles to excess: "the works of many modern painters, poets, and romance writers . . . teem with all sorts of terrific and horrific monsters and hobgoblins."[97] He goes on to quote the attempt of Sir William Chambers (the designer of Kew Gardens) "to introduce those charming delights of danger, pain, terror and astonishment into the art of landscape gardening". Undoubtedly Chambers's *Dissertation on Oriental Gardening* (1772) contains phantasmagoric descriptions of so-called Chinese gardens which excel in horrific details of gibbets, crosses, poisonous weeds, "scenes of terror", and the like[98]—but

[94] Coleridge may also have had Burke in mind when, referring to the history of fanaticism, he speaks of "the truth of the assertion, that deep feeling has a tendency to combine with obscure ideas, in preference to distinct and clear notions" (*Friend*, I, 177–8 n.).

[95] *The Picturesque*, p. 57.

[96] *Ibid.*, p. 58.

[97] *Analytical Inquiry*, III, i, 67.

[98] See C. Hussey, *The Picturesque*, pp. 157–8.

this emotional response to the business of laying out gardens had little to do with China. Chambers confessed in a letter that he passed off his own ideas as those of the Chinese.[99] But the hoax was not penetrated and the blame was fathered on Burke and the Orient.

More sober exponents of the art of gardening were certainly influenced by the *Enquiry*. Such a one was Thomas Whateley whose *Observations on Modern Gardening* (1770), according to Hussey,[100] became the text-book of gardening until the advent of the "Picturesque school" (of Uvedale Price and Repton) and its manifestoes in 1794. Whateley asserted that gardening "is entitled to a place of considerable rank among the liberal arts. It is as superior to landskip painting, as a reality to a representation."[101] Burke is present at once in the terms used to define the gardener's task: "to select and apply whatever is great, elegant, or characteristic" in natural scenes. "Great" or "elegant", "sublime" or "beautiful" are terms always at hand in Whateley's treatise. "The prevailing character of a wood is generally grandeur. . . . But the character of a grove is *beauty*";[102]

the roar and the rage of a torrent, its force, its violence, its impetuosity, tend to inspire terror; that terror, which, whether as cause or effect, is so nearly allied to sublimity;[103]

"the character of greatness, when divested of terror, is placid";[104] "greatness is as essential to the character of terror as to that of dignity; vast efforts in little objects are but ridiculous"[105]—such Burkean dicta abound in the *Observations*. Theory becoming practical advice, still in accord with the *Enquiry*, is evident in Whateley's comments provoked by the scene "at the New Weir on the Wye" (between Ross and Monmouth):

But marks of inhabitants must not be carried to the length of cultivation, which is too mild for the ruggedness of the place, and

99 J. Summerson, *Architecture in Britain 1530–1830* (1953), p. 271, n. 12.
100 *Op. cit.*, p. 152.
101 *Op. cit.* (4th edn., 1777) p. 1.
102 *Ibid.*, p. 46.
103 *Ibid.*, p. 62.
104 *Ibid.*, p. 102.
105 *Ibid.*, p. 106.

has besides an air of chearfulness inconsistent with the character of terror; a little inclination towards melancholy is generally acceptable, at least to the exclusion of all gaiety; and beyond that point, so far as to throw just a tinge of gloom upon the scene. For this purpose, the objects whose colour is obscure should be preferred; and those which are too bright may be thrown into shadow; the wood may be thickened, and the dark greens abound in it; if it is necessarily thin, yews and shabby firs should be scattered about it; and sometimes, to shew a withering or a dead tree, it may for a space be cleared entirely away.[106]

Whateley set out to produce in the observer of his gardens "a train of pleasing ideas"; the nature of these ideas was determined by the *Enquiry*; and the method used to excite them was that of the landscape gardener, in the tradition of William Shenstone at Leasowes, directed by Burke's dictum: "no work of art can be great, but as it deceives".[107]

When the advocates of the "picturesque"—particularly Uvedale Price—came to dominate the gardening scene, Burke's influence was perpetuated on account of the authoritative position he held with them. Even though they believed his analysis of the qualities of beauty led to insipidity[108]—and beauty was the great aim of the "improver" since the sublime could not be "created"—they invariably used Burke's theory as a starting-point for their own and invoked his authority and prestige whenever possible.

Burke's influence in architecture, in part at any rate, was also perpetuated through the refracting medium of Uvedale Price. Reynolds, in his 13th Discourse (1786), had indeed put his seal on the Gothic revival by urging that plans characterized by regularity ought to be abandoned in favour of those which appealed to the imagination; he insisted that architecture was capable of "filling the mind with great and sublime ideas"; and he quoted Vanbrugh with approval.[109] But it was Price (acknowledging Reynolds's lead), in his essay *On Architecture and Buildings*, who thoroughly analysed Vanbrugh's art—and it was Burke who provided Price with his standards and key-terms.

[106] *Op cit.*, pp. 110–11.
[107] *Enquiry*, p. 76.
[108] Cf. Uvedale Price, *Essays on the Picturesque*, I, 103.
[109] *Discourses* (1842), pp. 236–8.

Burke, Price affirms, had pointed out the "most efficient causes" of the sublime in buildings, "two of which are succession and uniformity".[110] He goes on to add, adapting Burke's first principles:

where the objects are such as are capable of inspiring awe or terror, there suspense and uncertainty are powerful causes of the sublime; and intricacy may, by those means, create no less grand effects than uniformity and succession.

From here, of course, he can argue that sublimity is present in Gothic architecture no less than in buildings characterized by succession and uniformity and by the "massiness" which Burke deemed essential. Vanbrugh's achievement at Blenheim was to unite Grecian "beauty and magnificence", Gothic "picturesqueness", and "the massive grandeur of a castle", Burke's principle of massiveness being "the foundation of grandeur".[111]

Later, Price turns to the beautiful in architecture. Again his standard of reference is the *Enquiry*. He says that on this topic Burke was not specific but left us to deduce the causes of architectural beauty from "the general tenor of his Essay".

The principles which he has there laid down are so just, and are so happily explained and enforced, that they may readily be applied to buildings, as to all other objects; though with certain exceptions and modifications, which arise from the nature of architecture.[112]

The chief exception involves "waving lines": though they are important in domes, arches, columns and so forth, "straight lines belong to [architecture's] very essence". Price then considers how far the temple of the Sibyl at Tivoli—generally recognized as possessing great beauty—measures up to Burke's definition of the beautiful. He finds that it has as many of the qualities listed by Burke (smallness, smoothness, delicacy, etc.) "as the particular principles of architecture will allow". In fact,

110 *Op. cit.*, II, 197–8.

111 *Ibid.*, II, 212. Burke himself appears to have foreseen the possibility that his principles might affect architectural practice. His tone occasionally is that of a man giving instructions for the erection of a "sublime building". Cf. *Enquiry*, p. 82.

112 *Ibid.*, II, 234.

with obvious and necessary modifications, the *Enquiry* was judged to provide valuable practical guidance to an architect.

Yet—to revert to the question of sublimity in building—Burke himself never recognized in Gothic architecture the outstanding illustration of the sublime he advocated: magnitude, apparent disorder, magnificent profusion of detail, the expression of immense energy, the suggestion of infinity through ornamental traceries, the awful gloom of the interior, and so on. Indeed, his sole reference to Gothicism reveals the common Augustan prejudices.[113]

Subsequent writers, however, saw in the *Enquiry* principles which made the Gothic preferable to the Grecian style. Uvedale Price has already been mentioned. Equally important in view of the ecclesiastical Gothicism of the nineteenth century are the views expressed in an essay by the Rev. John Milner, in a symposium, *Essays on Gothic Architecture* (1800).[114] Milner contributed an introductory letter—*Observations on the Means necessary for further illustrating the Ecclesiastical Architecture of the middle Ages*—in which he examines "the true principles of *the Sublime and Beautiful*, as applied to those sacred fabrics which are the undoubted masterpieces and glory of the pointed order."[115] His tone is that of a man making a discovery. Burke had been used earlier to justify the Gothic on aesthetic and not merely antiquarian grounds: Milner uses him to prove the superiority of Gothic over Wren's churches on the ground that they are more conducive to "prayer and contemplation".

There is no need to quote extensively from Milner's letter: as might be expected, having adopted Burke's definition of the sublime, he stresses the height and length, the artificial infinite, the solemn gloom and so forth, which are characteristic of Gothic churches. Milner is convinced that sublimity "forms their proper character"; he is chiefly concerned with their effect on "the mind of the spectator"; and consequently the *Enquiry* is of inestimable value in proving his case. Within forty years the Tractarian architectural societies were

113 *Enquiry*, p. 76.

114 Other contributors were Rev. Thomas Warton, Rev. J. Bentham, and Capt. F. Grose.

115 *Op. cit.*, p. xvi.

beginning to introduce as architectural, canons of criticism which were originally ecclesiastical.[116] It is interesting to speculate on Burke's contribution, through a writer like Milner, to making this development possible and its success assured.

When we turn to painting a similar story is to be told and two of the key-figures—Reynolds and Uvedale Price—reappear. In many ways Reynolds's *Discourses* are the most notable embodiment of eighteenth-century aesthetic principles but—*pace* Blake—important developments in pictorial art are foreshadowed in them. Certainly Burke's influence is present, though it can be overestimated. The only specific reference to the *Enquiry* occurs in a footnote; it is an afterthought implying that, in his "admirable treatise", Burke shows "the connection between the rules of art and the eternal and immutable dispositions of our passions".[117] But Reynolds follows Burke—to Blake's disgust—in allowing obscurity to be "one source of the sublime";[118] he rates intuition higher than reason;[119] he claims that the sublime overwhelms the mind and forbids minute criticism;[120] and he agrees with Burke in believing both that poetry frequently works by stimulating the reader's imagination to particularize "general indistinct expressions", and that the preliminary, unfinished sketch for a painting stimulates the imagination in the same way.[121]

Reynolds stood high in Uvedale Price's estimation: his *Discourses* were "the most original and impressive work that ever was published on his, or possibly on any art". Moreover, as a man, Reynolds was "a painter of a liberal and comprehensive mind, who . . . added extensive observation and reflection to practical execution": in a word, he was the ideal exemplar for the "improver".[122] Price never ceased to insist on the importance of painting for forming the taste of landscape gardeners. This insistence naturally stimulated an interest in both arts—gardening and painting—and Price's veneration for Burke, reinforced by the more indirect influence of Burke through Reynolds, gave the *Enquiry* considerable prestige

[116] See K. Clark, *The Gothic Revival* (1928), p. 201.
[117] *Op. cit.*, p. 160. [118] *Ibid.*, p. 114. [119] *Ibid.*, p. 222.
[120] *Ibid.*, p. 272. [121] *Ibid.*, pp. 160–1.
[122] *Essays on the Picturesque*, I, 236–7.

among painters in the late eighteenth and early nineteenth centuries.

Burke made his own personal contribution to this prestige through his patronage of painters and his general interest in the subject of painting. By an interesting accident he made protégés of two fellow Irishmen, George Barret and James Barry, one largely a painter of the beautiful and the other of the sublime. The lesser of the two, Barret, whom Burke persuaded to London about 1762–3 and eventually secured for him the post of Master Painter to Chelsea Hospital, made a great success with his landscapes; far inferior to Richard Wilson, he outdid him in popularity. Burke, writing to Barry, speaks of Barret's success:

> Barrett has fallen into the painting of views. It is the most called for, and the most lucrative part of his business. He is a wonderful observer of the accidents of nature, and produces every day something new from that source, and indeed is on the whole a delightful painter, and possessed of great resources.[123]

His work has all the smoothness Burke required of beauty; it also suffers from the lack of energy and vitality characterizing Burke's concept of beauty. The landscapes are the work of a competent artist; they are pleasant but tepid. The present Duke of Portland possesses a number of his paintings[124]—Barret was commissioned by the Portland family to paint a number of views and objects on the Welbeck estate—and the overriding impression they give is of smooth, glassy water, gently undulating country, flowing lines, insignificant, languid human figures, all gracefully presented in rather flat, mild colours. Possibly the most interesting example in the Portland collection is *Hazel Gap Plantation* (*c.* 1767) of which the catalogue description reads: "A stream in the foreground with wooded banks; nearly in the centre a boat, in which are two men, one fishing; swans to left and horses grazing on the bank to right."[125]

[123] James Barry, *Works* (1809), I, 89.

[124] I am indebted to his Grace for permission to inspect his private collection, and for generous hospitality.

[125] *Catalogue of the Pictures belonging to his Grace the Duke of Portland, at Welbeck Abbey, and in London* (1894), item no. 384.

The quality of the painting is suggested by this quite just description.

Of a different order, both as man and painter, was Burke's other protégé, Barry. The undoubted talents of this fiery, irascible and vain Irishman are receiving more of the attention they deserve, principally on account of his influence on Blake.[126] (He provides one channel by which Burke indirectly influenced his great adversary.) Burke was solely responsible for bringing Barry to London and was largely responsible for his being able to visit France and Italy. Barry's *Works* abound with tributes to his patron—"to the conversation of this truly great man, I am proud to acknowledge that I owe the best part of my education."[127] They did not, it is true, agree politically, and their views on aesthetics gradually diverged, yet it is difficult unreservedly to accept Blake's marginal comment to the effect that Burke "used to shew" Barry's *Pandora*, which had been painted for him, and say, "I gave Twenty Guineas for this horrible Dawb."[128] What is certain is that Barry, in his youth, was "captivated" by the *Enquiry* and had completely transcribed it before he knew even the identity of its author.[129] Many of his subsequent works, both literary and pictorial, bear the marks of this early enthusiasm. Writing to Burke when on his way to Italy Barry speaks of "the most awful and horridly grand, romantic, and picturesque scenes, that it is possible to conceive";[130] he writes of Ghiberti's "ideas of true beauty and perfection on the one hand, and of real grandeur and sublimity on the other";[131] in one of his lectures as Royal Academy Professor of Painting he clearly expected his students to understand by the "*artificial infinite*" the significance Burke gave to the term;[132] his conception of beauty has the femininity which marks that of Burke and, again like Burke, he thinks of "grandeur, majesty and sublimity" as of "a higher order" than beauty[133]—indeed, throughout his writings he gives evidence of the permanent effect of the *Enquiry* on his mind.

[126] Cf. Geoffrey Grigson, "Painters of the Abyss", *Architectural Review* (Oct. 1950), pp. 215–20; D. V. Erdman, *Blake Prophet Against Empire* (Princeton University Press, 1954), p. 37 ff.

[127] *Op. cit.*, II, 340. Cf. I, 153. [128] Blake, *Works*, p. 778. [129] *Works*, I, 10.
[130] *Ibid.*, I, 59. [131] *Ibid.*, I, 182. [132] *Ibid.*, I, 494. [133] *Ibid.*, I, 400.

On one subject Barry differed markedly from his patron. In his *Letter to the Dilletanti Society* (1793) he claims to give some new insights "which had escaped the penetration of the Abbe du Bos, of Mr. Edmund Burke, Mr. Harris, and other great writers who had treated this elegant subject."[134] The "elegant subject" concerned the relative merits of poetry and painting. Barry firmly places painting as the superior art: it "is the real art of wisdom and Poetry is only an account or relation of it, more or less animated as the poetry is more or less excellent."[135]

This clash of views was not of a kind to minimize the total influence of the *Enquiry* on Barry's work as a painter. It was almost inevitable that he should be attracted to the book and its theory. Apart from personal acquaintance with Burke himself—they met in 1763, only four years from the painstaking second edition—Barry felt a strong attraction towards "the immense, rugged and tremendous";[136] his "favourite" was "Nic Poussin";[137] and he was, in 1769, "a furious enthusiast for Michael Angelo".[138] Burke's influence is obvious, for example, in the engraving of an unpublished work, *Satan, Sin, and Death* (reproduced by Geoffrey Grigson in his article, *Painters of the Abyss*). It is a raw but vigorous interpretation of Milton's description, the chief elements in it being terror, an accentuated emotional intensity, the hugeness of the figures, and the general effect calculated to arouse the Burkean "delightful horror". Barry's *King Lear* is similarly in a grand manner: a titanic figure against a dark sky and a rocky background of waste. Grigson further mentions "the Magnasco-like, liquid horror" in Barry's painting of the moment in *Cymbeline* when Iachimo emerges from the trunk in Imogen's bedroom.[139] Another important element in producing Barry's "majestic" or sublime was sheer size. In 1791 he was at work on *The Birth of Pandora*, a painting to rival Raphael: the canvas was 120 inches by 216 inches. Indeed, according to Edwards, Barry "seldom painted any small pictures, for he seemed to entertain an idea that no work of art could be in a great style, unless it were of great

[134] *Works*, II, 144. [135] *Ibid.*, II, 586. [136] *Ibid.*, I, 20.
[137] *Ibid.*, I, 31. [138] *Ibid.*, I, 104.
[139] *Architectural Review* (Oct. 1950), p. 220.

dimensions."[140] Certainly the series of pictures in the Great Room of the Society of Arts was immense and crowded with figures, and, judging from Charles Brandion's drawing, *The Exhibition at the Royal Academy 1771*, where it is clearly to be seen, Barry's first Academy exhibit, *Adam and Eve*, was commanding if only by reason of its size.[141]

Burke may be held partly to blame for this stress on size in painting: in the *Enquiry* he sufficiently emphasizes "magnitude" as an element in sublimity. He did, however, insist that "Designs that are vast only by their dimensions, are always the sign of a common and low imagination."[142] His disciples tended to ignore the disclaimer and to strive after the effect of magnitude without heeding Burke's caution. It seems, however, that he was aware of the tendency, may perhaps have held himself partially responsible, and it is likely that he was the writer of an anonymous letter in 1783 commenting on Barry's *Account of a series of Pictures, in the Great Room of the Society of Arts*. In it he speaks of the "erroneous principle" widely prevalent:

> This is the confounding greatness of size with greatness of manner, and imagining that extent of canvass or weight of marble can contribute towards making a picture or a statue sublime. The only kind of sublimity which a painter or sculptor should aim at, is to express by certain proportions and positions of limbs and features, that strength and dignity of mind, and vigour and activity of body, which enable men to conceive and execute great actions: provided the space in which these are represented, is large enough for the artist to distinguish them clearly to the eye of the spectator, at the distance from which he intends his work to be seen. . . . The representation of gigantic and monstrous figures has nothing of sublimity either in poetry or painting, which entirely depend upon expression.[143]

Burke's principal object is to check "this taste for false sublime" among painters, but he takes the opportunity to condemn the same quality in Macpherson's *Ossian*:

[140] *Anecdotes of Painters* (1808), p. 310.

[141] See W. T. Whitley, *Artists and their Friends in England 1700–1799* (1928), I, 284.

[142] *Op. cit.*, p. 76.

[143] J. Barry, *Works*, I, 263–4.

> those miserable rhapsodies . . . have been received by many as standards of true taste and sublimity. . . . The consequence of this was the corrupting all true taste and introducing gigantic and extravagant tinsel, for easy dignity and natural sublimity.[144]

The attempt to create sublimity in art by means of vastness was continued into the nineteenth century by such a painter as John Martin. His *Belshazzar's Feast* (1821) has terror as the dominant motif; the picture is crowded with figures under a dark and menacing sky; the immensity of the pillars supporting the building and of the building itself is insisted on; and the whole painting occupies an area 62½ inches by 98 inches. The reactions of *The Edinburgh Review* prove that Burke's terms provided the natural idiom and his values the criteria for a criticism of such a painting over seventy years after the *Enquiry* was first published.

> The ruling sentiment of the present subject is *a sublime and supernatural awe*. . . . Vastness and strength powerfully excite a sense of awe and grandeur . . . and Mr. Martin has accordingly presented us with a hall of dimensions and gorgeous strength unparalleled. But when to the grand and the gigantic we add some powerful moral association,—when we give to it the hoariness of antiquity,—when we deepen its solemnity by the obscurity of night,—when, by concealing its limits, we lead the imagination to draw out the vast almost into the infinite,—then, indeed, do we awake to a sense of awe and sublimity, beneath which the mind seems overpowered.[145]

The Fall of Nineveh (1828)—on a canvas 84 inches by 134 inches—reveals similar characteristics of gloom (heightened by the brilliant red of the burning city), terror, vast buildings, the suggestion of supernatural vengeance, and so on—many elements, indeed, of Burke's sublime gone bad through exaggeration. James Ward's *Gordale Scar* (Tate Gallery, no. 1043)—on a canvas 131 inches by 166 inches—with its immense, black, towering cliffs surmounted by dark clouds and dominating a group of cattle, with a rushing stream falling in the centre of the cliffs, betrays the same signs of degeneracy.

An earlier painter of great calibre, who also felt Burke's influence, was J. H. Mortimer. With Barry and Fuseli he

144 *Ibid.*, I, 266.

145 *Op. cit.* (1829), XLIX, 471.

formed the group of painters in whom Blake was particularly interested. There is a certain irony in the fact that through these men Blake himself was tainted, however slightly, with the ideas of the *Enquiry* which he so despised. As Grigson and Erdman have shown, he undoubtedly owed his *Nebuchadnezzar* in great measure to Mortimer's drawing, *Nebuchadnezzar recovering his Reason*; his *Ordeal of Queen Emma* was also suggested, both in manner and subject, by Mortimer's *Edward the Confessor seizing the Treasures of his Mother.*[146] There would seem equally little doubt about Mortimer's own debt to Burke. As Edwards remarks, Mortimer's subjects were largely "all those kind of scenes, that personify 'Horrible Imaginings'",[147] and his "monsters" (Reynolds's term)[148] are marked by the hugeness, the gloom and terror, the power, and the emotional intensity which Burke prescribed for the sublime. His *Caliban* has a hideous face of great power and the cruel nails are intended to exploit feelings of terror; similarly his Nebuchadnezzar is a massive figure with a powerful, muscular body, again with fierce nails, shown against a background of rocky waste. There is here an artist of imaginative force conveying a personal vision, but one is sure that the *Enquiry* provided an essential formative influence.

There is even less doubt in the case of Henry Fuseli. How much weight Reynolds's estimate of Burke carried for Fuseli it is impossible to say, but certainly the latter is loud in his praise for the author of the *Discourses.*[149] However, Paul Ganz makes the unequivocal statement:

> The *Conjectures on Original Composition* of Edward Young . . . and the remarkable *Inquiry into . . . the Sublime and Beautiful* by Burke, . . . confirmed [Fuseli] in his views concerning the function of art and increased his self-confidence.[150]

Fuseli's prose-remains support such an assertion. His review of Cowper's *Homer* for the *Analytical Review*—he was a member of

[146] *Architectural Review* (Oct. 1950), p. 219; *Blake Prophet Against Empire*, pp. 44, 177.

[147] *Op. cit.*, p. 63.

[148] Blake, *Works*, p. 784.

[149] J. Knowles, *The Life and Writings of Henry Fuseli* (1831), II, 15.

[150] *The Drawings of Henry Fuseli* (1949), p. 30.

the publisher Johnson's political circle—contains the by now familiar Burkean terminology;[151] in his Lectures to the Royal Academy Fuseli claims that the effect of the "epic or sublime" manner in painting is that it "*astonishes*";[152] he is clearly of the opinion that it ought to excite the most powerful emotions the human mind is capable of feeling; and his "recipe" for a sublime figure is thoroughly Burkean. "Whatever connects the individual with the elements . . . is an instrument of sublimity",[153] is a statement whose significance becomes more evident when Fuseli gives concrete illustration. Macbeth, he says, is not made "an object of terror" simply by the accumulation of supernatural machinery in the play; "to render him so you must place him on a ridge, his downdashed eye absorbed by the murky abyss; surround the horrid vision with darkness, exclude its limits, and shear its light to glimpses." Here is, indeed, a cluster of Burkean notions: there is the terror, the obscurity, the infinity, the height, the sombre colour, and the emotional intensity which the *Enquiry* claims are essential to the sublime. Fuseli's drawing *The Bard* (from Gray's poem) contains some of these elements. The towering figure stands on a rocky ledge; his downward look and raised arms emphasize his elevated position; there is a suggestion of power in his personality; the ominous sky behind enhances the man's elemental grandeur and "connects him with the elements". But it is, perhaps, as (Kirke White's) "Genius of horror and romantic awe"[154] that Fuseli most obviously connects with the sublime of terror. Blake—a fervent admirer of Fuseli—spoke of "the gloom of a real terror" in his picture of Count Ugolino;[155] Grigson observes that Johnson's remark about Milton —"pleasure and terror are indeed the genuine sources of poetry"—is applicable to the spirit of Fuseli's interpretation.[156] The nature of his vision is illustrated by the famous work, *The Nightmare*. The intention of both the initial sketch (1781) and the subsequent painting (1782) is to arouse a pleasing terror in the onlooker: the grinning goblin crouching on the breast of a

[151] J. Knowles, *op. cit.*, I, 109. [152] *Ibid.*, II, 157.
[153] *Ibid.*, II, 225. [154] *Ibid.*, I, 432. [155] *Works*, p. 912.
[156] *Architectural Review* (Oct. 1950), p. 216. On this and other Johnsonian references quoted by Grigson see this introduction, pp. xci–xcii.

sleeping woman is indeed a terrifying sight. But it is not the crude horror of a Gothic novel; it is an exploitation of the intensity, not the crudity, of the imaginative experience; it is, in fact, an attempt to arouse from the particular occasion, "the strongest emotion which the mind is capable of feeling".[157]

The other painter for whom one can be sure the *Enquiry* was an important work is the water-colourist, David Cox. The strongest support for this claim is to be found in his *Treatise on Landscape Painting and Effect in Water Colours* (1813), a quotation from which will sufficiently indicate its main drift:

a Cottage or a Village scene requires a soft and simple admixture of tones, calculated to produce pleasure without astonishment; awakening all the delightful sensations of the bosom, without trenching on the nobler provinces of feeling. On the contrary, the structures of greatness and antiquity should be marked by a character of awful sublimity, suited to the dignity of the subject. . . . In the language of the pencil, as well as of the pen, sublime ideas are expressed by lofty and obscure images; such as in pictures, objects of fine majestic forms, lofty towers, mountains, lakes margined with stately trees, rugged rocks, and clouds rolling their shadowy forms in broad masses over the scene. Much depends on the classification of the objects, which should wear a magnificent uniformity; and much on the colouring, the tones of which should be deep and impressive.[158]

The reliance on the *Enquiry* in the passage quoted is too obvious to require detailed comment, though it is worth noticing that the Burkean sublime provides the yardstick and what may be classed as "the beautiful" (cottage or village scenes) is described by reference to it: ". . . calculated to produce pleasure *without astonishment*". He later says that abrupt lines produce a "grand" effect, and colouring in harmony with "gloomy majesty" produces "grandeur".[159] It is interesting to note here that it was Cox's practice to copy paintings by other men which caught his imagination: one of such works was Martin's *Belshazzar's Feast*.[160]

In his own work Cox appears to have attempted both the

[157] *Enquiry*, p. 39.

[158] *Op. cit.* (ed. A. L. Baldry, 1922), pp. 11–12.

[159] *Ibid.*, pp. 16, 17.

[160] Trenchard Cox, *David Cox* (1947), p. 78.

sublime and the beautiful. This is not to claim him as a slavish disciple of Burke, but simply to suggest that the *Enquiry* was an important factor in Cox's acquiring a personal idiom and realizing a personal vision. In his water-colour, *Buckingham House from the Green Park,*[161] the colours—predominantly green, brown, and pale blue—are what Burke would call "clean and fair", not "strong";[162] the lines are "even and horizontal" which, in contrast to the sublime, Cox believed would produce "serenity";[163] and there is a general "smoothness" about the whole picture, especially in the broad area of grass in the foreground and the large background of sky. Another attempt at the "beautiful" is to be seen in *The Wind*, a water-colour marked by the Burkean "gradual variation" among the mild colours, and no abruptness but rather curved and gentle lines. On the other hand several of the sepia drawings printed as an appendix to the *Treatise* are attempts at the sublime: the gaunt solidity of Kenilworth Castle shrouded with "gloomy majesty" (plate XXXIII); *Snowdon, North Wales* shows a dark mass of mountains with irregular outline under a threatening sky (plate XLIV); and *Twilight—Warwick Castle* has a foreground of dark water and trees with vague outline, in the background the huge mass of the castle obscurely featured but with an abruptly angled outline, and a dark mass of clouds across the whole scene (plate LIV). But one of the most impressive of Cox's "sublime" pictures is the water-colour, *The Challenge*, "in which a bull, bellowing as the rain beats down on a desolate moor, vies with the roar of a thunderstorm".[164] The Burkean elements are pronounced: the bull, expressly mentioned in the *Enquiry* as "frequently" having "a place in sublime descriptions" because of its destructive, terrifying power;[165] the awe-inspiring force of elemental nature; the desolation of the moor; and the suggestion of "excessive loudness [which] is sufficient to overpower the soul . . . and to fill it with terror".[166] It might well be that Cox was here expressing an individual mood and was beyond any specific literary direction, but it remains true that Burke's *Enquiry* appears to have contributed

161 Trenchard Cox, *David Cox,* Plate II.
162 *Enquiry*, p. 117.
163 *Treatise,* p. 16.
164 Trenchard Cox, *op. cit.*, p. 110.
165 *Op. cit.*, p. 65.
166 *Ibid.*, p. 82.

significantly to the achievement of a personal and powerful statement.

The final instance of the *Enquiry*'s direct influence in England to be quoted—its influence on Thomas Hardy[167]—possibly resulted from the increasing regard in the nineteenth century for Burke as a political thinker and a man of letters. George Henry Lewes's *Principles of Success in Literature* (already referred to)[168] was a posthumous collection (published in 1898) of articles written in the mid-sixties for *The Fortnightly Review*; in 1867 John Morley published his perceptive historical study of Burke; J. B. Robertson's *Lectures on Burke* appeared in 1869; Arnold made his claim for Burke as the greatest of English prose-writers;[169] and Leslie Stephen, in his *History of English Thought in the 18th century* (1876), accorded Burke especial prominence. Such a spate of publications could scarcely fail to create an interest in Burke for a voracious reader like Hardy, particularly when it was reinforced by personal acquaintance with two of the writers mentioned. Morley he met in 1869 as the publisher's reader of his first novel, and Stephen, whom he knew from about 1872–3, was "the man whose philosophy was to influence his own for many years, indeed, more than that of any other contemporary."[170] (And while it is principally to the 1870's that our attention must be directed, it is worth noticing that when Hardy first met Arnold, in 1880, it was the question of style that they discussed.[171])

This subject of style was one which evidently occupied a great deal of Hardy's attention in the mid-seventies, the time of writing *Far from the Madding Crowd* (1874) and *The Return of the Native* (1878). It was precisely for this reason and at this time that Burke's *Enquiry* became important to him, though his interest in it was not confined to a concern with style. In *Far from the Madding Crowd* occurs the statement: "It has been said that mere ease after torment is delight for a time."[172] On being

[167] I am greatly indebted here to Mr. S. F. Johnson, of the University of Columbia. See his letter to *T.L.S.*, 7 Dec. 1956.

[168] See p. lxxxii.

[169] In "The Literary Influence of Academies", *Cornhill Magazine*, Aug. 1864.

[170] F. E. Hardy, *The Life of Thomas Hardy* (1933), I, 132.

[171] *Ibid.*, I, 175.

[172] *Op. cit.*, Chap. 21.

challenged by Rebekah Owen, in 1893, about the source of the passage, Hardy at once replied: "Edmund Burke."[173] There can be little doubt but that Hardy was thinking of Burke's distinction, in Part I of the *Enquiry*, between delight and pleasure, the former being "the sensation which accompanies the removal of pain or danger". The ease with which Hardy introduced the reference into the novel and answered his interrogator several years later, is indicative of the thoroughness with which he had absorbed Burke's book.

The most explicit documentary evidence of his study of Burke is given by an entry concerning style in his notebook in 1875:

> Read again Addison, Macaulay, Newman, Sterne, Defoe, Lamb, Gibbon, Burke, *Times* leaders, etc., in a study of style. Am more and more confirmed in an idea I have long held . . . "Ars est celare artem". The whole secret of a living style and the difference between it and a dead style, lies in not having too much style—being, in fact, a little careless, or rather seeming to be, here and there.[174]

While the *Enquiry* is not specifically mentioned here it contains the Burkean dictum which most obviously coincides with the view of style expressed: "no work of art can be great, but as it deceives".[175] That the notebook entry in fact referred to the *Enquiry* cannot, of course, be proved, but it becomes the more likely when Hardy is seen to have this particular work very much in mind in writing *The Return of the Native* which was probably begun towards the end of the following year, 1876. In this novel, for example, he is at one point fascinated by the idea that there are persons who, "without clear ideas of the things they criticize, have yet had clear ideas of the relations of those things".[176] Mrs. Yeobright is such a person and, to illustrate his assertion about her, Hardy cites the examples of Blacklock, the blind poet, and Saunderson, the blind professor of mathematics. It is certain that these examples came straight from the *Enquiry*; Burke had used them to prove the same general point; and, especially over Saunderson, Hardy almost quotes Burke *verbatim*.[177]

173 Carl J. Weber, *Hardy and the Lady from Madison Square* (1952), p. 89.

174 F. E. Hardy, *op. cit.*, I, 138.

175 *Op. cit.*, p. 76.

176 *Op. cit.*, III, iii.

177 *Enquiry*, p. 169.

The most significant contribution, however, which Burke made to Hardy's achievement in the same novel was through his theory of sublimity. Had Hardy not read the *Enquiry* the famous description of Egdon Heath would have been other than it is. Hardy's view of the world, expressed particularly in the fifth and sixth paragraphs of the opening chapter, made him unusually appreciative of the Burkean sublime; Burke's "sublime" and "beautiful" in fact provided him with just the kind of sharply defined dualism he required.

Haggard Egdon appealed to a subtler and scarcer instinct, to a more recently learned emotion, than that which responds to the sort of beauty called charming and fair.

Indeed, it is a question if the exclusive reign of this orthodox beauty is not approaching its last quarter. The new Vale of Tempe may be a gaunt waste in Thule: human souls may find themselves in closer and closer harmony with external things wearing a sombreness distasteful to our race when it was young. The time seems near, if it has not actually arrived, when the chastened sublimity of a moor, a sea, a mountain will be all of nature that is absolutely in keeping with the moods of the more thinking among mankind.

That it is the Burkean sublime being evoked is made more certain by other references. Hardy describes Egdon as being dark and sombre, "exhaling darkness", obscure, "best felt when it could not clearly be seen", "majestic", and "grand in its simplicity"; he contrasts the sublimity of Egdon with "spots renowned for beauty of the accepted kind"; and the isolation, vastness, and awe-inspiring quality of the heath are ever implicit. There is no reason to doubt Burke's direct influence. Nor is there any doubt but that Burke's *Enquiry* made its finest contribution to imaginative literature through the stimulus it gave Thomas Hardy.

(ii) *France and Germany*

The impact made by the *Enquiry* in both France and Germany was immediate and forceful.[1] Diderot seems to have found that

[1] I am indebted in this section to G. Candrea, *Der Begriff des Erhabenen bei Burke und Kant* (Strassburg, 1894); W. G. Howard, "Burke among the forerunners of Lessing", *P.M.L.A.* (1907), XXII, 608–32; and W. Folkierski, *Entre le Classicisme et le Romantisme* (Paris, 1925).

the work echoed and formalized much of his own unsystematic thinking. In Germany, Lessing had become acquainted with it by November 1757, by January 1758 he had begun to translate it, and, most probably in the following year, he wrote his *Bemerkungen* on various points in it.[2] Moses Mendelssohn reviewed and summarized Burke's theory in 1758; Herder considered making a translation of it; Christian Garve published a translation in 1773; and Kant came under its influence. Mendelssohn appears to have been the key-figure: it was he who continuously (but unsuccessfully) urged Lessing to complete his translation; his was the review on which Kant probably based his early knowledge of Burke and which, partly at any rate, provoked his *Beobachtungen über das Gefühl des Schönen und Erhabenen* (1764).

Diderot was peculiarly ready for Burke's influence. He had made a free translation of Shaftesbury in *l'Essai sur le mérite et la vertu* (1745); in his *Lettres sur les aveugles* (1749) he had used as evidence—as Burke did in the *Enquiry*—the life and work of Saunderson and the discussion which followed Cheselden's operation on a boy blind from birth;[3] he considered intense emotion essential in art and detested formality and artificiality both in nature and in art; and his melancholy fitted him to respond to an aesthetic of dark, terrible sublimity. In all it would have been strange if Diderot had not been fascinated by Burke's theory.

Comments excited by the paintings of Claude Vernet in the *Salon de 1767* most clearly prove the impact of the *Enquiry* on Diderot.[4] Elsewhere (in the *Pensées détachées sur la peinture*) we find this description of the great landscape painter:

> Le grand paysagiste a son enthousiasme particulier; c'est une espèce d'horreur sacrée. Ses antres sont ténébreux et profonds; ses rochers escarpés menacent le ciel; les torrents en descendent avec fracas, ils rompent au loin le silence auguste de ses forêts. L'homme passe à travers de la demeure des démons et des dieux.[5]

[2] See *Sämtliche Schriften* (Leipzig, 1886–1924), XIV, 220 n.

[3] Cf. *Enquiry*, pp. 169, 144.

[4] A translation of the *Enquiry* appeared in Paris in 1765. See Appendix.

[5] *Œuvres complètes* (Paris, 1875–7), XII, 88.

Such a characteristic rhapsody makes it easy to understand why Vernet's paintings in the Salon of 1767 prompted Diderot to pour out his thoughts on the mysterious order of nature, the definition of beauty and virtue, and the conditions making for terror and sublimity. Burke's are the terms he uses for the latter: indeed his comments seem to consist of a précis of relevant parts of the *Enquiry*. Familiar phrases reappear in a French version:

Tout ce qui étonne l'âme, tout ce qui imprime un sentiment de terreur conduit au sublime. Une vaste plaine n'étonne pas comme l'océan, ni l'océan tranquille comme l'océan agité.

L'obscurité ajoute à la terreur.

La clarté est bonne pour convaincre; elle ne vaut rien pour émouvoir. La clarté, de quelque manière qu'on l'entende, nuit à l'enthousiasme.

Les idées de puissance ont aussi leur sublimité; mais la puissance qui menace émeut plus que celle qui protège. La magnificence n'est belle que dans le désordre.[6]

There can be no doubt but that these ideas and phrases—and there are many more parallels of image and idiom—came direct from the *Enquiry*. But there is no acknowledgment. Diderot was ready for and had absorbed Burke's ideas; he had given to them his peculiar verve; they had, in fact, become his own.

The case with Lessing is similar. While it is known that he read the *Enquiry*—his *Bemerkungen über Burkes philosophische Untersuchungen* is proof enough—in the major work, *Laocoön*, Lessing does not give Burke a single mention. Howard suggests that the absence of reference is due to Lessing's substantial agreement with Burke and since the *Laocoön* was a polemical work, taking issue with certain opponents, Lessing found no occasion to refer to his English predecessor.[7] Yet even in the *Bemerkungen*—if one excludes the title—Burke is not mentioned by name. The fact is that in this early work certain sections of the *Enquiry* serve as a springboard for Lessing's own ideas (on sublimity, beauty, delight, love and hatred), but he makes no

[6] *Ibid.*, XI, 146–8.

[7] *P.M.L.A.*, XXII, 618.

attempt to analyse the whole of Burke's theory. Nor does he examine Burke's views on the poetry-painting issue which was to be the focal point of the *Laocoön*. From the outset, then, Lessing seems to have discovered in the *Enquiry* a statement of fundamental principles which he could readily accept.[8] It is hazardous, therefore, to speak of Lessing's "indebtedness" to Burke: it is more accurate to claim that Burke confirmed views already held by the German critic and to describe Burke (as Howard does) as a "forerunner" of Lessing.

In the *Enquiry* and the *Laocoön* the two writers are not concerned with the same problem. The premises from which they work are also totally different. Poetry, for Burke, not being an imitative art, cannot be properly descriptive; its effectiveness rests on the intensity of the poet's conception and it works through suggestiveness, emotional connotations, the combination of elements of which we have no sensory experience, and so on. Lessing, on the other hand, maintains that words are appropriate for conveying succession in time, and that poetry is therefore best suited to a subject involving action and not description of static objects. Consequently his objection to descriptive poetry rests on the assumption that it cannot give an idea of co-existent totality: "the *co-existence* of the physical object comes into collision with the *consecutiveness* of speech".[9] Furthermore, though it may make clear, it cannot make interesting.[10]

However, much of what Burke has to say on the qualities of poetry and on the inadequacy of words to delineate objects, and the many contrasts he draws between the techniques and provinces of poetry and painting would appeal strongly to Lessing. Frequently in the *Laocoön* we are reminded of Burke. Lessing claims that he looks to the poet, not for precise knowledge of reality, but for "the effect which this knowledge,

[8] This claim is made in spite of Lessing's letter to Mendelssohn, 1758 (quoted by Bosanquet, *History of Aesthetic*, 4th edn., 1917, p. 203), in which he says that Burke's principles "are not worth much". Lessing goes on to add: "still his book is uncommonly useful as a collection of all the occurrences and perceptions which the philosophers must assume as indisputable in inquiries of this kind. He has collected all the materials for a good system. . . ."

[9] *Laocoön* (Everyman's edn., 1930), p. 63.

[10] *Ibid.*, pp. 60–1.

expressed in words, produces on [his] imagination".[11] A description of a beautiful woman by Ariosto may reveal the poet's understanding of the theory of proportion, his thorough knowledge of colour, and the like, but

What good is all this erudition and insight to us his readers who want to have the picture of a beautiful woman, who want to feel something of the soft excitement of the blood which accompanies the actual sight of beauty?[12]

By a remarkable coincidence Lessing quotes the same Homeric description as does Burke and draws substantially the same lesson from it.[13] He points out that Homer "refrains from all piecemeal delineation of physical beauties", but "what Homer could not describe in its component parts, he makes us feel in its working".[14] Burke distinguishes on the same grounds between "describing" (or exact imitation), the province of painting, and evoking "feeling", the province of poetry.

just as the wise poet showed beauty merely in its effect, which he felt he could not delineate in its component parts, so did the no less wise painter show us beauty by nothing else than its component parts and hold it unbecoming to his art to resort to any other method.

The remark might have come from either writer: it is from the *Laocoön*.[15] Similarly Burke claims—and Lessing echoes the claim—that poetry can present emotively objects of which we have had no sensory experience:

To represent an angel in a picture, you can only draw a beautiful young man winged; but what painting can furnish out any thing so grand as the addition of one word, "the angel of the *Lord*"?[16]

Earlier in the *Enquiry* he had made an analogous point with reference to the spirit which passed before the face of Job:

When painters have attempted to give us clear representations of these very fanciful and terrible ideas, they have I think almost always failed; insomuch that I have been at a loss, in all the pictures

[11] *Ibid.*, p. 76. Cf. *Enquiry*, p. 172.

[12] *Ibid.*, p. 77.

[13] "Coincidence" because Burke adds this description in the 2nd edition and it is likely that Lessing saw only the first.

[14] *Laocoön*, p. 79. Cf. *Enquiry*, p. 172.

[15] *Op. cit.*, p. 81.

[16] *Enquiry*, p. 174.

I have seen of hell, whether the painter did not intend something ludicrous.[17]

Lessing agreed completely. Figures which are superhumanly great and noble in poetry become, he says, degraded when translated into painting; translations of poetical obscurities are ludicrous, utterly evacuated of all positive and symbolic values.

With Kant the case is different again. Unlike Lessing, it is probable that he did not know the *Enquiry* at first hand when he wrote his *Beobachtungen*, but that he drew on Mendelssohn's review-summary; but, unlike Lessing and Diderot, when Kant wrote his mature work, the *Critique of Judgment* (1790), he gave Burke honourable mention. By that time Burke's sensationist theories represented a stage through which Kant had passed and which could conveniently be quoted as an inadequate solution to the problem of the sublime.

The "Observations"[18] are not, like the *Critique*, an analysis of the emotion of the sublime; they are rather a collection of aesthetic-ethical aperçus on the concept of the sublime. Relying on the method of observation, and claiming that aesthetic impressions are independent of intellectual perceptions, Kant examines the connections between the moral life and the aesthetic sensibility. He tries to determine how far the approval of the good can be traced back to the aesthetic judgment. Like Shaftesbury (but unlike Burke) Kant speaks of the beauty of virtue which becomes conscious only when we subordinate a love of self to the interest of benevolence. But the emotion which leads to true virtue he calls "the sense of beauty and dignity of human nature". It is plain, indeed, that certain detached ideas point forward to Kant's mature conception of the sublime; what is important here, however, is his method of getting an initial hold on this conception. The method is Burkean.

Kant examines, for instance, the sublime characteristics of the human body and decides that the large face of the individual, a brownish complexion and black eyes, together with the dignity of age, create an impression of sublimity. Such

[17] *Enquiry*, p. 63.

[18] *Sämtliche Werke* (ed. G. Hartenstein, Leipzig, 1867), II, 227 ff. See G. Candrea, *Der Begriff des Erhabenen bei Burke und Kant*, pp. 19–23.

physiological data, taken with certain isolated observations and phrases, point unmistakably to Burke's influence. Kant claims, with Burke, that the sublime causes a feeling of pleasure that at times is mixed with astonishment and even with terror. The sight of a snow-clad mountain, the description of a violent storm, or Milton's picture of hell, are sublime; so are the lonely shades of sacred groves, the night, or the idea of infinity. When Kant goes further and defines three types of sublimity—the awful, the lofty, and the splendid—we are again reminded of the *Enquiry*. The "awful" sublime is connected with horror, the feeling aroused by the profound loneliness of a desert; the "lofty" Kant illustrates by the calm admiration excited by the vast simplicity of the Pyramids; and the "splendid", connected with the impression created by magnificence, is illustrated by St. Peter's in Rome. While, then, Kant's conception of sublimity is broader than Burke's—it includes the feelings of admiration, respect, and reverence which Burke, while acknowledging, relegates to an inferior level[19]—the contribution made by the English writer is too marked to be gainsaid.

The *Critique* bears equally clear traces of Burke's influence but the theory is undoubtedly profounder and subtler. The transcendentalism puts it beyond anything Burke was capable of and it must be stated at once that there is a fundamental divergence between the two critics. Burke's theory is linked with the passions relating to self-preservation; it turns on pain and danger; and it conceives the sublime as provoking astonishment. To Kant astonishment is only the first stage. In his view we feel physically helpless in the face of fearsome natural objects, but because we are independent of nature the mind is conscious of its own essential power. Consequently, a feeling of physical inferiority is succeeded by a sense of intellectual or moral superiority. Once this basic difference is recognized, Burke's contribution can the better be determined.

Both Burke and Kant refuse to accept the sublime as a manifestation of the beautiful;[20] both agree that the sublime is to be found in objects which suggest "limitlessness";[21] to both,

[19] *Enquiry*, p. 57.
[20] *Critique* (transl. J. C. Meredith, Oxford, 1952), pp. 90–3.
[21] *Ibid.*, p. 90. Cf. *Enquiry*, pp. 73–4.

the sublime puts a strain on the imagination;[22] both writers recognize the importance of "succession";[23] each insists, though Kant more emphatically, that "instead of the object, it is rather the cast of the mind in appreciating it that we have to estimate as *sublime*";[24] and they agree that natural objects are sublime when they are "a source of fear", but Kant does not believe that "every object that is a source of fear is sublime".[25] It can, in fact, be claimed that Kant takes certain elements from Burke—by the time of the *Critique* he certainly knew the whole *Enquiry*—and embodies them in his own system. It must also be said that he points to the central weakness in Burke's empirical system: it depends purely on egoistic judgments, on the individual's appraisal of personal sensory experiences, and no universal laws can be laid down. Nevertheless, while he points out the limitations of the empirical method, Kant pays the highest possible tribute to his English predecessor. He acknowledges that "the empirical exposition of aesthetic judgments may be a first step towards accumulating the material for a higher investigation"—Burke, he affirms, "deserves to be called the foremost author in this method of treatment".[26]

[22] *Critique*, p. 91. Cf. *Enquiry*, pp. 75, 134–6, *et passim*.
[23] *Ibid.*, pp. 99–100. Cf. *Enquiry*, p. 74.
[24] *Ibid.*, p. 104. [25] *Ibid.*, p. 109. [26] *Ibid.*, pp. 132, 130.

NOTE ON THE TEXT

THE second edition, 1759, has provided the copy-text for this edition. Textual changes in editions after the second are limited to punctuation, spelling, and capitalization, and there is no reason to suppose that Burke had any hand in such alterations. His own preface to the second edition, and the obvious care with which he prepared that text (for style, emphasis, answers to reviews, etc.) make it authoritative. (The copy of the first edition in the Bodleian Library has been used for collation; the two minor occasions on which it differs from the British Museum copy have been noted.)[1]

In the textual notes all verbal changes between the first and second editions are given, and with the exception of two obvious errors in the latter,[2] its readings have been adopted throughout. Differences in spelling and capitalization have not been noted; changes in punctuation have been recorded only where they bear significantly on style and meaning; and, whereas eighteenth-century spelling has been retained, the few errors have been silently corrected. At the request of the publishers the periods at the ends of headings are omitted, and "SECTION" is used in place of "SECT.", an abbreviation which Burke employs throughout.

Greek quotations have been modernized typographically and taken from the standard Oxford texts.

Passages which were added in the second edition are indicated by angled brackets. Whenever Burke appears to be answering some criticism of the first edition by his additions in the second, the relevant quotation from the reviewer is

[1] See pp. 172, 173. Professor Todd informs me that at these two points the Harvard University Library copy follows the Bodleian, the Berg copy (New York Public Library) follows the British Museum, and the Shenstone copy (Harvard) is correct on both occasions.

[2] See pp. 157, 159.

given, without comment, in a note to the beginning of the addition.

Information which is given in the introduction is not repeated in the explanatory notes to the text.

The place of publication of works quoted is London, except as otherwise noted.

For the reader's convenience, the first-edition preface has been printed before the second. In the original editions both prefaces are in italics.

THE PREFACE TO THE FIRST EDITION

THE author hopes it will not be thought impertinent to say something of the motives which induced him to enter into the following enquiry. The matters which make the subject of it had formerly engaged a great deal of his attention. But he often found himself greatly at a loss; he found that he was far from having any thing like an exact theory of our passions, or a knowledge of their genuine sources; he found that he could not reduce his notions to any fixed or consistent principles; and he had remarked, that others lay under the same difficulties.

He observed that the ideas of the sublime and beautiful were frequently confounded; and that both were indiscriminately applied to things greatly differing, and sometimes of natures directly opposite. Even Longinus, in his incomparable discourse upon a part of this subject, has comprehended things extremely repugnant to each other, under one common name of the *Sublime*. The abuse of the word *Beauty*, has been still more general, and attended with still worse consequences.

Such a confusion of ideas must certainly render all our reasonings upon subjects of this kind extremely inaccurate and inconclusive. Could this admit of any remedy, I imagined it could only be from a diligent examination of our passions in our own breasts; from a careful survey of the properties of things which we find by experience to influence those passions; and from a sober and attentive investigation of the laws of nature, by which those properties are capable of affecting the body, and thus of exciting our passions. If this could be done, it was imagined that the rules deducible from such an enquiry might be applied to the imitative arts, and to whatever else they concerned, without much difficulty.

It is four years now since this enquiry was finished;[1] during which time the author found no cause to make any material alteration in his theory. He has shewn it to some of his friends, men of learning and candour,[2] who do not think it wholly unreasonable; and he now ventures to lay it before the public, proposing his notions as probable conjectures, not as things certain and indisputable; and if he has any where expressed himself more positively, it was owing to inattention.

[1] 1st edn. published 21 April 1757 (R. Straus, *Robert Dodsley*, 1910, p. 362).

[2] See Introduction, p. xxii.

THE PREFACE TO THE SECOND EDITION

I HAVE endeavoured to make this edition[1] something more full and satisfactory than the first. I have sought with the utmost care, and read with equal attention, every thing which has appeared in publick against my opinions; I have taken advantage of the candid liberty of my friends; and if by these means I have been better enabled to discover the imperfections of the work, the indulgence it has received, imperfect as it was, furnished me with a new motive to spare no reasonable pains for its improvement. Though I have not found sufficient reason, or what appeared to me sufficient, for making any material change in my theory, I have found it necessary in many places to explain, illustrate and enforce it. I have prefixed an introductory discourse concerning Taste; it is a matter curious in itself; and it leads naturally enough to the principal enquiry. This with the other explanations has made the work considerably larger; and by increasing its bulk has, I am afraid added to its faults; so that notwithstanding all my attention, it may stand in need of a yet greater share of indulgence than it required at its first appearance.

They who are accustomed to studies of this nature will expect, and they will allow too for many faults. They know that many of the objects of our enquiry are in themselves obscure and intricate; and that many others have been rendered so by affected refinements or false learning; they know that there are many impediments in the subject, in the prejudices of others, and even in our own, that render it a matter of no small difficulty to shew in a clear light the genuine face of nature. They know that whilst the mind is intent on the general scheme of things, some particular parts must be neglected; that we must often submit the style to the matter, and frequently give up the praise of elegance, satisfied with being clear.

[1] Published 10 January 1759 (R. Straus, *Robert Dodsley*, p. 367).

The characters of nature are legible it is true; but they are not plain enough to enable those who run, to read them. We must make use of a cautious, I had almost said, a timorous method of proceeding. We must not attempt to fly, when we can scarcely pretend to creep. In considering any complex matter, we ought to examine every distinct ingredient in the composition, one by one; and reduce every thing to the utmost simplicity; since the condition of our nature binds us to a strict law and very narrow limits. We ought afterwards to re-examine the principles by the effect of the composition, as well as the composition by that of the principles. We ought to compare our subject with things of a similar nature, and even with things of a contrary nature; for discoveries may be, and often are made by the contrast, which would escape us on the single view. The greater number of these comparisons we make, the more general and the more certain our knowledge is like to prove, as built upon a more extensive and perfect induction.

If an enquiry thus carefully conducted, should fail at last of discovering the truth, it may answer an end perhaps as useful, in discovering to us the weakness of our own understanding. If it does not make us knowing, it may make us modest. If it does not preserve us from error, it may at least from the spirit of error, and may make us cautious of pronouncing with positiveness or with haste, when so much labour may end in so much uncertainty.

I could wish that in examining this theory, the same method were pursued which I endeavoured to observe in forming it. The objections, in my opinion, ought to be proposed, either to the several principles as they are distinctly considered, or to the justness of the conclusion which is drawn from them. But it is common to pass over both the premises and conclusion in silence, and to produce as an objection, some poetical passage which does not seem easily accounted for upon the principles I endeavour to establish.[2] This manner of proceeding I should think very improper. The task would be infinite, if we could establish no principle until we had previously unravelled the

[2] Cf. *The Critical Review* (1757), III, 369–70; *The Literary Magazine* (1757), II, 186–7.

complex texture of every image or description to be found in poets and orators. And though we should never be able to reconcile the effect of such images to our principles, this can never overturn the theory itself, whilst it is founded on certain and indisputable facts. A theory founded on experiment and not assumed, is always good for so much as it explains. Our inability to push it indefinitely is no argument at all against it. This inability may be owing to our ignorance of some necessary *mediums*; to a want of proper application; to many other causes besides a defect in the principles we employ. In reality the subject requires a much closer attention, than we dare claim from our manner of treating it.

If it should not appear on the face of the work, I must caution the reader against imagining that I intended a full dissertation on the Sublime and Beautiful. My enquiry went no further than to the origin of these ideas. If the qualities which I have ranged under the head of the Sublime be all found consistent with each other, and all different from those which I place under the head of Beauty; and if those which compose the class of the Beautiful have the same consistency with themselves, and the same opposition to those which are classed under the denomination of Sublime, I am in little pain whether any body chuses to follow the name I give them or not, provided he allows that what I dispose under different heads are in reality different things in nature. The use I make of the words may be blamed as too confined or too extended; my meaning cannot well be misunderstood.

To conclude; whatever progress may be made towards the discovery of truth in this matter, I do not repent the pains I have taken in it. The use of such enquiries may be very considerable. Whatever turns the soul inward on itself, tends to concenter its forces, and to fit it for greater and stronger flights of science. By looking into physical causes our minds are opened and enlarged; and in this pursuit whether we take or whether we lose our game, the chace is certainly of service. *Cicero*, true as he was to the Academic philosophy, and consequently led to reject the certainty of physical as of every other kind of knowledge, yet freely confesses its great importance to the human understanding: "*Est animorum ingeniorumque nostrorum naturale quoddam quasi pabulum consideratio contemplatioque naturæ.*"[3] If we can direct the lights we derive from such exalted speculations, upon the humbler field of the imagination, whilst we investigate the springs and trace the courses of our passions, we may not only communicate to the taste a sort of philosophical solidity, but we may reflect back on the severer sciences some of the graces and elegancies of taste, without which the greatest proficiency in those sciences will always have the appearance of something illiberal.

[3] *Academicorum Priorum*, II, 127 (misquoted). The Academic philosophers —Arcesilaus, Carneades, and others—were followers of Plato who stressed the sceptical elements in his thought and denied the possibility of certain knowledge. Cicero was converted to the Academic school as a young man when Philo of Larissa, then its leader, visited Rome.

THE CONTENTS

[a] *between the . . . Pleasure.*] *between Pain and Pleasure*

[b] *Recapitulation*] *The Recapitulation*

[c] *SECTION XIX. The Conclusion.*] *SECTION XIX. SECTION XX. The same SECTION XXI. The Conclusion*

PART II

PART III

[d] *Passion*] *Passions*

[e] [*IV.*]] *V.*

[f] *SECTION VIII. . . . Magnitude*] *SECTION VIII. Infinity SECTION IX. The same SECTION X. Succession and Uniformity SECTION XI. The effect of Succession and Uniformity in Building SECTION XII. Magnitude*

PART IV

[g] *SECTION XXVI. Taste*] *SECTION XXVI. Continued SECTION XXVII. Taste*

PART V

[h] *in*] *by*
[i] *Why*] *The cause why*

INTRODUCTION ON TASTE[1]

ON a superficial view, we may seem to differ very widely from each other in our reasonings, and no less in our pleasures: but notwithstanding this difference, which I think to be rather apparent than real, it is probable that the standard both of reason and Taste is the same in all human creatures. For if there were not some principles of judgment as well as of sentiment common to all mankind, no hold could possibly be taken either on their reason or their passions, sufficient to maintain the ordinary correspondence of life. It appears indeed to be generally acknowledged, that with regard to truth and falsehood there is something fixed. We find people in their disputes continually appealing to certain tests and standards which are allowed on all sides, and are supposed to be established in our common nature. But there is not the same obvious concurrence in any uniform or settled principles which relate to Taste. It is even commonly supposed that this delicate and aerial faculty, which seems too volatile to endure even the chains of a definition, cannot be properly tried by any test, nor regulated by any standard. There is so continual a call for the exercise of the reasoning faculty, and it is so much strengthened by perpetual contention, that certain maxims of right reason seem to be tacitly settled amongst the most ignorant. The learned have improved on this rude science, and reduced those maxims into a system. If Taste has not been so happily cultivated, it was not that the subject was barren, but that the labourers were few or negligent; for to say the truth, there are not the same interesting motives to impel us to fix the one, which urge us to ascertain the other. And after all, if men differ in their opinion concerning such matters, their difference is not attended with the same important consequences, else I make no doubt but that the logic of Taste, if I may be allowed

1 See Introduction, pp. xxvii–xxxix.

the expression, might very possibly be as well digested, and we might come to discuss matters of this nature with as much certainty, as those which seem more immediately within the province of mere reason. And indeed it is very necessary at the entrance into such an enquiry, as our present, to make this point as clear as possible; for if Taste has no fixed principles, if the imagination is not affected according to some invariable and certain laws, our labour is like to be employed to very little purpose; as it must be judged an useless, if not an absurd undertaking, to lay down rules for caprice, and to set up for a legislator of whims and fancies.

The term Taste, like all other figurative terms, is not extremely accurate: the thing which we understand by it, is far from a simple and determinate idea in the minds of most men, and it is therefore liable to uncertainty and confusion. I have no great opinion of a definition, the celebrated remedy for the cure of this disorder. For when we define, we seem in danger of circumscribing nature within the bounds of our own notions, which we often take up by hazard, or embrace on trust, or form out of a limited and partial consideration of the object before us, instead of extending our ideas to take in all that nature comprehends, according to her manner of combining. We are limited in our enquiry by the strict laws to which we have submitted at our setting out.

——*Circa vilem patulumque morabimur orbem*
Unde pudor proferre pedem vetat aut operis lex.[2]

A definition may be very exact, and yet go but a very little way towards informing us of the nature of the thing defined; but let the virtue of a definition be what it will, in the order of things, it seems rather to follow than to precede our enquiry, of which it ought to be considered as the result. It must be acknowledged that the methods of disquisition and teaching may be sometimes different, and on very good reason undoubtedly; but for my part, I am convinced that the method of teaching which approaches most nearly to the method of investigation, is incomparably the best; since not content with serving up a few barren and lifeless truths, it leads to the stock

[2] Horace, *De Arte Poetica*, ll. 132, 135 (misquoted).

on which they grew; it tends to set the reader himself in the track of invention, and to direct him into those paths in which the author has made his own discoveries, if he should be so happy as to have made any that are valuable.

But to cut off all pretence for cavilling, I mean by the word Taste no more than that faculty, or those faculties of the mind which are affected with, or which form a judgment of the works of imagination and the elegant arts. This is, I think, the most general idea of that word, and what is the least connected with any particular theory. And my point in this enquiry is to find whether there are any principles, on which the imagination is affected, so common to all, so grounded and certain, as to supply the means of reasoning satisfactorily about them. And such principles of Taste, I fancy there are; however paradoxical it may seem to those, who on a superficial view imagine, that there is so great a diversity of Tastes both in kind and degree, that nothing can be more indeterminate.

All the natural powers in man, which I know, that are conversant about external objects, are the Senses; the Imagination; and the Judgment. And first with regard to the senses. We do and we must suppose, that as the conformation of their organs are nearly, or altogether the same in all men, so the manner of perceiving external objects is in all men the same, or with little difference. We are satisfied that what appears to be light to one eye, appears light to another; that what seems sweet to one palate, is sweet to another; that what is dark and bitter to this man, is likewise dark and bitter to that; and we conclude in the same manner of great and little, hard and soft, hot and cold, rough and smooth; and indeed of all the natural qualities and affections of bodies. If we suffer ourselves to imagine, that their senses present to different men different images of things, this sceptical proceeding will make every sort of reasoning on every subject vain and frivolous, even that sceptical reasoning itself, which had persuaded us to entertain a doubt concerning the agreement of our perceptions. But as there will be very little doubt that bodies present similar images to the whole species, it must necessarily be allowed, that the pleasures and the pains which every object excites in one man, it must raise in all mankind, whilst it operates naturally, simply, and by its proper powers only; for if we deny this, we must imagine, that the same cause operating in the same manner, and on subjects of the same kind, will produce different effects, which would be highly absurd. Let us first consider this point in the sense of Taste, and the rather as the faculty in question has taken its name from that sense. All men are agreed to call vinegar sour, honey sweet, and aloes bitter; and as they are all agreed in finding these qualities in those objects, they do not in the least differ concerning their effects with regard to pleasure and pain. They all concur in calling sweetness pleasant, and sourness and bitterness unpleasant. Here there is no diversity in their sentiments; and that there is not appears fully from the consent of all men in the metaphors which are taken from the sense of Taste. A sour temper, bitter expressions, bitter curses, a bitter fate, are terms well and strongly understood by all. And we are altogether as well understood when we say, a sweet disposition, a sweet person, a sweet condition, and the like. It is confessed, that custom, and some other causes, have made many deviations from the natural pleasures or pains which belong to these several Tastes; but then the power of distinguishing between the natural and the acquired relish remains to the very last. A man frequently comes to prefer the Taste of tobacco to that of sugar, and the flavour of vinegar to that of milk; but this makes no confusion in Tastes, whilst he is sensible that the tobacco and vinegar are not sweet, and whilst he knows that habit alone has reconciled his palate to these alien pleasures. Even with such a person we may speak, and with sufficient precision, concerning Tastes. But should any man be found who declares, that to him tobacco has a Taste like sugar, and that he cannot distinguish between milk and vinegar; or that tobacco and vinegar are sweet, milk bitter, and sugar sour, we immediately conclude that the organs of this man are out of order, and that his palate is utterly vitiated. We are as far from conferring with such a person upon Tastes, as from reasoning concerning the relations of quantity with one who should deny that all the parts together were equal to the whole. We do not call a man of this kind wrong in his notions, but absolutely mad. Exceptions of this sort in either way, do not at all impeach our general rule, nor make us conclude that men have various principles concerning the relations of quantity, or the Taste of things. So that when it is said, Taste cannot be disputed, it can only mean, that no one can strictly answer what pleasure or pain some particular man may find from the Taste of some particular thing. This indeed cannot be disputed; but we may dispute, and with sufficient clearness too, concerning the things which are naturally pleasing or disagreeable to the sense. But when we talk of any peculiar or acquired relish, then we must know the habits, the prejudices, or the distempers of this particular man, and we must draw our conclusion from those.

This agreement of mankind is not confined to the Taste solely. The principle of pleasure derived from sight is the same in all. Light is more pleasing than darkness. Summer, when the earth is clad in green, when the heavens are serene and bright, is more agreeable than winter, when every thing makes a different appearance. I never remember that any thing beautiful, whether a man, a beast, a bird, or a plant, was ever shewn, though it were to an hundred people, that they did not all immediately agree that it was beautiful, though some might have thought that it fell short of their expectation, or that other things were still finer. I believe no man thinks a goose to be more beautiful than a swan, or imagines that what they call a Friezland hen excels a peacock. It must be observed too, that the pleasures of the sight are not near so complicated, and confused, and altered by unnatural habits and associations, as the pleasures of the Taste are; because the pleasures of the sight more commonly acquiesce in themselves; and are not so often altered by considerations which are independent of the sight itself. But things do not spontaneously present themselves to the palate as they do to the sight; they are generally applied to it, either as food or as medicine; and from the qualities which they possess for nutritive or medicinal purposes, they often form the palate by degrees, and by force of these associations. Thus opium is pleasing to Turks, on account of the agreeable delirium it produces. Tobacco is the delight of Dutchmen, as it diffuses a torpor and pleasing stupefaction. Fermented spirits please our common people, because they banish care, and all consideration of future or present evils. All of these would lie absolutely neglected if their properties had originally gone no further than the Taste; but all these, together with tea and coffee, and some other things, have past from the apothecary's shop to our tables, and were taken for health long before they were thought of for pleasure. The effect of the drug has made us use it frequently; and frequent use, combined with the agreeable effect, has made the Taste itself at last agreeable. But this does not in the least perplex our reasoning; because we distinguish to the last the acquired from the natural relish. In describing the Taste of an unknown fruit, you would scarcely say, that it had a sweet and pleasant flavour like tobacco, opium, or garlic, although you spoke to those who were in the constant use of these drugs, and had great pleasure in them. There is in all men a sufficient remembrance of the original natural causes of pleasure, to enable them to bring all things offered to their senses to that standard, and to regulate their feelings and opinions by it. Suppose one who had so vitiated his palate as to take more pleasure in the Taste of opium than in that of butter or honey, to be presented with a bolus of squills; there is hardly any doubt but that he would prefer the butter or honey to this nauseous morsel, or to any other bitter drug to which he had not been accustomed; which proves that his palate was naturally like that of other men in all things, that it is still like the palate of other men in many things, and only vitiated in some particular points. For in judging of any new thing, even of a Taste similar to that which he has been formed by habit to like, he finds his palate affected in the natural manner, and on the common principles. Thus the pleasure of all the senses, of the sight, and even of the Taste, that most ambiguous of the senses, is the same in all, high and low, learned and unlearned.

Besides the ideas, with their annexed pains and pleasures, which are presented by the sense; the mind of man possesses a sort of creative power of its own; either in representing at pleasure the images of things in the order and manner in which they were received by the senses, or in combining those images in a new manner, and according to a different order. This power is called Imagination; and to this belongs whatever is called wit, fancy, invention, and the like. But it must be observed, that this power of the imagination is incapable of producing any thing absolutely new; it can only vary the disposition of those ideas which it has received from the senses.[3] Now the imagination is the most extensive province of pleasure and pain, as it is the region of our fears and our hopes, and of all our passions that are connected with them; and whatever is calculated to affect the imagination with these commanding ideas, by force of any original natural impression, must have the same power pretty equally over all men. For since the imagination is only the representative of the senses, it can only be pleased or displeased with the images from the same principle on which the sense is pleased or displeased with the realities; and consequently there must be just as close an agreement in the imaginations as in the senses of men. A little attention will convince us that this must of necessity be the case.

But in the imagination, besides the pain or pleasure arising from the properties of the natural object, a pleasure is perceived from the resemblance, which the imitation has to the original; the imagination, I conceive, can have no pleasure but what results from one or other of these causes. And these causes operate pretty uniformly upon all men, because they operate by principles in nature, and which are not derived from any particular habits or advantages. Mr. Locke very justly and finely observes of wit, that it is chiefly conversant in tracing resemblances; he remarks at the same time, that the business of judgment is rather in finding differences.[4] It may perhaps appear, on this supposition, that there is no material distinction between the wit and the judgment, as they both seem to result from different operations of the same faculty of *comparing*. But in reality, whether they are or are not dependent on the same power of the mind, they differ so very materially in many respects, that a perfect union of wit and judgment is one of the rarest things in the world. When two distinct objects are unlike to each other, it is only what we expect; things are in

[3] Cf. Locke, *An Essay concerning Human Understanding*, II, ii, 2; II, xii, 2; etc.

[4] *Essay*, II, xi, 2. The idea was popular before Locke; it appears in Hobbes, *Leviathan*, I, 8, and *Human Nature*, X, 4. (See J. E. Spingarn, *Critical Essays of the 17th Century*, Oxford, 1908, I, xxix.)

their common way; and therefore they make no impression on the imagination: but when two distinct objects have a resemblance, we are struck, we attend to them, and we are pleased. The mind of man has naturally a far greater alacrity and satisfaction in tracing resemblances than in searching for differences; because by making resemblances we produce *new images*, we unite, we create, we enlarge our stock; but in making distinctions we offer no food at all to the imagination; the task itself is more severe and irksome, and what pleasure we derive from it is something of a negative and indirect nature. A piece of news is told me in the morning; this, merely as a piece of news, as a fact added to my stock, gives me some pleasure. In the evening I find there was nothing in it. What do I gain by this, but the dissatisfaction to find that I had been imposed upon? Hence it is, that men are much more naturally inclined to belief than to incredulity. And it is upon this principle, that the most ignorant and barbarous nations have frequently excelled in similitudes, comparisons, metaphors, and allegories, who have been weak and backward in distinguishing and sorting their ideas. And it is for a reason of this kind that Homer and the oriental writers, though very fond of similitudes, and though they often strike out such as are truly admirable, they seldom take care to have them exact; that is, they are taken with the general resemblance, they paint it strongly, and they take no notice of the difference which may be found between the things compared.

Now as the pleasure of resemblance is that which principally flatters the imagination, all men are nearly equal in this point, as far as their knowledge of the things represented or compared extends. The principle of this knowledge is very much accidental, as it depends upon experience and observation, and not on the strength or weakness of any natural faculty; and it is from this difference in knowledge that what we commonly, though with no great exactness, call a difference in Taste proceeds. A man to whom sculpture is new, sees a barber's block, or some ordinary piece of statuary; he is immediately struck and pleased, because he sees something like an human figure; and entirely taken up with this likeness, he does not at all attend to its defects. No person, I believe, at the first time of seeing a piece of imitation ever did. Some time after, we suppose that this novice lights upon a more artificial work of the same nature; he now begins to look with contempt on what he admired at first; not that he admired it even then for its unlikeness to a man, but for that general though inaccurate resemblance which it bore to the human figure. What he admired at different times in these so different figures, is strictly the same; and though his knowledge is improved, his Taste is not altered. Hitherto his mistake was from a want of knowledge in art, and this arose from his inexperience; but he may be still deficient from a want of knowledge in nature. For it is possible that the man in question may stop here, and that the masterpiece of a great hand may please him no more than the middling performance of a vulgar artist; and this not for want of better or higher relish, but because all men do not observe with sufficient accuracy on the human figure to enable them to judge properly of an imitation of it. And that the critical Taste does not depend upon a superior principle in men, but upon superior knowledge, may appear from several instances. The story of the ancient painter and the shoemaker is very well known. The shoemaker set the painter right with regard to some mistakes he had made in the shoe of one of his figures, and which the painter, who had not made such accurate observations on shoes, and was content with a general resemblance, had never observed.[5] But this was no impeachment to the Taste of the painter, it only shewed some want of knowledge in the art of making shoes. Let us imagine, that an anatomist had come into the painter's working room. His piece is in general well done, the figure in question in a good attitude, and the parts well adjusted to their various movements; yet the anatomist, critical in his art, may observe the swell of some muscle not quite just in the peculiar action of the figure. Here the anatomist observes what the painter had not observed, and

[5] This story is told of the Greek painter Apelles, in Pliny, *Historia Naturalis*, XXXV, 84–5. It also appears in Roger De Piles, *Abregé de la vie Des Peintres* (Paris, 1699), pp. 125–6. This work was translated into English in 1706; a second edition in 1744 may have been Burke's source (see pp. 80–1). A contemporary reference to the story of Apelles is found in Johnson, *Rambler* No. 4 (31 March 1750).

he passes by what the shoemaker had remarked. But a want of the last critical knowledge in anatomy no more reflected on the natural good Taste of the painter, or of any common observer of his piece, than the want of an exact knowledge in the formation of a shoe. A fine piece of a decollated head of St. John the Baptist was shewn to a Turkish emperor; he praised many things, but he observed one defect; he observed that the skin did not shrink from the wounded part of the neck.[6] The sultan on this occasion, though his observation was very just, discovered no more natural Taste than the painter who executed this piece, or than a thousand European connoisseurs who probably never would have made the same observation. His Turkish majesty had indeed been well acquainted with that terrible spectacle, which the others could only have represented in their imagination. On the subject of their dislike there is a difference between all these people, arising from the different kinds and degrees of their knowledge; but there is something in common to the painter, the shoemaker, the anatomist, and the Turkish emperor, the pleasure arising from a natural object, so far as each perceives it justly imitated; the satisfaction in seeing an agreeable figure; the sympathy proceeding from a striking and affecting incident. So far as Taste is natural, it is nearly common to all.

In poetry, and other pieces of imagination, the same parity may be observed. It is true, that one man is charmed with Don Bellianis,[7] and reads Virgil coldly; whilst another is transported

[6] The painter in this story was Gentile Bellini (*c.* 1421–1508). The story appears in Carlo Ridolfi, *Le Maraviglie Dell'Arte* (Venice, 1648), I, 40, and also in De Piles, *Abregé de la vie Des Peintres*, pp. 250–1 (English translation, 1744, p. 158). Burke does not quite complete the story: the Emperor, Mahomet II, to prove the validity of his criticism, ordered a slave to be beheaded so that Bellini might see how the skin shrank back from the wound.

[7] Geronimo Fernandez, *Historia del valeroso é invencible Principe don Belianis de Grecia* (Burgos, 1547–79). Part I of this work was translated into English (by "L.A.") in 1598; other parts were added in 1664 and 1672, and the whole collected by Francis Kirkman in 1673: *The Famous and Delectable History of Don Bellienis of Greece*. This last was probably Burke's source. H. Thomas, *Spanish and Portuguese Romances of Chivalry* (Cambridge, 1920, pp. 256–62) gives an account of the history of the romance and says that

with the Eneid, and leaves Don Bellianis to children. These two men seem to have a Taste very different from each other; but in fact they differ very little. In both these pieces, which inspire such opposite sentiments, a tale exciting admiration is told; both are full of action, both are passionate, in both are voyages, battles, triumphs, and continual changes of fortune. The admirer of Don Bellianis perhaps does not understand the refined language of the Eneid, who if it was degraded into the style of the Pilgrim's Progress, might feel it in all its energy, on the same principle which made him an admirer of Don Bellianis.

In his favourite author he is not shocked with the continual breaches of probability, the confusion of times, the offences against manners, the trampling upon geography; for he knows nothing of geography and chronology, and he has never examined the grounds of probability. He perhaps reads of a shipwreck on the coast of Bohemia;[8] wholly taken up with so interesting an event, and only solicitous for the fate of his hero, he is not in the least troubled at this extravagant blunder. For why should he be shocked at a shipwreck on the coast of Bohemia, who does not know but that Bohemia may be an island in the Atlantic ocean? and after all, what reflection is this on the natural good Taste of the person here supposed?

So far then as Taste belongs to the imagination, its principle is the same in all men; there is no difference in the manner of their being affected, nor in the causes of the affection; but in the *degree* there is a difference, which arises from two causes principally; either from a greater degree of natural sensibility, or from a closer and longer attention to the object. To illustrate this by the procedure of the senses in which the same difference is found, let us suppose a very smooth marble table to be set before two men; they both perceive it to be smooth, and they are both pleased with it, because of this quality. So far they agree. But suppose another, and after that another table, the latter still smoother than the former, to be set before them. It

the English versions were popular in Ireland in the eighteenth century. (See also Introduction, p. xvi, and A. P. I. Samuels, *Early Life . . . of Burke*, Cambridge, 1923, pp. 45–8.)

[8] Shakespeare, *The Winter's Tale*, III, iii, 2.

is now very probable that these men, who are so agreed upon what is smooth, and in the pleasure from thence, will disagree when they come to settle which table has the advantage in point of polish. Here is indeed the great difference between Tastes, when men come to compare the excess or diminution of things which are judged by degree and not by measure. Nor is it easy, when such a difference arises, to settle the point, if the excess or diminution be not glaring. If we differ in opinion about two quantities, we can have recourse to a common measure, which may decide the question with the utmost exactness; and this I take it is what gives mathematical knowledge a greater certainty than any other. But in things whose excess is not judged by greater or smaller, as smoothness and roughness, hardness and softness, darkness and light, the shades of colours, all these are very easily distinguished when the difference is any way considerable, but not when it is minute, for want of some common measures which perhaps may never come to be discovered. In these nice cases, supposing the acuteness of the sense equal, the greater attention and habit in such things will have the advantage. In the question about the tables, the marble polisher will unquestionably determine the most accurately. But notwithstanding this want of a common measure for settling many disputes relative to the senses and their representative the imagination, we find that the principles are the same in all, and that there is no disagreement until we come to examine into the preeminence or difference of things, which brings us within the province of the judgment.

So long as we are conversant with the sensible qualities of things, hardly any more than the imagination seems concerned; little more also than the imagination seems concerned when the passions are represented, because by the force of natural sympathy they are felt in all men without any recourse to reasoning, and their justness recognized in every breast. Love, grief, fear, anger, joy, all these passions have in their turns affected every mind; and they do not affect it in an arbitrary or casual manner, but upon certain, natural and uniform principles. But as many of the works of imagination are not confined to the representation of sensible objects, nor to efforts upon the passions, but extend themselves to the manners, the characters, the actions, and designs of men, their relations, their virtues and vices, they come within the province of the judgment, which is improved by attention and by the habit of reasoning. All these make a very considerable part of what are considered as the objects of Taste; and Horace sends us to the schools of philosophy and the world for our instruction in them.[9] Whatever certainty is to be acquired in morality and the science of life; just the same degree of certainty have we in what relates to them in works of imitation. Indeed it is for the most part in our skill in manners, and in the observances of time and place, and of decency in general, which is only to be learned in those schools to which Horace recommends us, that what is called Taste by way of distinction, consists; and which is in reality no other than a more refined judgment. On the whole it appears to me, that what is called Taste, in its most general acceptation, is not a simple idea, but is partly made up of a perception of the primary pleasures of sense, of the secondary pleasures of the imagination, and of the conclusions of the reasoning faculty, concerning the various relations of these, and concerning the human passions, manners and actions. All this is requisite to form Taste, and the ground-work of all these is the same in the human mind; for as the senses are the great originals of all our ideas,[10] and consequently of all our pleasures, if they are not uncertain and arbitrary, the whole ground-work of Taste is common to all, and therefore there is a sufficient foundation for a conclusive reasoning on these matters.

Whilst we consider Taste, merely according to its nature and species, we shall find its principles entirely uniform; but the degree in which these principles prevail in the several individuals of mankind, is altogether as different as the principles themselves are similar. For sensibility and judgment, which are the qualities that compose what we commonly call a *Taste*, vary exceedingly in various people. From a defect in the former of these qualities, arises a want of Taste; a weakness in the

[9] *De Arte Poetica*, ll. 309 ff. (Burke may have had in mind the Earl of Roscommon's translation, ll. 340 ff.)

[10] Cf. Locke, *Essay*, II, i, 3, *et passim*.

latter, constitutes a wrong or a bad one. There are some men formed with feelings so blunt, with tempers so cold and phlegmatic, that they can hardly be said to be awake during the whole course of their lives. Upon such persons, the most striking objects make but a faint and obscure impression. There are others so continually in the agitation of gross and merely sensual pleasures, or so occupied in the low drudgery of avarice, or so heated in the chace of honours and distinction, that their minds, which had been used continually to the storms of these violent and tempestuous passions, can hardly be put in motion by the delicate and refined play of the imagination. These men, though from a different cause, become as stupid and insensible as the former; but whenever either of these happen to be struck with any natural elegance or greatness, or with these qualities in any work of art, they are moved upon the same principle.

The cause of a wrong Taste is a defect of judgment. And this may arise from a natural weakness of understanding (in whatever the strength of that faculty may consist) or, which is much more commonly the case, it may arise from a want of proper and well-directed exercise, which alone can make it strong and ready. Besides that ignorance, inattention, prejudice, rashness, levity, obstinacy, in short, all those passions, and all those vices which pervert the judgment in other matters, prejudice it no less in this its more refined and elegant province. These causes produce different opinions upon every thing which is an object of the understanding, without inducing us to suppose, that there are no settled principles of reason. And indeed on the whole one may observe, that there is rather less difference upon matters of Taste among mankind, than upon most of those which depend upon the naked reason; and that men are far better agreed on the excellence of a description in Virgil, than on the truth or falsehood of a theory of Aristotle.

A rectitude of judgment in the arts which may be called a good Taste, does in a great measure depend upon sensibility; because if the mind has no bent to the pleasures of the imagination, it will never apply itself sufficiently to works of that species to acquire a competent knowledge in them. But, though a degree of sensibility is requisite to form a good judgment, yet a good judgment does not necessarily arise from a quick sensibility of pleasure; it frequently happens that a very poor judge, merely by force of a greater complexional sensibility, is more affected by a very poor piece, than the best judge by the most perfect; for as every thing new, extraordinary, grand, or passionate is well calculated to affect such a person, and that the faults do not affect him, his pleasure is more pure and unmixed; and as it is merely a pleasure of the imagination, it is much higher than any which is derived from a rectitude of the judgment; the judgment is for the greater part employed in throwing stumbling blocks in the way of the imagination, in dissipating the scenes of its enchantment, and in tying us down to the disagreeable yoke of our reason: for almost the only pleasure that men have in judging better than others, consists in a sort of conscious pride and superiority, which arises from thinking rightly; but then, this is an indirect pleasure, a pleasure which does not immediately result from the object which is under contemplation. In the morning of our days, when the senses are unworn and tender, when the whole man is awake in every part, and the gloss of novelty fresh upon all the objects that surround us, how lively at that time are our sensations, but how false and inaccurate the judgments we form of things? I despair of ever receiving the same degree of pleasure from the most excellent performances of genius which I felt at that age, from pieces which my present judgment regards as trifling and contemptible. Every trivial cause of pleasure is apt to affect the man of too sanguine a complexion: his appetite is too keen to suffer his Taste to be delicate; and he is in all respects what Ovid says of himself in love,

Molle meum levibus cor est violabile telis,
Et semper causa est, cur ego semper amem.[11]

One of this character can never be a refined judge; never what the comic poet calls *elegans formarum, spectator.*[12] The excellence and force of a composition must always be imperfectly estimated from its effect on the minds of any, except we know the temper and character of those minds. The most powerful effects of poetry and music have been displayed, and perhaps are still displayed, where these arts are but in a very low and imperfect

[11] *Heroides,* XV, 79–80 (misquoted).

[12] Terence, *Eunuchus,* l. 566.

state. The rude hearer is affected by the principles which operate in these arts even in their rudest condition; and he is not skilful enough to perceive the defects. But as the arts advance towards their perfection, the science of criticism advances with equal pace, and the pleasure of judges is frequently interrupted by the faults which are discovered in the most finished compositions.

Before I leave this subject I cannot help taking notice of an opinion which many persons entertain, as if the Taste were a separate faculty of the mind, and distinct from the judgment and imagination; a species of instinct by which we are struck naturally, and at the first glance, without any previous reasoning with the excellencies, or the defects of a composition.[13] So far as the imagination and the passions are concerned, I believe it true, that the reason is little consulted; but where disposition, where decorum, where congruity are concerned, in short wherever the best Taste differs from the worst, I am convinced that the understanding operates and nothing else; and its operation is in reality far from being always sudden, or when it is sudden, it is often far from being right. Men of the best Taste by consideration, come frequently to change these early and precipitate judgments which the mind from its aversion to neutrality and doubt loves to form on the spot. It is known that the Taste (whatever it is) is improved exactly as we improve our judgment, by extending our knowledge, by a steady attention to our object, and by frequent exercise. They who have not taken these methods, if their Taste decides quickly, it is always uncertainly; and their quickness is owing to their presumption and rashness, and not to any sudden irradiation that in a moment dispels all darkness from their minds. But they who have cultivated that species of knowledge which makes the object of Taste, by degrees and habitually attain not only a soundness, but a readiness of judgment, as men do by the same methods on all other occasions. At first they are obliged to spell, but at last they read with ease and with celerity: but this celerity of its operation is no proof, that the Taste is a distinct faculty. Nobody I believe has attended the course of a discussion, which turned upon matters within the

[13] See Introduction, p. xxxi.

sphere of mere naked reason, but must have observed the extreme readiness with which the whole process of the argument is carried on, the grounds discovered, the objections raised and answered, and the conclusions drawn from premises, with a quickness altogether as great as the Taste can be supposed to work with; and yet where nothing but plain reason either is or can be suspected to operate. To multiply principles for every different appearance, is useless, and unphilosophical too in a high degree.

This matter might be pursued much further; but it is not the extent of the subject which must prescribe our bounds, for what subject does not branch out to infinity? it is the nature of our particular scheme, and the single point of view in which we consider it, which ought to put a stop to our researches.

A PHILOSOPHICAL ENQUIRY INTO THE ORIGIN OF OUR IDEAS OF THE SUBLIME AND BEAUTIFUL

Part One

SECTION I
NOVELTY

THE first and the simplest emotion which we discover in the human mind, is Curiosity. By curiosity, I mean whatever desire we have for, or whatever pleasure we take in novelty. We see children perpetually running from place to place to hunt out something new; they catch with great eagerness, and with very little choice, at whatever comes before them; their attention is engaged by every thing, because every thing has, in that stage of life, the charm of novelty to recommend it. But as those things which engage us merely by their novelty, cannot attach us for any length of time, curiosity is the most superficial of all the affections; it changes its object perpetually; it has an appetite which is very sharp, but very easily satisfied; and it has always an appearance of giddiness, restlessness and anxiety. Curiosity from its nature is a very active principle; it quickly runs over the greatest part of its objects, and soon exhausts the variety which is commonly to be met with in nature; the same things make frequent returns, and they return with less and less of any agreeable effect. In short, the occurrences of life, by the time we come to know it a little, would be incapable of affecting the mind with any other sensations than those of loathing and weariness, if many things were not adapted to affect the mind by means of other powers besides novelty in them, and of other passions besides curiosity in ourselves. These powers and passions shall be considered in their place. But whatever these powers are, or upon what principle soever they affect the mind, it is absolutely necessary that they should not be exerted in those things which a daily and vulgar use have brought into a stale unaffecting familiarity. Some degree of novelty must be one of the materials in every instrument which works upon the mind; and curiosity blends itself more or less with all our passions.

SECTION II

PAIN and PLEASURE

It seems then necessary towards moving the passions of people advanced in life to any considerable degree, that the objects designed for that purpose, besides their being in some measure new, should be capable of exciting pain or pleasure from other causes. Pain and pleasure are simple ideas, incapable of definition.[1] People are not liable to be mistaken in their feelings, but they are very frequently wrong in the names they give them, and in their reasonings about them. Many are[j] of opinion, that pain arises necessarily from the removal of some pleasure; as they think pleasure does from the ceasing or diminution of some pain.[2] For my part I am rather inclined to imagine, that pain and pleasure in their most simple and natural manner of affecting, are each of a positive nature, and by no means necessarily dependent on each other for their existence. The human mind is often, and I think it is for the most part, in a state neither of pain nor pleasure, which I call a state of indifference. When I am carried from this state into a state of actual pleasure, it does not appear necessary that I should pass through the medium of any sort of pain. If in such a state of indifference, or ease, or tranquillity, or call it what you please, you were to be suddenly entertained with a concert of music; or suppose some object of a fine shape, and bright lively[k] colours to be presented before you; or imagine your smell is gratified with the fragrance of a rose; or if without any previous thirst you were to drink of some pleasant kind of wine; or to taste of some sweetmeat without being hungry; in all the several senses, of hearing, smelling, and tasting, you undoubtedly find a pleasure; yet if I enquire into the state of your mind previous to these gratifications, you will hardly tell me that they found you in any kind of pain; or having satisfied these several senses with their several pleasures, will you say that any pain has succeeded, though the pleasure is absolutely over? Suppose on the other hand, a man in the same state of

[j] *Many are*] *Many people are*

[k] *bright lively*] *bright and lively*

[1] Cf. Locke, *Essay*, II, vii, 1.

[2] See Burke's note to p. 34.

indifference, to receive a violent blow, or to drink of some bitter potion, or to have his ears wounded with some harsh and grating sound; here is no removal of pleasure; and yet here is felt, in every sense which is affected, a pain very distinguishable. It may be said perhaps, that the pain in these cases had its rise from the removal of the pleasure which the man[l] enjoyed before, though that pleasure was of so low a degree as to be perceived only by the removal. But this seems to me a subtilty,[m] that is not discoverable in nature. For if, previous to the pain, I do not feel any actual pleasure, I have no reason to judge that any such thing exists; since pleasure is only pleasure as it is felt. The same may be said of pain, and with equal reason. I can never persuade myself that pleasure and pain are mere relations, which can only exist as they are contrasted: but I think I can discern clearly that there are positive pains and pleasures, which do not at all depend upon each other. Nothing is more certain to my own feelings than this. There is nothing which I can distinguish in my mind with more clearness than the three states, of indifference, of pleasure, and of pain. Every one of these I can perceive without any sort of idea of its relation to any thing else. Caius is afflicted with a fit of the cholic; this man is actually in pain; stretch Caius upon the rack, he will feel a much greater pain; but does this pain of the rack arise from the removal of any pleasure? or is the fit of the cholic a pleasure or a pain just as we are pleased to consider it?

SECTION III

The difference between the removal of PAIN and positive PLEASURE

We shall carry this proposition yet a step further. We shall venture to propose, that pain and pleasure are not only, not necessarily dependent for their existence on their mutual diminution or removal, but that, in reality, the diminution or ceasing of pleasure does not operate like positive pain; and that the removal or diminution of pain, in its effect has very little

[l] *the man*] *he*

[m] *removal. But . . . subtilty,*] *removal; but this seems to me to be a subtilty,*

resemblance to positive pleasure.* The former of these propositions will, I believe, be much more readily allowed than the latter; because it is very evident that pleasure, when it has run its career, sets us down very nearly where it found us. Pleasure of every kind quickly satisfies; and when it is over, we relapse into indifference, or rather we fall into a soft tranquillity, which is tinged with the agreeable colour of the former sensation. I own, it is not at first view so apparent, that the removal of a great pain does not resemble positive pleasure: but let us recollect in what state we have found our minds upon escaping some imminent danger, or on being released from the severity of some cruel pain. We have on such occasions found, if I am not much mistaken, the temper of our minds in a tenor very remote from that which attends the presence of positive pleasure; we have found them in a state of much sobriety, impressed with a sense of awe, in a sort of tranquillity shadowed with horror. The fashion of the countenance and the gesture of the body on such occasions is so correspondent to this state of mind, that any person, a stranger to the cause of the appearance, would rather judge us under some consternation, than in the enjoyment of any thing like positive pleasure.

> ὡς δ' ὅτ' ἂν ἄνδρ' ἄτη πυκινὴ λάβῃ, ὅς τ' ἐνὶ πάτρῃ
> φῶτα κατακτείνας ἄλλων ἐξίκετο δῆμον,
> ἀνδρὸς ἐς ἀφνειοῦ, θάμβος δ' ἔχει εἰσορόωντας,
>
> Iliad. 24.[3]

> *As when a wretch, who conscious of his crime,*
> *Pursued for murder from his native clime,*
> *Just gains some frontier, breathless, pale, amaz'd;*
> *All gaze, all wonder!*[4]

This striking appearance of the man whom Homer supposes to have just escaped an imminent danger, the sort of mixt passion of terror and surprize, with which he affects the spectators,

* Mr. Locke [essay on human understanding, l. 2. c. 20. section 16.] thinks that the removal or lessening of a pain is considered and operates as a pleasure, and the loss or diminishing of pleasure as a pain. It is this opinion which we consider here.

[3] *Iliad*, XXIV, 480–2.

[4] Pope, *Iliad*, XXIV, 590–3 (misquoted).

paints very strongly the manner in which we find ourselves affected upon occasions any way similar. For when we have suffered from any violent emotion, the mind naturally continues in something like the same condition, after the cause which first produced it has ceased to operate. The[n] tossing of the sea remains after the storm; and when this remain of horror has entirely subsided, all the passion, which the accident raised, subsides along with it; and the mind returns to its usual state of indifference. In short, pleasure (I mean any thing either in the inward sensation, or in the outward appearance like pleasure from a positive cause) has never, I imagine, its origin from the removal of pain or danger.

SECTION IV

Of DELIGHT and PLEASURE, as opposed to each other

But shall we therefore say, that the removal of pain or its diminution is always simply painful? or affirm that the cessation or the lessening of pleasure is always attended itself with a pleasure? by no means. What I advance is no more than this; first, that there are pleasures and pains of a positive and independent nature; and secondly, that the feeling which results from the ceasing or diminution of pain does not bear a sufficient resemblance to positive pleasure to have it considered as of the same nature, or to entitle it to be known by the same name; and thirdly, that[o] upon the same principle the removal or qualification of pleasure has no resemblance to positive pain. It is certain that the former feeling (the removal or moderation of pain) has something in it far from distressing, or disagreeable in its nature. This feeling, in many cases so agreeable, but in all so different from positive pleasure, has no name which I know; but that hinders not its

[n] *operate. The*] *operate; the*

[o] *and thirdly, that*] *and that*

being a very real one, and very different from all others. [5]⟨It is most certain, that every species of satisfaction or pleasure, how different soever in its manner of affecting, is of a positive nature in the mind of him who feels it. The affection is undoubtedly positive; but the cause may be, as in this case it certainly is, a sort of *Privation*. And it is very reasonable that we should distinguish by some term two things so distinct in nature, as a pleasure that is such simply, and without any relation, from that pleasure, which cannot exist without a relation, and that too a relation to pain. Very extraordinary it would be, if these affections, so distinguishable in their causes, so different in their effects, should be confounded with each other, because vulgar use has ranged them under the same general title.⟩ Whenever I have occasion to speak of this species of relative pleasure, I call[p] it *Delight*; and I shall take the best care I can, to use that word in no other sense. I am satisfied the word is not commonly used in this appropriated signification; but I thought it better to take up a word already known, and to limit its signification, than to introduce a new one which would not perhaps incorporate so well with the language.[6] I should never have presumed the least[q] alteration in our words, if the nature of the language, framed for the purposes of business rather than those of philosophy, and the nature of my subject that leads me out of the common track of discourse, did not in a manner necessitate me to it. I shall make use of this liberty with all possible caution. As I make use of the word *Delight* to express

[p] *speak of . . . call*] *speak of it, I shall call*
[q] *presumed the least*] *presumed to attempt the least*

[5] *Literary Magazine*, II, 183: "But surely the removal of a toothach, is pleasure to all intents and purposes; it induces a train of pleasing ideas in the mind, such as satisfaction with our present state, etc. and pleasure is equally positive whether it begins in the mind, or is conveyed thither by agreeable bodily sensation. In like manner the removal of pleasure is positive pain, as the absence of a fine woman to whom we are attached, etc. The truth is, pain and pleasure may subsist independently, and also reciprocally induce each other." See also *The Monthly Review* (1757), XVI, 474–5 n.

[6] Cf. Dryden, *Defence of the Epilogue* (Mermaid Series, 1949, I, 220): "There is yet another way of improving language . . . that is, by applying received words to a new signification."

the sensation which accompanies the removal of pain or danger; so when I speak of positive pleasure, I shall for the most part call it simply *Pleasure*.

SECTION V

JOY and GRIEF

It must be observed, that the cessation of pleasure affects the mind three ways. If it simply ceases, after having continued a proper time, the effect is *indifference*; if it be abruptly broken off, there ensues an uneasy sense called *disappointment*; if the object be so totally lost that there is no chance of enjoying it again, a passion arises in the mind, which is called *grief*.[7] Now there is none of these, not even grief, which is the most violent, that I think has any resemblance to positive pain. The person who grieves, suffers his passion to grow upon him; he indulges it, he loves it: but this never happens in the case of actual pain, which no man ever willingly endured for any considerable time. That grief should be willingly endured, though far from a simply pleasing sensation, is not so difficult to be understood. It is the nature of grief to keep its object perpetually in its eye, to present it in its most pleasurable views, to repeat all the circumstances that attend it, even to the last minuteness;[r] to go back to every particular enjoyment, to dwell upon each, and to find a thousand new perfections in all, that were not sufficiently understood before; in grief, the *pleasure* is still uppermost; and the affliction we suffer has no resemblance to absolute pain, which is always odious, and which we endeavour to shake off as soon as possible. The Odyssey of Homer, which abounds with so many natural and affecting images, has none more striking than those which Menelaus raises of the calamitous fate of his friends, and his own manner of feeling it. He owns indeed, that he often gives himself some intermission from such melancholy reflections, but he observes too, that melancholy as they are, they give him pleasure.

[r] *that attend . . . minuteness;*] *that attended it, even to the least minuteness,*

[7] The definition of "grief" is reminiscent of Locke's definition of "sorrow" (*Essay*, II, xx, 8).

ἀλλ' ἔμπης πάντας μὲν ὀδυρόμενος καὶ ἀχεύων
πολλάκις ἐν μεγάροισι καθήμενος ἡμετέροισιν
ἄλλοτε μέν τε γόῳ φρένα τέρπομαι, ἄλλοτε δ' αὖτε
παύομαι· αἰψηρὸς δὲ κόρος κρυεροῖο γόοιο.[8]

Still in short intervals of pleasing woe,
Regardful of the friendly dues I owe,
I to the glorious dead, for ever dear,
Indulge *the tribute of a* grateful *tear.*[9]

HOM. Od. 4.

On the other hand, when we recover our health, when we escape an imminent danger, is it with joy that we are affected? The sense on these occasions is far from that smooth and voluptuous satisfaction which the assured prospect of pleasure bestows. The delight which arises from the modifications of pain, confesses the stock from whence it sprung, in its solid, strong, and severe nature.

SECTION VI

Of the passions which belong to SELF-PRESERVATION

Most of the ideas which are capable of making a powerful impression on the mind, whether simply of Pain or Pleasure, or of the modifications of those, may be reduced very nearly to these two heads, *self-preservation* and *society*; to the ends of one or the other of which all our passions are calculated to answer. The passions which concern self-preservation, turn mostly on *pain* or *danger*. The ideas of *pain*, *sickness*, and *death*, fill the mind with strong emotions of horror; but *life* and *health*, though they put us in a capacity of being affected with pleasure, they make no such impression by the simple enjoyment. The passions therefore which are conversant about the preservation of the individual, turn chiefly on *pain* and *danger*, and they are the most powerful of all the passions.

[8] *Odyssey*, IV, 100–103.

[9] Pope, *Odyssey*, IV, 127–30.

SECTION VII

Of the SUBLIME

Whatever is fitted in any sort to excite the ideas of pain, and danger, that is to say, whatever is in any sort terrible, or is conversant about terrible objects, or operates in a manner analogous to terror, is a source of the *sublime*; that is, it is productive of the strongest emotion which the mind is capable of feeling. [10]⟨I say the strongest emotion, because I am satisfied the ideas of pain are much more powerful than those which enter on the part of pleasure. Without all doubt, the torments which we may be made to suffer, are much greater in their effect on the body and mind, than any pleasures which the most learned voluptuary could suggest, or than the liveliest imagination, and the most sound and exquisitely sensible body could enjoy. Nay I am in great doubt, whether any man could be found who would earn a life of the most perfect satisfaction, at the price of ending it in the torments, which justice inflicted in a few hours on the late unfortunate regicide in France.[11] But as pain is stronger in its operation than pleasure, so death

[10] *Literary Magazine*, II, 183: "But surely this is false philosophy: the brodequin of *Ravilliac*, and the iron bed of *Damien* are capable of exciting alarming ideas of terror, but cannot be said to hold anything of the sublime. Besides, why are our other passions to be excluded? cannot the sublime consist with ambition? it is perhaps in consequence of this very passion, grafted in us, for the wisest purposes by the author of our existence, that we are capable of feeling the sublime in the degree we do; of delighting in everything that is magnificent, of preferring the sun to a farthing candle, that by proceeding from greater to still greater, we might at last fix our imagination on him who is the supreme of all. And this perhaps is the true source of the sublime, which is always greatly heightened when any of our passions are strongly agitated, such as terror, grief, rage, indignation, admiration, love, etc. By the strongest of these the sublime will be enforced, but it will consist with any of them."

[11] Robert Francis Damiens (1714–57) who attempted the life of Louis XV, 5 Jan. 1757, and was put to death, after barbarous tortures, by *écartèlement*, on 28 March. (See F. Ravaisson, *Archives de la Bastille*, Paris, 1866–91, XVI, 472–80.) Damiens's execution figured prominently in English periodicals: see *Literary Magazine*, II, 1–4; *Monthly Review* (1757), XVII, 57–78. He is mentioned by Goldsmith, *Citizen of the World*, Letter V, and *The Traveller*, l. 436.

is in general a much more affecting idea than pain; because there are very few pains, however exquisite, which are not preferred to death; nay, what generally makes pain itself, if I may say so, more painful, is, that it is considered as an emissary of this king of terrors.〉 When danger or pain press too nearly, they are incapable of giving any delight, and are simply terrible; but at certain distances, and with certain modifications, they may be, and they are delightful, as we every day experience. The cause of this I shall endeavour to investigate hereafter.

SECTION VIII

Of the passions which belong to SOCIETY

The other head under which I class our passions, is that of *society*, which may be divided into two sorts. 1. The society of the *sexes*, which answers the purposes of propagation; and next, that more *general society*, which we have with men and with other animals, and which we may in some sort be said to have even with the inanimate world. The passions belonging to the preservation of the individual, turn wholly on pain and danger; those which belong to *generation*, have their origin in gratifications and *pleasures*; the pleasure most directly belonging to this purpose is of a lively character, rapturous and violent, and confessedly the highest pleasure of sense; yet the absence of this so great an enjoyment, scarce amounts to an uneasiness; and except at particular times, I do not think it affects at all. When men describe in what manner they are affected by pain and danger; they do not dwell on the pleasure of health and the comfort of security, and then lament the *loss* of these satisfactions: the whole turns upon the actual pains and horrors which they endure. But if you listen to the complaints of a forsaken lover, you observe, that he insists largely on the pleasures which he enjoyed, or hoped to enjoy, and on the perfection of the object of his desires; it is the *loss* which is always uppermost in his mind.[12] The violent effects produced by love, which has

[12] In 1744 Burke was intimately acquainted with a "forsaken lover" whose "*loss*" resulted in suicide (Samuels, *Early Life*, pp. 50–2).

sometimes been even wrought up to madness, is no objection to the rule which we seek to establish. When men have suffered their imaginations to be long affected with any idea, it so wholly engrosses them as to shut out by degrees almost every other, and to break down every partition of the mind which would confine it. Any idea is sufficient for the purpose, as is evident from the infinite variety of causes which give rise to madness: but this at most can only prove, that the passion of love is capable of producing very extraordinary effects, not that its extraordinary emotions have any connection with positive pain.

SECTION IX

The final cause of the difference between the passions belonging to SELF-PRESERVATION, and those which regard the SOCIETY of the SEXES

The final cause of the difference in character between the passions which regard self-preservation, and those which are directed to the multiplication of the species, will illustrate the foregoing remarks yet further; and it is, I imagine, worthy of observation even upon its own account. As the performance of our duties of every kind depends upon life, and the performing them with vigour and efficacy depends upon health, we are very strongly affected with whatever threatens the destruction of either; but as we were not made to acquiesce in life and health, the simple enjoyment of them is not attended with any real pleasure, lest satisfied with that, we should give ourselves over to[s] indolence and inaction. On the other hand, the generation of mankind is a great purpose, and it is requisite that men should be animated to the pursuit of it by some great incentive. It is therefore attended with a very high pleasure; but as it is by no means designed to be our constant business, it is not fit that the absence of this pleasure should be attended with any considerable pain. The difference between men and brutes in this point, seems to be remarkable. Men are at all times pretty equally disposed to the pleasures of love, because they are to be guided by reason in the time and manner of

[s] *give ourselves over to*] *give up ourselves to*

indulging them. Had any great pain arisen from the want of this satisfaction, reason, I am afraid, would find great difficulties in the performance of its office. But brutes who obey laws, in the execution of which their own reason has but little share, have their stated seasons; at such times it is not improbable that the sensation from the want is very troublesome, because the end must be then answered, or be missed in many, perhaps for ever; as the inclination returns only with its season.

SECTION X

Of BEAUTY

The passion which belongs to generation, merely as such, is lust only; this is evident in brutes, whose passions are more unmixed, and which pursue their purposes more directly than ours. The only distinction they observe with regard to their mates, is that of sex. It is true, that they stick severally to their own species in preference to all others. But[t] this preference, I imagine, does not arise from any sense of beauty which they find in their species, as Mr. Addison supposes,[13] but from a law of some other kind to which they are subject; and this we may fairly conclude, from their apparent want of choice amongst those objects to which the barriers of their species have confined them. But man, who is a creature adapted to a greater variety and intricacy of relation, connects with the general passion, the idea of some *social* qualities, which direct and heighten the appetite which he has in common with all other animals; and as he is not designed like them to live at large, it is fit that he should have something to create a preference, and fix his choice; and this in general should be some sensible quality; as no other can so quickly, so powerfully, or so surely produce its effect. The object therefore of this mixed passion which we call love, is the *beauty* of the *sex*. Men are carried to the sex in general, as it is the sex, and by the common law of nature; but they are attached to particulars by personal *beauty*. I call beauty a social quality; for where women

[t] *others. But*] *others; but*

[13] *Spectator* No. 413.

and men, and not only they, but when other animals give us a sense of joy and pleasure in beholding them, (and there are many that do so) they inspire us with sentiments of tenderness and affection towards their persons; we like to have them near us, and we enter willingly into a kind of relation with them, unless we should have strong reasons to the contrary. But to what end, in many cases, this was designed, I am unable to discover; for I see no greater reason for a connection between man and several animals who are attired in so engaging a manner, than between him and some others who entirely want this attraction, or possess it in a far weaker degree. But it is probable, that providence did not make even this distinction, but with a view to some great end, though we cannot perceive distinctly what it is, as his wisdom is not our wisdom, nor our ways his ways.

SECTION XI
SOCIETY and SOLITUDE

The second branch of the social passions, is that which administers to *society in general.* With regard to this, I observe, that society, merely as society, without any particular heightenings, gives us no positive pleasure in the enjoyment; but absolute and entire *solitude,* that is, the total and perpetual exclusion from all society, is as great a positive pain as can almost be conceived. Therefore in the balance between the pleasure of general *society,* and the pain of absolute solitude, *pain* is the predominant idea. But the pleasure of any particular social enjoyment outweighs very considerably the uneasiness caused by the want of that particular enjoyment; so that the strongest sensation, relative to the habitudes of *particular society,* are sensations of pleasure. Good company, lively conversations, and the endearments of friendship, fill the mind with great pleasure; a temporary solitude on the other hand, is itself agreeable. This may perhaps prove, that we are creatures designed for contemplation as well as action; since solitude as well as society has its pleasures; as from the former observation we may discern, that an entire life of solitude contradicts the purposes of our being, since death itself is scarcely an idea of more terror.

SECTION XII

SYMPATHY, IMITATION, and AMBITION

Under this denomination of society, the passions are of a complicated kind, and branch out into a variety of forms agreeable to that variety[u] of ends they are to serve in the great chain of society. The three principal links in this chain are *sympathy*, *imitation*, and *ambition.*

SECTION XIII

SYMPATHY

It is by the first of these passions that we enter into the concerns of others; that we are moved as they are moved, and are never suffered to be indifferent spectators of almost any thing which men can do or suffer. For sympathy must be considered as a sort of substitution, by which we are put into the place of another man, and affected in many respects[v] as he is affected; so that this passion may either partake of the nature of those which regard self-preservation, and turning upon pain may be a source of the sublime; or it may turn upon ideas of pleasure; and then, whatever has been said of the social affections, whether they regard society in general, or only some particular modes of it, may be applicable here. It is by this principle chiefly that poetry, painting, and other affecting arts, transfuse their passions from one breast to another, and are often capable of grafting a delight on wretchedness, misery, and death itself. It is a common observation, that objects which in the reality would shock, are in tragical, and such like representations, the source of a very high species of pleasure. This taken as a fact, has been the cause of much reasoning.[14] The satisfaction has been commonly attributed, first, to the comfort we receive in considering that so melancholy a story is no more than a

[u] *forms agreeable . . . variety*] *forms agreeably to the great variety*

[v] *in many respects*] *in a good measure*

[14] Cf. Aristotle, *Poetics*, IV, XIV (ed. Hamilton Fyfe, Oxford, 1940, pp. 9, 37); Addison, *Spectator* No. 418.

fiction; and next, to the contemplation of our own freedom from the evils which we see represented. I am afraid it is a practice much too common in inquiries of this nature, to attribute the cause of feelings which merely arise from the mechanical structure of our bodies, or from the natural frame and constitution of our minds, to certain conclusions of the reasoning faculty on the objects presented to us; for I should imagine, that[w] the influence of reason in producing our passions is nothing near so extensive as it is[x] commonly believed.

SECTION XIV

The effects of SYMPATHY in the distresses of others

To examine this point concerning the effect of tragedy in a proper manner, we must previously consider, how we are affected by the feelings of our fellow creatures in circumstances of real distress. I am convinced we have a degree of delight, and that no small one, in the real misfortunes and pains of others; for let the affection be what it will in appearance, if it does not make us shun such objects, if on the contrary it induces us to approach them, if it makes us dwell upon them, in this case I conceive we must have a delight or pleasure of some species or other in contemplating objects of this kind. Do we not read the authentic histories of scenes of this nature with as much pleasure as romances or poems, where the incidents are fictitious? The prosperity of no empire, nor the grandeur of no king, can so agreeably affect in the reading, as the ruin of the state of Macedon, and the distress of its unhappy prince.[15] Such a catastrophe touches us in history as much as the destruction of Troy does in fable. Our delight in cases of this kind, is very greatly heightened, if the sufferer be some excellent

[w] *I should . . . that*] *I have some reason to apprehend, that*

[x] *as it is*] *as is*

[15] Most probably a reference to the break-up of the Macedonian empire among the Successors of Alexander, and to the circumstances of his death (323 B.C.).

person who sinks under an unworthy fortune. Scipio and Cato are both virtuous characters; but we are more deeply affected by the violent death of the one, and the ruin of the great cause he adhered to, than with the deserved triumphs and uninterrupted prosperity of the other;[16] for terror is a passion which always produces delight when it does not press too close, and pity is a passion accompanied with pleasure, because it arises from love and social affection. Whenever we are formed by nature to any active purpose, the passion which animates us to it, is attended with delight, or a pleasure of some kind, let the subject matter be what it will; and as our Creator has designed we should be united by the bond of sympathy, he has strengthened that bond by a proportionable delight; and there most where[y] our sympathy is most wanted, in the distresses of others. If this passion was simply painful, we would shun with the greatest care all persons and places that could excite such a passion; as, some who are so far gone in indolence as not to endure any strong impression actually do. But the case is widely different with the greater part of mankind; there is no spectacle we so eagerly pursue, as that of some uncommon and grievous calamity; so that whether the misfortune is before our eyes, or whether they are turned back to it in history, it always touches with delight. This is[z] not an unmixed delight, but blended with no small uneasiness. The delight we have in such things, hinders us from shunning scenes of misery; and the pain we feel, prompts us to relieve ourselves in relieving those who suffer; and all this antecedent to any reasoning, by an instinct that works us to its own purposes, without our concurrence.

[y] *united by . . . where*] *united together by so strong a bond as that of sympathy, he has therefore twisted along with it a proportionable quantity of this ingredient; and always in the greatest proportion where*

[z] *delight. This is*] *delight; but it is*

[16] Publius Cornelius Scipio Africanus (236–184 B.C.), the conqueror of Carthage, who defeated Hannibal at Zama in 202. Marcus Portius Cato (Uticensis) (95–46 B.C.), the prominent Stoic and opponent of Caesar, who committed suicide after defeat at Utica in 46. Using the word "cause" Burke may have had in mind Lucan's famous line: "Victrix causa deis placuit, sed victa Catoni" (*Pharsalia*, I, 128).

SECTION XV

Of the effects of TRAGEDY

It is thus in real calamities. In imitated distresses the only difference is the pleasure resulting from the effects of imitation; for it is never so perfect, but we can perceive it is an imitation, and on that principle are somewhat pleased with it. And indeed in some cases we derive as much or more pleasure from that source than from the thing itself. But then I imagine we shall be much mistaken if we attribute any considerable part of our satisfaction in tragedy to a consideration that tragedy is a deceit, and its representations no realities. The nearer it approaches the reality, and the further it removes us from all idea of fiction, the more perfect is its power. But be its power of what kind it will, it never approaches to what it represents. Chuse a day on which to represent the most sublime and affecting tragedy we[a] have; appoint the most favourite actors; spare no cost upon the scenes and decorations; unite the greatest efforts of poetry, painting and music; and when you have collected your audience, just at the moment when their minds are erect with expectation, let it be reported that a state criminal of high rank is on the point of being executed in the adjoining square;[17] in a moment the emptiness of the theatre would demonstrate the comparative weakness of the imitative arts, and proclaim the triumph of the real sympathy. I believe that this notion of our having a simple pain in the reality, yet a delight in the representation, arises from hence, that we do not sufficiently distinguish what we would by no means chuse to do, from what we should be eager enough to see if it was once done. We delight in seeing things, which so far from doing, our heartiest wishes would be to see redressed. This noble

[a] *tragedy we*] *tragedy which we*

[17] Burke's illustration was most likely prompted by the extraordinary popular interest shown in the execution of Lord Lovat (9 April 1747). Burke himself was fully acquainted with the details of the trial and execution: on 28 April 1747 the Trinity College "Club" heard and debated an "Oration" from its President (William Dennis) on the subject. (See Samuels, *Early Life*, p. 231.)

capital, the pride of England and of Europe, I believe no man is so strangely wicked as to desire to see destroyed by a conflagration or an earthquake, though he should be removed himself to the greatest distance from the danger.[18] But suppose such a fatal accident to have happened, what numbers from all parts would croud to behold the ruins, and amongst them many who would have been content never to have seen London in its glory? Nor is it either in real or fictitious distresses, our immunity from them which produces our delight; in my own mind I can discover nothing like it. I apprehend that this mistake is owing to a sort of sophism, by which we are frequently imposed upon; it arises from our not distinguishing between what is indeed a necessary condition to our doing or suffering any thing in general, and[b] what is the *cause* of some particular act. If a man kills me with a sword, it is a necessary condition to this that we should have been both of us alive before the fact; and yet it would be absurd to say, that our being both living creatures was the cause of his crime and of my death. So it is certain, that it is absolutely necessary my life should be out of any imminent hazard before I can take a delight in the sufferings of others, real or imaginary, or indeed in any thing else from any cause whatsoever. But then it is a sophism to argue from thence, that this immunity is the cause of my delight either on these or on any occasions. No one can distinguish such a cause of satisfaction in his own mind I believe; nay when we do not suffer any very acute pain, nor are exposed to any imminent danger of our lives, we can feel for others, whilst we suffer ourselves; and often then most when we are softened by affliction; we see with pity even distresses which we would accept in the place of our own.

[b] *thing in general, and*] *thing, and*

[18] A possible allusion to the earthquakes felt in London on 8 Feb. and 8 March 1750, and to the vast exodus from the city caused by the prophecy that it would be entirely destroyed by a further earthquake on 8 April. (See *The Gentleman's Magazine* (1750), XX, 184; Dixon Wecter, "The Missing Years in Burke's Biography", *P.M.L.A.*, LIII, 1102, n. 2.)

SECTION XVI

IMITATION

The second passion belonging to society is imitation, or, if you will, a desire of imitating, and consequently a pleasure in it. This passion arises from much the same cause with sympathy. For as sympathy makes us take a concern in whatever men feel, so this affection prompts us to copy whatever they do; and consequently we have a pleasure in imitating, and in whatever belongs to imitation merely as it is such, without any intervention of the reasoning faculty, but solely from our natural constitution, which providence has framed in such a manner as to find either pleasure or delight according to the nature of the object, in whatever regards the purposes of our being. It is by imitation far more than by precept that we learn every thing; and what we learn thus we acquire not only more effectually, but more pleasantly. This forms our manners, our opinions, our lives. It is one of the strongest links of society; it is a species of mutual compliance which all men yield to each other, without constraint to themselves, and which is extremely flattering to all. Herein it is that painting and many other agreeable arts have laid one of the principal foundations of their power. And since by its influence on our manners and our passions it is of such great consequence, I[c] shall here venture to lay down a rule, which may inform us with a good degree of certainty when we are to attribute the power of the arts, to imitation, or to our pleasure in[d] the skill of the imitator merely, and when to sympathy, or some other cause in conjunction with it. When the object represented in poetry or painting is such, as we could have no desire of seeing in the reality;[e] then I may be sure that its power in poetry or painting is owing to the power of imitation, and to no cause operating in the thing itself. So it is with most of the pieces which the painters call still life. In these a cottage, a dunghill, the meanest and most ordinary utensils of the kitchen, are capable of giving us pleasure. But when the object of the painting or poem is such as we should run to see if real, let it affect us with what

[c] *power. And . . . I*] *power. I* [d] *in*] *of* [e] *in the reality;*] *in reality;*

odd sort of sense it will, we may rely upon it, that the power of the poem or picture is more owing to the nature of the thing itself than to the mere effect of imitation, or to a consideration of the skill of the imitator however excellent. Aristotle has spoken so much and so solidly upon the force of imitation in his poetics, that it makes any further discourse upon this subject the less necessary.[19]

SECTION XVII
AMBITION

Although imitation is one of the great instruments used by providence in bringing our nature towards its perfection, yet if men gave themselves up to imitation entirely, and each followed the other, and so on in an eternal circle, it is easy to see that there never could be any improvement amongst them. Men must remain as brutes do, the same at the end that they are at this day, and that they were in the beginning of the world. To prevent this, God has planted in man a sense of ambition, and a satisfaction arising from the contemplation of his excelling his fellows in something deemed valuable amongst them. It is this passion that drives men to all the ways we see in use of signalizing themselves, and that tends to make whatever excites in a man the idea of this distinction so very pleasant. It has been so strong as to make very miserable men take comfort that they were supreme in misery; and certain it is, that where we cannot distinguish ourselves by something excellent, we begin to take a complacency in some singular infirmities, follies, or defects of one kind or other. It is on this principle that flattery is so prevalent; for flattery is no more than what raises in a man's mind an idea of a preference which he has not. Now whatever either on good or upon bad grounds tends to raise a man in his own opinion, produces a sort of swelling and triumph that is extremely grateful to the human mind; and this swelling is never more perceived, nor operates with more force, than when without danger we are conversant with terrible objects, the mind always claiming to itself some part of

[19] *Poetics*, IV *et passim.*

the dignity and importance of the things which it contemplates. Hence[f] proceeds what Longinus has observed of that glorying and sense of inward greatness, that always fills the reader of such passages in poets and orators as are sublime;[20] it is what every man must have felt in himself upon such occasions.

SECTION XVIII
The RECAPITULATION

To draw the whole of what has been said into a few distinct points. The passions which belong to self-preservation, turn on pain and danger; they are simply painful when their causes immediately affect us; they are delightful when we have an idea of pain and danger, without being actually in such circumstances; this delight I have not called pleasure, because it turns on pain, and because it is different enough from any idea of positive pleasure. Whatever excites this delight, I call *sublime*. The passions belonging to self-preservation are the strongest of all the passions.

The[g] second head to which the passions are referred with[h] relation to their final cause, is society. There are two sorts of societies. The first is, the society of sex. The passion belonging to this is called love, and it contains a mixture of lust; its object is the beauty of women. The other is the great society with man and all other animals. The passion subservient to this is called likewise love, but it has no mixture of lust, and its object is beauty; which is a name I shall apply to all such qualities in things as induce in us a sense of affection and tenderness, or some other passion the most nearly resembling these. The passion of love has its rise in positive pleasure; it is, like all things which grow out of pleasure, capable of being mixed with a mode of uneasiness, that is, when an idea of its object is excited in the mind with an idea at the same time of having irretrievably lost it. This mixed sense of pleasure I have not called *pain*, because it turns upon actual pleasure, and because

[f] *the things . . . Hence*] *the objects with which it is conversant; hence*

[g] *the passions. The*] *the passions. SECTION XIX. The*

[h] *with*] *in*

[20] *On the Sublime*, VII.

it is both in its cause and in most of its effects of a nature altogether different.

Next[i] to the general passion we have for society, to a choice in which we are directed by the pleasure we have in the object, the particular passion under this head called sympathy has the greatest extent. The nature of this passion is to put us in the place of another in whatever circumstance he is in, and to affect us in a like manner; so that this passion may, as the occasion requires, turn either on pain or pleasure; but with the modifications mentioned in some cases in section 11. As to imitation and preference nothing more need be said.

SECTION XIX[j]

The CONCLUSION

I believed that an attempt to range and methodize some of our most leading passions, would be a good preparative to such an enquiry as we are going to make in[k] the ensuing discourse. The passions I have mentioned are almost the only ones which it can be necessary to consider in our present design; though [l] the variety of the passions is great, and worthy in every branch of that variety of an attentive investigation. The more accurately we search into the human mind, the stronger traces we every where find of his wisdom who made it. If a discourse on the use of the parts of the body may be considered as an hymn to the Creator; the use of the passions, which are the organs of the mind, cannot be barren of praise to him, nor unproductive to ourselves of that noble and uncommon union of science and admiration, which a contemplation of the works of infinite wisdom alone can afford to a rational mind; whilst referring to him whatever we find of right, or good, or fair in ourselves, discovering his strength and wisdom even in our own weakness and imperfection, honouring them where we discover them clearly, and adoring their profundity where we are lost in our search, we may be inquisitive without impertinence, and elevated without pride; we may be admitted, if I may dare to

[i] *different. Next*] *different. SECTION XX. The same. Next*

[j] *SECTION XIX.*] *SECTION XXI.*

[k] *to such . . . in*] *to an enquiry of the nature of that which is to be attempted in*

[l] *to consider . . . though*] *to our present design to consider; though*

say so, into the counsels of the Almighty by a consideration of his works. The[m] elevation of the mind ought to be the principal end of all our studies, which if they do not in some measure effect, they are of very little service to us. But besides this great purpose, a consideration of the rationale of our passions seems to me very necessary for all who would affect them upon solid and sure principles. It is not enough to know them in general; to affect them after a delicate manner, or to judge properly of any work designed to affect them, we should know the exact boundaries of their several jurisdictions; we should pursue them through all their variety of operations, and pierce into the inmost, and what might appear inaccessible parts of our nature,

Quod latet arcanâ non enarrabile fibrâ.[21]

Without all this it is possible for a man after a confused manner sometimes to satisfy his own mind of the truth of his work; but he can never have a certain determinate rule to go by, nor can he ever make his propositions sufficiently clear to others. Poets, and orators, and painters, and those who cultivate other branches of the liberal arts, have without this critical knowledge succeeded well in their several provinces, and will succeed; as among artificers there are many machines made and even invented without any exact knowledge of the principles they are governed by. It is, I own, not uncommon to be wrong in theory and right in practice; and we are happy that it is so. Men often act right from their feelings, who afterwards reason but ill on them from principle; but as it is impossible to avoid an attempt at such reasoning, and equally impossible to prevent its having some influence on our practice, surely it is worth taking some pains to have it just, and founded on the basis of sure experience. We might expect that the artists themselves would have been our surest guides; but the artists have[n] been too much occupied in the practice; the philosophers have done little, and what they have done, was mostly with a view

[m] *The*] *This*

[n] *experience. We . . . have*] *experience. The artists themselves, who might be most relied on here, have*

[21] Persius, *Satires*, V, 29.

to their own schemes and systems; and as for those called critics, they have generally sought the rule of the arts in the wrong place; they sought it among poems, pictures, engravings, statues and buildings. But art can never give the rules that make an art. This is, I believe, the reason why artists in general, and poets principally, have been confined in so narrow a circle; they have been rather imitators of one another than of nature; and this with so faithful an uniformity, and to so remote an antiquity, that it is hard to say who gave the first model. Critics follow them, and therefore can do little as guides. I can judge but poorly of any thing whilst I measure it by no other standard than itself. The true standard of the arts is in every man's power; and an easy observation of the most common,[o] sometimes of the meanest things in nature, will give the truest lights, where the greatest sagacity and industry that slights such observation, must leave us in the dark, or what is worse, amuse and mislead us by false lights. In an enquiry, it is almost every thing to be once in a right road. I am satisfied I have done but little by these observations considered in themselves; and I never should have taken the pains to digest them, much less should I have ever ventured to publish them, if I was not convinced that nothing tends more to the corruption of science than to suffer it to stagnate. These waters must be troubled before they can exert their virtues. A man who works beyond the surface of things, though he may be wrong himself, yet he clears[p] the way for others, and may chance to make even his errors subservient to the cause of truth. In the following parts I shall enquire what things they are that cause in us the affections of the sublime and beautiful, as in this I have considered the affections themselves. I only desire one favour; that no part of this discourse may be judged of by itself and independently of the rest; for I am sensible I have not disposed my materials to abide the test of a captious controversy, but of a sober and even forgiving examination; that they are not armed at all points for battle; but dressed to visit those who are willing to give a peaceful entrance to truth.

The end of the First Part.

[o] *most common,*] *commonest,* [p] *yet he clears*] *yet clears*

A PHILOSOPHICAL ENQUIRY INTO THE ORIGIN OF OUR IDEAS OF THE SUBLIME AND BEAUTIFUL

Part Two

SECTION I

Of the passion caused by the SUBLIME

THE passion caused by the great and sublime in *nature*, when those causes operate most powerfully, is Astonishment; and astonishment is that state of the soul, in which all its motions are suspended, with some degree of horror.* In this case the mind is so entirely filled with its object, that it cannot entertain any other, nor by consequence reason on that object which employs it. Hence arises the great power of the sublime, that far from being produced by them, it anticipates our reasonings, and hurries us on by an irresistible force. Astonishment, as I have said, is the effect of the sublime in its highest degree; the inferior effects are admiration, reverence and respect.

SECTION II

TERROR

No passion so effectually robs the mind of all its powers of acting and reasoning as fear. †For fear being an apprehension of pain or death, it operates in a manner that resembles actual pain. Whatever therefore is terrible, with regard to sight, is sublime too, whether this cause of terror, be endued with greatness of dimensions or not; for it is impossible to look on any thing as trifling, or contemptible, that may be dangerous. There are many animals, who though far from being large, are yet capable of raising ideas of the sublime, because they are considered as objects of terror. As serpents and poisonous animals of almost all kinds. And[q] to things of great dimensions, if we annex an[r] adventitious idea of terror, they become without comparison greater. A level plain[s] of a vast extent on land, is certainly no mean idea; the prospect of such a plain may be as extensive as a prospect of the ocean; but can it ever fill the

* Part 1, sections 3, 4, 7. † Part 4, sections 3, 4, 5, 6.

[q] *And*] *Even* [r] *an*] *any* [s] *A level plain*] *An even plain*

mind with any thing so great as the ocean itself? This[t] is owing to several causes, but it is owing to none more than this,[u] that the ocean is an object of no small terror. [1]⟨Indeed terror is in all cases whatsoever, either more openly or latently the ruling principle of the sublime. Several languages bear a strong testimony to the affinity of these ideas. They frequently use the same word, to signify indifferently the modes of astonishment or admiration and those of terror. *Θάμβος* is in greek, either fear or wonder; *δεινός* is terrible or respectable; *αἰδέω*, to reverence or to fear. *Vereor* in latin, is what *αἰδέω* is in greek. The Romans used the verb *stupeo*, a term which strongly marks the state of an astonished mind, to express the effect either of simple fear, or of astonishment; the word *attonitus*, (thunder-struck) is equally expressive of the alliance of these ideas; and do not the french *etonnement*, and the english *astonishment* and *amazement*, point out as clearly the kindred emotions which attend fear and wonder? They who have a more general knowledge of languages, could produce, I make no doubt, many other and equally striking examples.⟩

SECTION III

OBSCURITY

To make any thing very terrible, obscurity† seems in general to be necessary. When we know the full extent of any danger, when we can accustom our eyes to it, a great deal of the

† Part 4, sections 14, 15, 16.

[t] *itself? This*] *itself? this* [u] *than this,*] *than to this,*

[1] *Literary Magazine*, II, 185 (referring initially to p. 57, ll., 3–4): "But astonishment is perhaps that state of the soul, when the powers of the mind are suspended with wonder. Horror may tincture it, and love may enliven it. . . . Longinus's account of the sublime is, we apprehend, very just: it is not built on any single passion; though they may all serve to inflame that pathetic enthusiasm, which in conjunction with an exalted thought, serves to hurry away the mind with great rapidity from itself. Terror is therefore a great addition, and in like manner so are all the other passions, grief, love, rage, indignation, ambition, compassion etc."

apprehension vanishes. Every one will be sensible of this, who considers how greatly night adds to our dread, in all cases of danger, and how much the notions of ghosts and goblins, of which none can form clear ideas, affect minds, which give credit to the popular tales concerning such sorts of beings. Those despotic governments, which are founded on the passions of men, and principally upon the passion of fear, keep their chief as much as may be from the public eye. The policy has been the same in many cases of religion. Almost all the heathen temples were dark.[2] Even in the barbarous temples of the Americans at this day, they keep their idol in a dark part of the hut, which is consecrated to his worship. For this purpose too the druids performed all their ceremonies in the bosom of the darkest woods, and in the shade of the oldest and most spreading oaks. No person seems better to[v] have understood the secret of heightening, or of setting terrible things, if I may use the expression, in their strongest light by the force of a judicious obscurity, than Milton. His description of Death in the second book is admirably studied; it is astonishing with what a gloomy pomp, with what a significant and expressive uncertainty of strokes and colouring he has finished the portrait of the king of terrors.

The other shape,
If shape it might be called that shape had none
Distinguishable, in member, joint, or limb;
Or substance might be called that shadow seemed,
For each seemed either; black he stood as night;
Fierce as ten furies; terrible as hell;
And shook a deadly dart. What seemed his head
The likeness of a kingly crown had on.[3]

In this description all is dark, uncertain, confused, terrible, and sublime to the last degree.

[v] *seems better to*] *seems to*

[2] Cf. F. Hutcheson, *An Inquiry into the Original of our Ideas of Beauty and Virtue* (1725), p. 76: "The cunning of the *Heathen Priests* might make such obscure Places the Scene of the fictitious Appearances of their *Deitys*."

[3] *Paradise Lost*, II, 666–73 (misquoted).

SECTION IV

Of the difference between CLEARNESS and OBSCURITY with regard to the passions

It is one thing to make an idea clear, and another to make it *affecting* to the imagination. If I make a drawing of a palace, or a temple, or a landscape, I present a very clear idea of those objects; but then (allowing for the effect of imitation which is something) my picture can at most affect only as the palace, temple, or landscape would have affected in the reality. On the other hand, the most lively and spirited verbal description I can give, raises a very obscure and imperfect *idea* of such objects; but then it is in my power to raise a stronger *emotion* by the description than I could do by the best painting. This experience constantly evinces. The proper manner of conveying the *affections* of the mind from one to another, is by words; there is a great insufficiency in all other methods of communication; and[w] so far is a clearness of imagery from being absolutely necessary to an influence upon the passions, that they may be considerably operated upon without presenting any image at all, by certain sounds adapted to that purpose; of which we have a sufficient proof in the acknowledged and powerful effects of instrumental music. In reality a great clearness helps but little towards affecting the passions, as it is in some sort an enemy to all enthusiasms whatsoever.

SECTION [IV][x]

The same subject continued

There are two verses in Horace's art of poetry that seem to contradict this opinion, for which reason I shall take a little more pains in clearing it up. The verses are,

Segnius inritant animos demissa per aurem
Quam quæ sunt oculis subjecta fidelibus.[4]

[w] *and*] *nay*

[x] *SECTION* [*IV*].] *SECTION V.*

[4] *De Arte Poetica*, ll. 180–1.

On this the abbe du Bos founds a criticism, wherein he gives painting the preference to poetry in the article of moving the passions; principally on account of[y] the greater *clearness* of the ideas it represents.[5] I believe this excellent judge was led into this mistake (if it be a mistake) by his system, to which he found it more conformable than I imagine it will be found to experience. I know several who admire and love painting, and yet who regard the objects of their admiration in that art, with coolness enough, in comparison of that warmth with which they are animated by affecting pieces of poetry or rhetoric. Among the common sort of people, I never could perceive that painting had much influence on their passions. It is true that the best sorts of painting, as well as the best sorts of poetry, are not much understood in that sphere. But it is most certain, that their passions are very strongly roused by a fanatic preacher, or by the ballads of Chevy-chase,[6] or the children in the wood, and by other little popular poems and tales that are current in that rank of life. I do not know of any paintings, bad or good, that produce the same effect. So that poetry with all its obscurity, has a more general as well as a more powerful dominion over the passions than the other art. And I think there are reasons in nature why the obscure idea, when properly conveyed, should be more affecting than the clear. It is our ignorance of things that causes all our admiration, and chiefly excites our passions. Knowledge and acquaintance make the most striking causes affect but little. It is thus with the vulgar, and all men are as the vulgar in what they do not understand. The ideas of eternity, and infinity, are among the most affecting we have, and yet perhaps there is nothing of which we really understand so little, as of infinity and eternity. We do not[z] any where meet a more sublime description than this justly celebrated one of Milton, wherein he gives the portrait of Satan with a dignity so suitable to the subject.

[y] *passions; principally . . . of*] *passions; and that on account principally of*
[z] *do not*] *don't*

[5] *Réflexions Critiques Sur La Poësie et Sur La Peinture* (Paris, 6th edn., 1755), I, 416 ff.

[6] Addison had written on *Chevy Chase* in *Spectator* Nos. 70 and 74.

He above the rest
In shape and gesture proudly eminent
Stood like a tower; his form had yet not lost
All her original brightness, nor appeared
Less than archangel ruin'd, and th' excess
Of glory obscured: as when the sun new ris'n
Looks through the horizontal misty air
Shorn of his beams; or from behind the moon
In dim eclipse disastrous twilight sheds
On half the nations; and with fear of change
Perplexes monarchs.[7]

Here is a very noble picture; and in what does this poetical picture consist? in images of a tower, an archangel, the sun rising through mists, or in an eclipse, the ruin of monarchs, and the revolutions of kingdoms. The mind is hurried out of itself, by a croud of great and confused images; which affect because they are crouded and confused. For separate them, and you lose much of the greatness, and join them, and you infallibly lose the clearness. The images raised by poetry are always of this obscure kind; though in general the effects of poetry, are by no means to be attributed to the images it raises; which point we shall examine more at large hereafter.* But painting, when we have allowed for the pleasure[a] of imitation, can only affect simply by the images it presents; and[b] even in painting a judicious obscurity in some things contributes to the effect of the picture; because the images in painting are exactly similar to those in nature; and in nature dark, confused, uncertain images have a greater power on the fancy to form the grander passions than those have which are more clear and determinate. But where and when this observation may be applied to practice, and how far it shall be extended, will be better deduced from the nature of the subject, and from the occasion, than from any rules that can be given.

* Part 5.

[a] *painting, when . . . pleasure*] *painting, with only the superadded pleasure*
[b] *and*] *but*

[7] *Paradise Lost*, I, 589–99. (For another view of this passage see R. Payne Knight, *An Analytical Inquiry into the Principles of Taste*, 2nd edn., 1805, III, i, 89.)

[8]⟨I am sensible that this idea has met with opposition, and is likely still to be rejected by several. But let it be considered that hardly any thing can strike the mind with its greatness, which does not make some sort of approach towards infinity; which nothing can do whilst we are able to perceive its bounds; but to see an object distinctly, and to perceive its bounds, is one and the same thing. A clear idea is therefore another name for a little idea. There is a passage in the book of Job amazingly sublime, and this sublimity is principally due to the terrible uncertainty of the thing described. *In thoughts from the visions of the night, when deep sleep falleth upon men, fear came upon me and trembling, which made all my bones to shake. Then a spirit passed before my face. The hair of my flesh stood up. It stood still*, but I could not discern the form thereof; *an image was before mine eyes; there was silence; and I heard a voice,—Shall mortal man be more just than God?*[9] We are first prepared with the utmost solemnity for the vision; we are first terrified, before we are let even into the obscure cause of our emotion; but when this grand cause of terror makes its appearance, what is it? is it not, wrapt up in the shades of its own incomprehensible darkness, more aweful, more striking, more terrible, than the liveliest description, than the clearest painting could possibly represent it? When painters have attempted to give us clear representations of these very fanciful and terrible ideas, they have I think almost always failed; insomuch that I have been at a loss, in all the pictures I have seen of hell, whether the painter did not intend something ludicrous. Several painters have handled a subject of this kind, with a view of assembling as many horrid phantoms as their

[8] *Literary Magazine*, II, 185: "Obscurity, our author observes, increases the sublime, which is certainly very just; but from thence erroneously infers, that clearness of imagery is unnecessary to affect the passions; but surely nothing can move but what gives ideas to the mind. . . . Our author . . . combats the opinion of the *Abbé du Bos* . . . but surely the reason he gives is not a very good one: he gives the preference to poetry on account of its obscurity. Whereas it should be on account of its greater perspicuity, its amplifications, and its being at liberty to select a greater variety of circumstances, in order to make its exhibitions more vivid and striking." *Monthly Review*, XVI, 477 n.: "Distinctness of imagery has ever been held productive of the sublime. . . ."

[9] *Job*, IV, 13–17.

imagination could suggest; but all the designs I have chanced to meet of the temptations of St. Anthony, were rather a sort of odd wild grotesques, than any thing capable of producing a serious passion.[10] In all these subjects poetry is very happy. Its apparitions, its chimeras, its harpies, its allegorical figures, are grand and affecting; and though Virgil's Fame,[11] and Homer's Discord,[12] are obscure, they are magnificent figures. These figures in painting would be clear enough, but I fear they might become ridiculous.

SECTION V

POWER

Besides these things which *directly* suggest the idea of danger, and those which produce a similar effect from a mechanical cause, I know of nothing sublime which is not some modification of power. And this branch rises as naturally as the other two branches, from terror, the common stock of every thing that is sublime. The idea of power at first view, seems of the class of these indifferent ones, which may equally belong to pain or to pleasure. But in reality, the affection arising from the idea of vast power, is extremely remote from that neutral character. For first, we must remember,* that the idea of pain, in its highest degree, is much stronger than the highest degree of pleasure; and that it preserves the same superiority through all the subordinate gradations. From hence it is, that where the chances for equal degrees of suffering or enjoyment are in any

* Part 1, section 7.

[10] The "Temptations of St. Anthony" was a popular subject for grotesque treatment among Dutch, Flemish, and Spanish painters of the sixteenth and seventeenth centuries (e.g. Brueghel, Teniers, Ribera). There is also a version by Salvator Rosa. (See A. B. Jameson, *Sacred and Legendary Art*, 1848, II, 381–3.)

[11] *Aeneid*, IV, 173 ff.

[12] *Iliad*, IV, 440–5. (Longinus uses this reference as an illustration: *On the Sublime*, IX.)

sort equal, the idea of the suffering must always be prevalent. And indeed the ideas of pain, and above all of death, are so very affecting, that whilst we remain in the presence of whatever is supposed to have the power of inflicting either, it is impossible to be perfectly free from terror. Again, we know by experience, that for the enjoyment of pleasure, no great efforts of power are at all necessary; nay we know, that such efforts would go a great way towards destroying our satisfaction: for pleasure must be stolen, and not forced upon us; pleasure follows the will; and therefore we are generally affected with it by many things of a force greatly inferior to our own. But pain is always inflicted by a power in some way superior, because we never submit to pain willingly. So that strength, violence, pain and terror, are ideas that rush in upon the mind together. Look at a man, or any other animal of prodigious strength, and what is your idea before reflection? Is it that this strength will be subservient to you, to your ease, to your pleasure, to your interest in any sense? No; the emotion you feel is, lest this enormous strength should be employed to the purposes of* rapine and destruction. That power derives all its sublimity from the terror with which it is generally accompanied, will appear evidently from its effect in the very few cases, in which it may be possible to strip a considerable degree of strength of its ability to hurt. When you do this, you spoil it of every thing sublime, and it immediately becomes contemptible. An ox is a creature of vast strength; but he is an innocent creature, extremely serviceable, and not at all dangerous; for which reason the idea of an ox is by no means grand. A bull is strong too; but his strength is of another kind; often very destructive, seldom (at least amongst us) of any use in our business; the idea of a bull is therefore great, and it has frequently a place in sublime descriptions, and elevating comparisons. Let us look at another strong animal in the two distinct lights in which we may consider him. The horse in the light of an useful beast, fit for the plough, the road, the draft, in every social useful light the horse has nothing of the sublime; but is it thus that we are affected with him, *whose neck is cloathed with thunder, the glory*

* Vide Part 3, section 21.

of whose nostrils is terrible, who swalloweth the ground with fierceness and rage, neither believeth that it is the sound of the trumpet?[13] In this description the useful character of the horse entirely disappears, and the terrible and sublime blaze out together. We have continually about us animals of a strength that is considerable, but not pernicious. Amongst these we never look for the sublime: it comes upon us in the gloomy forest, and in the howling wilderness, in the form of the lion, the tiger, the panther, or rhinoceros. Whenever strength is only useful, and employed for our benefit or our pleasure, then it is never sublime; for nothing can act agreeably to us, that does not act in conformity to our will; but to act agreeably to our will, it must be subject to us; and therefore can never be the cause of a grand and commanding conception. The description of the wild ass, in Job, is worked up into no small sublimity, merely by insisting on his freedom, and his setting mankind at defiance; otherwise the description of such an animal could have had nothing noble in it. *Who hath loosed* (says he) *the bands of the wild ass? whose house I have made the wilderness, and the barren land his dwellings. He scorneth the multitude of the city, neither regardeth he the voice of the driver. The range of the mountains is his pasture.*[14] The magnificent description of the unicorn and of leviathan in the same book, is full of the same heightening circumstances. *Will the unicorn be willing to serve thee? canst thou bind the unicorn with his band in the furrow? wilt thou trust him because his strength is great?——Canst thou draw out leviathan with an hook? will he make a covenant with thee? wilt thou take him for a servant for ever? shall not one be cast down even at the sight of him?*[15] In short, wheresoever we find strength, and in what light soever we look upon power, we shall all along observe the sublime the concomitant of terror, and contempt the attendant on a strength that is subservient and innoxious. The race of dogs in many of their

[13] *Job*, XXXIX, 19b, 20b, 24 (misquoted). Lowth quotes this passage to prove his contention that *Job* "is adapted in every respect to the incitement of terror; and . . . is universally animated with the true spirit of sublimity" (*Lectures on the Sacred Poetry of the Hebrews*, transl. G. Gregory, 1787, II, 428, 424).

[14] *Job*, XXXIX, 5b–8a (misquoted).

[15] *Ibid.*, XXXIX, 9a, 10a, 11a; XLI, 1a, 4, 9b.

kinds, have generally a competent degree of strength and swiftness; and they exert these, and other valuable qualities which they possess, greatly to our convenience and pleasure. Dogs are indeed the most social, affectionate, and amiable animals of the whole brute creation; but love approaches much nearer to contempt than is commonly imagined; and accordingly, though we caress dogs, we borrow from them an appellation of the most despicable kind, when we employ terms of reproach; and this appellation is the common mark of the last vileness and contempt in every language. Wolves have not more strength than several species of dogs; but on account of their unmanageable fierceness, the idea of a wolf is not despicable; it is not excluded from grand descriptions and similitudes. Thus we are affected by strength, which is *natural* power. The power which arises from institution in kings and commanders, has the same connection with terror. Sovereigns are frequently addressed with the title of *dread majesty*. And it may be observed, that young persons little acquainted with the world, and who have not been used to approach men in power, are commonly struck with an awe which takes away the free use of their faculties. *When I prepared my seat in the street* (says Job) *the young men saw me, and hid themselves.*[16] Indeed so natural is this timidity with regard to power, and so strongly does it inhere in our constitution, that very few are able to conquer it, but by mixing much in the business of the great world, or by using no small violence to their natural dispositions. [17] I know some people are of opinion, that no awe, no degree of terror, accompanies the idea of power, and have hazarded to affirm, that we can contemplate the idea of God himself without any such emotion. I purposely avoided when I first considered this subject, to introduce the idea of that great and tremendous being, as an example in an argument so

16 *Job*, XXIX, 7b–8a.

17 *Monthly Review*, XVI, 475 n.: "It is certain, we can have the most sublime ideas of the Deity, without imagining him a God of terror. Whatever raises our esteem of an object described, must be a powerful source of sublimity; and esteem is a passion nearly allied to love: Our astonishment at the sublime as often proceeds from an increased love, as from an increased fear."

light as this; though it frequently occurred to me, not as an objection to, but as a strong confirmation of my notions in this matter. I hope, in what I am going to say, I shall avoid presumption, where it is almost impossible for any mortal to speak with strict propriety. I say then, that whilst we consider the Godhead merely as he is an object of the understanding, which forms a complex idea of power, wisdom, justice, goodness, all stretched to a degree far exceeding the bounds of our comprehension, whilst we consider the divinity in this refined and abstracted light, the imagination and passions are little or nothing affected. But because we are bound by the condition of our nature to ascend to these pure and intellectual ideas, through the medium of sensible images, and to judge of these divine qualities by their evident acts and exertions, it becomes extremely hard to disentangle our idea of the cause from the effect by which we are led to know it. Thus when we contemplate the Deity, his attributes and their operation coming united on the mind, form a sort of sensible image, and as such are capable of affecting the imagination. Now, though in a just idea of the Deity, perhaps none of his attributes are predominant, yet to our imagination, his power is by far the most striking. Some reflection, some comparing is necessary to satisfy us of his wisdom, his justice, and his goodness; to be struck with his power, it is only necessary that we should open our eyes. But whilst we contemplate so vast an object, under the arm, as it were, of almighty power, and invested upon every side with omnipresence, we shrink into the minuteness of our own nature, and are, in a manner, annihilated before him. And though a consideration of his other attributes may relieve in some measure our apprehensions; yet no conviction of the justice with which it is exercised, nor the mercy with which it is tempered, can wholly remove the terror that naturally arises from a force which nothing can withstand. If we rejoice, we rejoice with trembling; and even whilst we are receiving benefits, we cannot but shudder at a power which can confer benefits of such mighty importance. When the prophet David contemplated the wonders of wisdom and power, which are displayed in the œconomy of man, he seems to be struck with a sort of divine horror, and cries out, *fearfully and wonderfully am I made!*[18] An heathen poet has a sentiment of a similar nature; Horace looks upon it as the last effort of philosophical fortitude, to behold without terror and amazement, this immense and glorious fabric of the universe.

> *Hunc solem, et stellas, et decedentia certis*
> *Tempora momentis, sunt qui formidine nulla*
> *Imbuti spectent.*[19]

Lucretius is a poet not to be suspected of giving way to superstitious terrors; yet when he supposes the whole mechanism of nature laid open by the master of his philosophy, his transport on this magnificent view which he has represented in the colours of such bold and lively poetry, is overcast with a shade of secret dread and horror.

> *His tibi me rebus quædam Divina voluptas*
> *Percipit, adque horror, quod sic Natura tua vi*
> *Tam manifesta patet ex omni parte retecta.*[20]

But the scripture alone can supply ideas answerable to the majesty of this subject. In the scripture, wherever God is represented as appearing or speaking, every thing terrible in nature is called up to heighten the awe and solemnity of the divine presence. The psalms, and the prophetical books, are crouded with instances of this kind. *The earth shook* (says the psalmist) *the heavens also dropped at the presence of the Lord.*[21] And what is remarkable, the painting preserves the same character, not only when he is supposed descending to take vengeance upon the wicked, but even when he exerts the like plenitude of power in acts of beneficence to mankind. *Tremble, thou earth! at the presence of the Lord; at the presence of the God of Jacob; which turned the rock into standing water, the flint into a fountain of waters!*[22] It were endless to enumerate all the passages both in the sacred

[18] *Psalms*, CXXXIX, 14 (misquoted). Lowth comments on this psalm at the end of a lecture which emphasizes the praise of God's power in Hebrew poetry: "It celebrates the omniscience of the Deity, and the incomparable art and design displayed in the formation of the human body" (*Lectures*, II, 283).

[19] *Epistles*, I, vi, 3–5.

[20] *De Rerum Natura*, III, 28–30 (misquoted).

[21] *Psalms*, LXVIII, 8 (misquoted).

[22] *Ibid.*, CXIV, 7–8 (misquoted).

and profane writers, which establish the general sentiment of mankind, concerning the inseparable union of a sacred and reverential awe, with our ideas of the divinity. Hence the common maxim, *primos in orbe deos fecit timor.*[23] This maxim may be, as I believe it is, false with regard to the origin of religion. The maker of the maxim saw how inseparable these ideas were, without considering that the notion of some great power must be always precedent to our dread of it. But this dread must necessarily follow the idea of such a power, when it is once excited in the mind. It is on this principle that true religion has, and must have, so large a mixture of salutary fear; and that false religions have generally nothing else but fear to support them. Before the christian religion had, as it were, humanized the idea of the divinity, and brought it somewhat nearer to us, there was very little said of the love of God. The followers of Plato have something of it, and only something.[24] The other writers of pagan antiquity, whether poets or philosophers, nothing at all. And they who consider with what infinite attention, by what a disregard of every perishable object, through what long habits of piety and contemplation it is, any man is able to attain an entire love and devotion to the Deity, will easily perceive, that it is not the first, the most natural, and the most striking effect which proceeds from that idea. Thus we have traced power through its several gradations unto the highest of all, where our imagination is finally lost; and we find terror quite throughout the progress, its inseparable companion, and growing along with it, as far as we can possibly trace them. Now as power is undoubtedly a capital source of the sublime, this will point out evidently from whence its energy is derived, and to what class of ideas we ought to unite it.〉

[23] Cf. Statius, *Thebaid*, III, 661.

[24] E.g. Plotinus: "Because the Soul is different from God, and yet springs from him, she loves him of necessity . . . it is natural for the Soul to love God and to desire union with him, as the daughter of a noble father feels a noble love." (W. R. Inge, *The Philosophy of Plotinus*, 3rd edn., 1941, II, 140.) Burke may well have been led to Plotinus through reading the Cambridge Platonist, Ralph Cudworth. Cudworth's *True Intellectual System of the Universe* (1743) was among items listed in the Sale Catalogue of Burke's library (item no. 138).

SECTION VI

PRIVATION

All *general* privations are great, because they are all terrible; *Vacuity*, *Darkness*, *Solitude* and *Silence*. With what a fire of imagination, yet with what severity of judgment, has Virgil amassed all these circumstances where he knows that all the images of a tremendous dignity ought to be united, at the mouth of hell! where before he unlocks the secrets of the great deep, he seems to be seized with a religious horror, and to retire astonished at the boldness of his own design.

Dii quibus imperium est animarum, umbræq; silentes!
Et Chaos, et Phlegethon! loca nocte silentia *late?*
Sit mihi fas audita loqui! sit numine vestro
Pandere res alta terra et caligine *mersas!*
Ibant obscuri, sola *sub* nocte, *per* umbram,
Perque domos Ditis[c] vacuas, *et* inania *regna.*[25]

Ye subterraneous gods! whose aweful sway
The gliding ghosts, and silent *shades obey;*
O Chaos hoar! and Phlegethon profound!
Whose solemn empire stretches wide around;
Give me, ye great tremendous powers, to tell
Of scenes and wonders in the depth[d] *of hell;*
Give me your mighty secrets to display
From those black *realms of darkness to the day.*

PITT.[26]

Obscure *they went through dreary* shades *that led*
Along the waste *dominions of the* dead.

DRYDEN.[27]

[c] *Ditis*] *dites*

[d] *depth*] *depths*

[25] *Aeneid*, VI, 264–9 (misquoted).

[26] *Aeneid* (1740), VI, 371–8.

[27] *Aeneid* (1697), VI, 378–9.

SECTION VII
VASTNESS

Greatness† of dimension, is a powerful cause of the sublime. This is too evident, and the observation too common, to need any illustration; it[e] is not so common, to consider in what ways greatness of dimension, vastness of extent, or quantity, has the most striking effect. For certainly, there are ways, and modes, wherein the same quantity of extension shall produce greater effects than it is found to do in others. Extension is either in length, height, or depth. Of these the length strikes least; an hundred yards of even ground will never work such an effect as a tower an hundred yards high, or a rock or mountain of that altitude. I am apt to imagine likewise, that height is less grand than depth; and that we are more struck at looking down from a precipice, than at looking up at an object of equal height, but of that I am not very positive. A perpendicular has more force in forming the sublime, than an inclined plane; and the effects of a rugged and broken surface seem stronger than where it is smooth and polished. It would carry us out of our way to enter in this place into the cause of these appearances; but[f] certain it is they afford a large and fruitful field of speculation. ⟨However, it may not be amiss to add to these remarks upon magnitude; that, as the great extreme of dimension is sublime, so the last extreme of littleness is in some measure sublime likewise; when we attend to the infinite divisibility of matter, when we pursue animal life into these excessively small, and yet organized beings, that escape the nicest inquisition of the sense, when we push our discoveries yet downward, and consider those creatures so many degrees yet smaller, and the still diminishing scale of existence, in tracing which the imagination is lost as well as the sense, we become amazed and confounded at the wonders of minuteness; nor can we distinguish in its effect this extreme of littleness from the vast itself. For division must be infinite as well as

† Part 4, section 9.

[e] *illustration; it*] *illustration; but it*

[f] *enter in . . . but*] *enter into the cause of these appearances here; but*

addition; because the idea of a perfect unity can no more be arrived at, than that of a compleat whole to which nothing may be added.〉

SECTION VIII

INFINITY

Another source of the sublime, is *infinity*; if it does not rather belong[g] to the last. Infinity has a tendency to fill the mind with that sort of delightful horror, which is the most genuine effect, and truest test of the sublime. There are scarce any things which can become the objects of our senses that are really, and in their own nature infinite. But the eye not being able to perceive the bounds of many things, they seem to be infinite, and they produce the same effects as if they were really so. We are deceived in the like manner, if the parts of some large object are so continued to any indefinite number, that the imagination meets no check which may hinder its extending them at pleasure.

Whenever[h] we repeat any idea frequently, the mind by a sort of mechanism repeats it long after the first cause has ceased to operate.*[28] After whirling about; when we sit down, the objects about us still seem to whirl. After a long succession of noises, as the fall of waters, or the beating of forge hammers, the hammers beat and the water roars in the imagination long after the first sounds have ceased to affect it; and they die away at last by gradations which are scarcely perceptible. If you hold up a strait pole, with your eye to one end, it will seem extended

* Part 4, section 12.

[g] *rather belong*] *rather in some sort belong*

[h] *at pleasure. Whenever*] *at pleasure. SECTION IX. The same. Whenever*

[28] In the passage which follows Burke may have been indebted to David Hartley who—in his *Observations on Man* (5th edn., 1810), I, 9–11—discusses the way that "Sensations remain in the Mind for a short time after the sensible Objects are removed." It is interesting to note that, in the course of his discussion, Hartley quotes the passage from Newton's *Opticks* which Burke probably had in mind at p. 138.

to a length almost incredible.* Place[i] a number of uniform and equidistant marks on this pole, they will cause the same deception, and seem multiplied without end. The senses strongly affected in some one manner, cannot quickly change their tenor, or adapt themselves to other things; but they continue in their old channel until the strength of the first mover decays. This is the reason of an appearance very frequent in madmen; that they remain whole days and nights, sometimes whole years, in the constant repetition of some remark, some complaint, or song; which having struck powerfully on their disordered imagination, in the beginning of their phrensy, every repetition reinforces it with new strength; and the hurry of their spirits, unrestrained by the curb of reason, continues[j] it to the end of their lives.

SECTION IX[k]

SUCCESSION and UNIFORMITY

Succession and *uniformity* of parts, are what constitute the artificial infinite. 1. *Succession*; which is requisite that the parts may be continued so long, and in such a direction, as by their frequent impulses on the sense to impress the imagination with an idea of their progress beyond their actual limits. 2. *Uniformity*; because if the figures of the parts should be changed, the imagination at every change finds a check; you are presented at every alteration with the termination of one idea, and the beginning of another; by which means it becomes impossible to continue that uninterrupted progression, which alone can stamp on bounded objects the character of infinity.† It is in

* Part 4, section 14.[29]

† Mr. Addison, in the Spectators concerning the pleasures of the

[i] *extended to. . . . Place*] *extended to almost an incredible length. Place*

[j] *spirits, unrestrained . . . continues*] *spirits unrestrained, the curb of reason continues*

[k] *SECTION IX.*] *SECTION X.*

[29] This note should presumably read: "Part 4, section 13."

this kind of artificial infinity, I believe, we ought to look for the cause why a rotund has such a noble effect. For in a rotund, whether it be a building or a plantation, you can no where fix a boundary; turn which way you will, the same object still seems to continue, and the imagination has no rest. But the parts must be uniform as well as circularly disposed, to give this figure its full force; because any difference, whether it be in the disposition, or in the figure, or even in the colour of the parts, is highly prejudicial to the idea of infinity, which every change must check and interrupt, at every alteration commencing a new series. On[l] the same principles of succession and uniformity, the grand appearance of the ancient heathen temples, which were generally oblong forms, with a range of uniform pillars on every side, will be easily accounted for. From the same cause also may[m] be derived the grand effect of the isles in many of our own old cathedrals. The form of a cross used in some churches seems to me not so eligible, as the parallelogram of the ancients; at least I imagine it is not so proper for the outside. For, supposing the arms of the cross every way equal, if you stand in a direction parallel to any of the side walls, or colonnades, instead of a deception that makes the building more extended than it is, you are cut off from a considerable part (two thirds) of its *actual* length; and to prevent all possibility of progression, the arms of the cross taking a new direction, make a right angle with the beam, and thereby wholly turn[n] the imagination from the repetition of the former idea. Or suppose the spectator placed where he may take a direct view of such a building; what will be the consequence? the necessary consequence will[o] be, that a good part of the basis of each angle, formed by the intersection of the arms of the cross, must be inevitably lost; the whole must of course assume a broken unconnected figure; the lights must be

imagination, thinks it is, because in the rotund at one glance you see half the building.[30] This I do not imagine to be the real cause.

[l] *new series. On*] *new series. SECTION XI. The effect of succession and uniformity in BUILDING. On*

[m] *cause also may*] *cause may*

[n] *arms . . . make . . . turn*] *arm . . . makes . . . turns*

[o] *will*] *must*

[30] *Spectator* No. 415.

unequal, here strong, and there weak; without that noble gradation, which the perspective always effects on parts disposed uninterruptedly in a right line. Some or all of these objections, will lie against every figure of a cross, in whatever view you take it. I exemplified them in the Greek cross in which these faults appear the most strongly; but they appear in some degree in all sorts of crosses. Indeed there is nothing more prejudicial to the grandeur of buildings, than to abound in angles; a fault obvious in many;[p] and owing to an inordinate thirst for variety, which, whenever it prevails, is sure to leave very little true taste.

SECTION X[q]

Magnitude in BUILDING

To the sublime in building, greatness of dimension seems requisite; for on a few parts, and those small, the imagination cannot rise to any idea of infinity. No greatness in the manner can effectually compensate for the want of proper dimensions. There is no danger of drawing men into extravagant designs by this rule; it carries its own caution along with it. Because too great a length in buildings[r] destroys the purpose of greatness which it was intended to promote; the[s] perspective will lessen it in height as it gains in length; and will bring it at last to a point; turning the whole figure into a sort of triangle, the poorest in its effect of almost any figure, that can be presented to the eye. I have ever observed, that colonnades and avenues of trees of a moderate length, were without comparison far grander, than when they were suffered to run to immense distances. A true artist should put a generous deceit on the spectators, and effect the noblest designs by easy methods. Designs that are vast only by their dimensions, are always the sign of a common and low imagination. No work of art can be great, but as it deceives; to be otherwise is the prerogative of nature only. A good eye will fix the medium betwixt an excessive length, or height, (for the same objection lies against

[p] *in many;*] *in very many;*
[q] *SECTION X.*] *SECTION XII.*
[r] *buildings*] *building*
[s] *promote; the*] *promote, as the*

both), and a short or broken quantity; and perhaps it might be ascertained to a tolerable degree of exactness, if it was my purpose to descend far into the particulars of any art.

SECTION XI[t]

INFINITY in pleasing OBJECTS

Infinity, though of another kind, causes much of our pleasure in agreeable, as well as of our delight in sublime images. The spring is the pleasantest of the seasons; and the young of most animals, though far from being compleatly fashioned, afford a more agreeable sensation than the full grown; because the imagination is entertained with the promise of something more, and does not acquiesce in the present object of the sense. In unfinished sketches of drawing, I have often seen[u] something which pleased me beyond the best finishing; and this I believe proceeds from the cause I have just now assigned.

SECTION XII[v]

DIFFICULTY

*Another source of greatness is *Difficulty*. When any work seems to have required immense force and labour to effect it, the idea is grand. Stonehenge, neither for disposition nor ornament, has any thing admirable; but those huge rude masses of stone, set on end, and piled each on other, turn the mind on the immense force necessary for such a work. Nay the rudeness of the work increases this cause of grandeur, as it excludes the idea of art, and contrivance; for dexterity produces another sort of effect which is different enough from this.

* Part 4, sections 4, 5, 6.

t *SECTION XI.*] *SECTION XIII.*

u *have often seen*] *have seen*

v *SECTION XII.*] *SECTION XIV.*

SECTION XIII[w]

MAGNIFICENCE

Magnificence is likewise a source of the sublime. A great profusion of things[x] which are splendid or valuable in themselves, is *magnificent.* The starry heaven, though it occurs so very frequently to our view, never fails to excite an idea of grandeur. This cannot be owing to any thing in the stars themselves, separately considered. The number is certainly the cause. The apparent disorder augments the grandeur,[y] for the appearance of care is highly contrary to our ideas of magnificence. Besides, the stars lye in such apparent confusion, as makes[z] it impossible on ordinary occasions to reckon them. This gives them the advantage of a sort of infinity.[31] In works of art, this kind of grandeur, which consists in multitude, is to be very cautiously admitted; because, a[a] profusion of excellent things is not to be attained, or with too much difficulty; and, because in many cases this splendid confusion would[b] destroy all use, which should be attended to in most of the works of art with the greatest care; besides it[c] is to be considered, that unless you can produce an appearance of infinity by your disorder, you will have disorder only without magnificence. There are, however, a sort of fireworks, and some other things, that in this way succeed well, and are truly grand. ⟨There are also many descriptions in the poets and orators which owe their sublimity to a richness and profusion of images, in which the mind is so dazzled as to make it impossible to attend to that exact coherence and agreement of the allusions, which we should require on every other occasion. I do not now remember a more striking example of this, than the description which is given of the king's army in the play of Henry the fourth;

[w] *SECTION XIII.*] *SECTION XV.*
[x] *of things*] *of any things*
[y] *the grandeur,*] *it,*
[z] *makes*] *make*
[a] *because, a*] *because, first, a*
[b] *too much . . . would*] *too great difficulty; secondly, because in many cases it would*
[c] *care; besides it*] *care; and with regard to disorder in the disposition, it*

[31] For a similar idea see Locke, *Essay*, II, xvii, 9.

All furnished, all in arms,
All plumed like ostriches that with the wind
Baited like eagles having lately bathed:
As full of spirit as the month of May,
And gorgeous as the sun in Midsummer,
Wanton as youthful goats, wild as young bulls.
I saw young Harry with his beaver on
Rise from the ground like feathered Mercury;
And vaulted with such ease into his seat
As if an angel dropped down from the clouds
To turn and wind a fiery Pegasus.[32]·

In that excellent book so remarkable for the vivacity of its descriptions, as well as the solidity and penetration of its sentences, the Wisdom of the son of Sirach, there is a noble panegyric on the high priest Simon the son of Onias; and it is a very fine example of the point before us.

How was he honoured in the midst of the people, in his coming out of the sanctuary! He was as the morning star in the midst of a cloud, and as the moon at the full: as the sun shining upon the temple of the Most High, and as the rainbow giving light in the bright clouds: and as the flower of roses in the spring of the year; as lillies by the rivers of waters, and as the frankincense tree in summer; as fire and incense in the censer; and as a vessel of gold set with precious stones; as a fair olive tree budding forth fruit, and as a cypress which groweth up to the clouds. When he put on the robe of honour, and was clothed with the perfection of glory, when he went up to the holy altar, he made the garment of holiness honourable. He himself stood by the hearth of the altar compassed with his brethren round about, as a young cedar in Libanus, and as palm trees compassed they him about. So were all the sons of Aaron in their glory, and the oblations of the Lord in their hands, &c.〉[33]

SECTION XIV[d]

LIGHT

Having considered extension, so far as it is capable of raising ideas of greatness; *colour* comes next under consideration. All

[d] *SECTION XIV.*] *SECTION XVI.*

[32] *Henry IV*, Pt. I, IV, i, 97–109 (misquoted).

[33] *Ecclesiasticus*, L, 5–13 (misquoted).

colours depend on *light*. Light therefore ought previously to be examined, and with it, its opposite, darkness. With regard to light; to make it a cause capable of producing the sublime, it must be attended with some circumstances, besides its bare faculty of shewing other objects. Mere light is too common a thing to make a strong impression on the mind, and without a strong impression nothing can be sublime. But such a light as that of the sun, immediately exerted on the eye, as it overpowers the sense, is a very great idea. Light of an inferior strength to this, if it moves with great celerity, has the same power; for lightning is certainly productive of grandeur, which it owes chiefly to the extreme velocity of its motion. A quick transition from light to darkness, or from darkness to light, has yet a greater effect. But darkness is more productive of sublime ideas than light.[e] ⟨Our great poet was convinced of this; and indeed so full was he of this idea, so entirely possessed with the power of a well managed darkness, that, in describing the appearance of the Deity, amidst that profusion of magnificent images, which the grandeur of his subject provokes him to pour out upon every side, he is far from forgetting the obscurity which surrounds the most incomprehensible of all beings, but

> ——*With the majesty of* darkness *round*
> *Circles his throne.*[34]

And what is no less remarkable, our author had the secret of preserving this idea, even when he seemed to depart the farthest from it, when he describes the light and glory which flows from the divine presence; a light which by its very excess is converted into a species of darkness,

> Dark *with excessive* light *thy skirts appear.*[35]

Here is an idea not only poetical in an high degree, but strictly and philosophically just. Extreme light, by overcoming the organs of sight, obliterates all objects, so as in its effect exactly to resemble darkness. After looking for some time at the sun, two black spots, the impression which it leaves, seem to

[e] *than light.*] *than light, as has been suggested in the second section of this part.*

[34] Milton, *Paradise Lost*, II, 266–7 (misquoted).

[35] *Ibid.*, III, 380 (misquoted).

dance before our eyes. Thus are two ideas as opposite as can be imagined reconciled in the extremes of both; and both in spite of their opposite nature brought to concur in producing the sublime. And this is not the only instance wherein the opposite extremes operate equally in favour of the sublime, which in all things abhors mediocrity.〉

SECTION XV[f]

Light in BUILDING

As the management of light is a matter of importance in architecture, it is worth enquiring, how far this remark is applicable to building. I[g] think then, that all edifices calculated to produce an idea of the sublime, ought rather to be dark and gloomy, and this for two reasons; the first is, that darkness itself on other occasions is known by experience to have a greater effect on the passions than light. The second is, that to make an object very striking, we should make it as different as possible from the objects with which we have been immediately conversant; when therefore you enter a building, you cannot pass into a greater light than you had in the open air; to go into one some few degrees less luminous, can[h] make only a trifling change; but to make the transition thoroughly striking, you ought to pass from the greatest light, to as much darkness as is consistent with the uses of architecture. At night the contrary rule will hold, but for the very same reason; and the more highly a room is then illuminated, the grander will the passion be.

SECTION XVI[i]

COLOUR considered as productive of the SUBLIME

Among colours, such as are soft, or cheerful, (except perhaps a strong red which is cheerful) are unfit to produce grand images. An immense mountain covered with a shining green turf, is

[f] *SECTION XV.*] *SECTION XVII.* [g] *to building. I*] *to that purpose. I*

[h] *less luminous, can*] *less, can*

[i] *SECTION XVI.*] *SECTION XVIII.*

nothing in this respect, to one dark and gloomy; the cloudy sky is more grand than the blue; and night more sublime and solemn than day. Therefore in historical painting, a gay or gaudy drapery, can never have a happy effect: and in buildings, when the highest degree of the sublime is intended, the materials and ornaments ought neither to be white, nor green, nor yellow, nor blue, nor of a pale red, nor violet, nor spotted, but of sad and fuscous colours, as black, or brown, or deep purple, and the like. Much of gilding, mosaics, painting or statues, contribute but little to the sublime. This rule need not be put in practice, except where an uniform degree of the most striking sublimity is to be produced, and that in every particular; for it ought to be observed, that this melancholy kind of greatness, though it be certainly the highest, ought not to be studied in all sorts of edifices, where yet grandeur must be studied; in such cases the sublimity must be drawn from the other sources; with a strict caution however against any thing light and riant; as nothing so effectually deadens the whole taste of the sublime.

SECTION XVII[j]

SOUND and LOUDNESS

The eye is not the only organ of sensation, by which a sublime passion may be produced. Sounds have a great power in these as in most other passions. I do not mean words, because words do not affect simply by their sounds, but by means altogether different. Excessive loudness alone is sufficient to overpower the soul, to suspend its action, and to fill it with terror. The noise of vast cataracts, raging storms, thunder, or artillery, awakes a great and aweful sensation in the mind, though we can observe no nicety or artifice in those sorts of music. The shouting of multitudes has a similar effect; and by the sole strength of the sound, so amazes and confounds the imagination, that in this staggering, and hurry of the mind, the best established tempers can scarcely forbear being borne down, and joining in the common cry, and common resolution of the croud.[36]

[j] *SECTION XVII.*] *SECTION XVIII.*

[36] See Introduction, p. xvii.

SECTION XVIII[k]

SUDDENNESS

A sudden beginning, or sudden cessation of sound of any considerable force, has the same power. The attention is roused by this; and the faculties driven forward, as it were, on their guard. Whatever either in sights or sounds makes the transition from one extreme to the other easy, causes no terror, and consequently can be no cause of greatness. In every thing sudden and unexpected, we are apt to start; that is, we have a perception of danger, and our nature rouses us to guard against it. It may be observed, that a single sound of some strength, though but of short duration, if repeated after intervals, has a grand effect. Few things are more aweful than the striking of a great clock, when the silence of the night prevents the attention from being too much dissipated. The same may be said of a single stroke on a drum, repeated with pauses; and of the successive firing of cannon at a distance; all the effects mentioned in this section have causes very nearly alike.

SECTION XIX[l]

INTERMITTING

A low, tremulous, intermitting sound, though it seems in some respects opposite to that just mentioned, is productive of the sublime. It is worth while to examine this a little. The fact itself must be determined by every man's own experience, and reflection. I[m] have already observed, that* night increases our terror more perhaps than any thing else; it is our nature, that, when we do not know what may happen to us, to fear the worst that can happen us; and hence it is, that uncertainty is so terrible, that we often seek to be rid of it, at the hazard of a certain mischief. Now some low, confused, uncertain sounds, leave us in the same fearful anxiety concerning their causes,

* Section 3.

[k] *SECTION XVIII.*] *SECTION XIX.*
[l] *SECTION XIX.*] *SECTION XX.*
[m] *reflection. I*] *reflection only. I*

that no light, or an uncertain light does concerning the objects that surround us.

Quale per incertam lunam sub luce maligna
Est iter in silvis.——[37]
——*A faint shadow of uncertain light,*
Like as a lamp, whose life doth fade away;
Or as the moon cloathed with cloudy night
Doth shew to him who walks in fear and great affright.
SPENSER.[38]

But a light now appearing, and now leaving us, and so off and on, is even more terrible than total darkness; and a sort of uncertain sounds are, when the necessary dispositions concur, more alarming than a total silence.

SECTION XX[n]

The cries of ANIMALS

Such sounds as imitate the natural inarticulate voices of men, or any[o] animals in pain or danger, are capable of conveying great ideas; unless it be the well known voice of some creature, on which we are used to look with contempt. The angry tones of wild beasts are equally capable of causing a great and aweful sensation.

Hinc exaudiri gemitus, iræque leonum
Vincla recusantum, et sera sub nocte rudentum;
Setigerique sues, atque in presepibus ursi
Sævire; et formæ magnorum ululare luporum.[39]

It might seem that these modulations of sound carry some connection with the nature of the things they represent, and are not merely arbitrary; because the natural cries of all animals, even of those animals with whom we have not been acquainted, never fail to make themselves sufficiently understood; this cannot be said of language. The modifications of sound, which may be productive of the sublime, are almost

[n] *SECTION XX.*] *SECTION XXI.*

[o] *any*] *any other*

[37] Virgil, *Aeneid*, VI, 270–1.

[38] *Faerie Queene*, II, vii, 29 (misquoted).

[39] Virgil, *Aeneid*, VII, 15–18.

infinite. Those I have mentioned, are only a few instances to shew, on what principle they are all built.

SECTION XXI[p]

SMELL and TASTE. BITTERS and STENCHES

Smells, and *Tastes*, have some share too, in ideas of greatness; but it is a small one, weak in its nature, and confined in its operations. I shall only observe, that no smells or tastes can produce a grand sensation, except excessive bitters, and intolerable stenches. It is true, that these affections of the smell and taste, when they are in their full force, and lean directly upon the sensory, are simply painful, and accompanied with no sort of delight; but when they are moderated, as in a description or narrative, they become sources of the sublime as genuine as any other, and upon the very same principle of a moderated pain. "A cup of bitterness;" to drain the bitter "cup of fortune;" the bitter apples of "Sodom." These are all ideas suitable to a sublime description. Nor is this passage of Virgil without sublimity, where the stench of the vapour in Albunea conspires so happily with the sacred horror and gloominess of that prophetic forest.

> *At rex sollicitus monstrorum oraculi fauni*
> *Fatidici genitoris adit, lucosque sub alta*
> *Consulit Albunea, nemorum quæ maxima sacro*
> *Fonte sonat;* sævamque exhalat opaca Mephitim.[40]

In the sixth book, and in a very sublime description, the poisonous exhalation of Acheron is not forgot, nor does it at all disagree with the other images amongst which it is introduced.

> *Spelunca* alta *fuit*, vastoque immanis *hiatu*
> *Scrupea, tuta* lacu nigro, *nemorumque* tenebris,
> *Quam super haud ullæ poterant impune volantes*
> *Tendere iter pennis*, talis sese halitus atris
> Faucibus effundens supera ad convexa ferebat.[41]

[p] *SECTION XXI.*] *SECTION XXIII.*

[40] *Aeneid*, VII, 81–4 (misquoted).

[41] *Aeneid*, VI, 237–41.

I have added these examples, because some friends, for whose judgment I have great deference, were[q] of opinion, that if the sentiment stood nakedly by itself, it would be subject at first view to burlesque and ridicule; but this I imagine would principally arise from considering the bitterness and stench in company with mean and contemptible ideas, with which it must be owned they are often united; such an union degrades the sublime in all other instances as well as in those. But it is one of the tests by which the sublimity of an image is to be tried, not whether it becomes mean when associated with mean ideas; but whether, when united with images of an allowed grandeur, the whole composition is supported with dignity. Things which are terrible are always great; but when things possess disagreeable qualities, or such as have indeed some degree of danger, but of a danger easily overcome, they are merely *odious*, as toads and spiders.

SECTION XXII[r]

FEELING. PAIN

Of *Feeling* little more can be said, than that the idea of bodily pain, in all the modes and degrees of labour, pain, anguish, torment, is productive of the sublime; and nothing else in this sense can produce it. I need not give here any fresh instances, as those given in the former sections abundantly illustrate a remark, that in reality wants only an attention to nature, to be made by every body.

Having thus run through the causes of the sublime with reference to all the senses, my first observation, (section 7.) will be found very nearly true; that the sublime is an idea belonging to self-preservation. That it is therefore one of the most affecting we have. That its strongest emotion is an emotion of distress, and that no† pleasure from a positive cause belongs[s] to it. Number-

† Vide section 6, part 1.

[q] *friends, for . . . were*] *friends to whose judgment I defer were*
[r] *SECTION XXII.*] *SECTION XXIV.*
[s] *no† pleasure . . . belongs*] *no† positive or absolute pleasure belongs*

less examples besides those mentioned, might be brought in support of these truths, and many perhaps useful consequences drawn from them.———

Sed fugit interea, fugit irrevocabile tempus,
Singula dum capti circumvectamur amore.[42]

[42] Virgil, *Georgics*, III, 284–5 (misquoted).

A

PHILOSOPHICAL ENQUIRY

INTO THE ORIGIN

OF OUR IDEAS

OF THE SUBLIME

AND BEAUTIFUL

Part Three

SECTION I

Of BEAUTY[t]

IT is my design to consider beauty as distinguished from the sublime; and in the course of the enquiry, to examine how far it is consistent with it. But previous to this, we must take a short review of the opinions already entertained of this quality; which I think are hardly to be reduced to any fixed principles; because men are used to talk of beauty in a figurative manner, that is to say, in a manner extremely uncertain, and indeterminate. By beauty I mean, that quality or those qualities in bodies by which they cause love, or some passion similar to it. ⟨I confine this definition to the merely sensible qualities of things, for the sake of preserving the utmost simplicity in a subject which must always distract us, whenever we take in those various causes of sympathy which attach us to any persons or things from secondary considerations, and not from the direct force which they have merely on being viewed. I likewise distinguish love, by which I mean that satisfaction which arises to the mind upon contemplating any thing beautiful, of whatsoever nature it may be, from desire or lust; which is an energy of the mind, that hurries us on to the possession of certain objects, that do not affect us as they are beautiful, but by means altogether different. We shall have a strong desire for a woman of no remarkable beauty; whilst the greatest beauty in men, or in other animals, though it causes love, yet excites nothing at all of desire. Which shews that beauty, and the passion caused by beauty, which I call love, is different from desire, though desire may sometimes operate along with it; but it is to this latter that we must attribute those violent and tempestuous passions, and the consequent emotions of the body which attend what is called love in some of its ordinary acceptations, and not to the effects of beauty merely as it is such.⟩

[t] *Part III. . . . BEAUTY.*] *Part III. Of BEAUTY. SECTION I.*

SECTION II

Proportion not the cause of BEAUTY in VEGETABLES

Beauty hath usually been said[u] to consist in certain proportions of parts. On[v] considering the matter, I have great reason to doubt, whether beauty be at all an idea belonging to proportion.[1] Proportion relates almost wholly to convenience, as every idea of order seems to do; and it must therefore be considered as a creature of the understanding, rather than a primary cause acting on the senses and imagination. It is not by the force of long attention and enquiry that we find any object to be beautiful; beauty demands no assistance from our reasoning; even the will is unconcerned; the appearance of beauty as effectually causes some degree of love in us, as the application of ice or fire produces the ideas of heat or cold. To gain something like a satisfactory conclusion in this point, it were well to examine, [2]⟨what proportion is; since several who make use of that word, do not always seem to understand very clearly the force of the term, nor to have very distinct ideas concerning the thing itself. Proportion is the measure of relative quantity. Since all quantity is divisible, it is evident that every distinct part into which any quantity is divided, must bear some relation to the other parts or to the whole. These relations give an origin to the idea of proportion. They are discovered by mensuration, and they are the objects of mathematical enquiry.

[u] *Beauty hath . . . said*] *Beauty is usually said* [v] *parts. On*] *parts; on*

[1] Plotinus rejects the notion that symmetry is the essence of beauty (W. R. Inge, *The Philosophy of Plotinus*, II, 214 ff). See p. 70 n.

[2] *Critical Review*, III, 366–7: "Proportion is not limited to one relation of parts, or one set of dimensions. Proportion is symmetry, and symmetry may be maintained under a variety of figures." *Literary Magazine*, II, 187: "Proportion is not beauty itself but one of its efficient qualities. A partial beauty may be seen, that is to say an handsome face, or an handsome leg, but, we apprehend, a beautiful and entire whole never existed without proportion and fitness. This we think so apparent that it need not be insisted on."

But whether any part of any determinate quantity be a fourth, or a fifth, or a sixth, or a moiety of the whole; or whether it be of equal length with any other part, or double its length, or but one half, is a matter merely indifferent to the mind; it stands neuter in the question: and it is from this absolute indifference and tranquillity of the mind, that mathematical speculations derive some of their most considerable advantages; because there is nothing to interest the imagination; because the judgment sits free and unbiassed to examine the point. All proportions, every arrangement of quantity is alike to the understanding, because the same truths result to it from all; from greater, from lesser; from equality and inequality. But surely beauty is no idea belonging to mensuration; nor has it any thing to do with calculation and geometry. If it had, we might then point out some certain measures which we could demonstrate to be beautiful, either as simply considered, or as related to others; and we could call in those natural objects, for whose beauty we have no voucher but the sense, to this happy standard, and confirm the voice of our passions by the determination of our reason. But since we have not this help, let us see whether proportion can in any sense be considered as the cause of beauty, as hath been so generally, and by some so confidently affirmed. If proportion be one of the constituents of beauty, it must derive that power either from some natural properties inherent in certain measures, which operate mechanically; from the operation of custom; or from the fitness which some measures have to answer some particular ends of conveniency. Our business therefore is to enquire, whether the parts of those objects which are found beautiful in the vegetable or animal kingdoms, are constantly so formed according to such certain measures, as may serve to satisfy us that their beauty results from those measures, on the principle of a natural mechanical cause; or from custom; or in fine, from their fitness for any determinate purposes. I intend to examine this point under each of these heads in their order. But before I proceed further, I hope it will not be thought amiss, if I lay down the rules which governed me in this enquiry, and which have misled me in it if I have gone astray. 1. If two bodies produce the same or a similar effect on the mind, and on examination they are found to agree in some of their properties, and to differ in others; the common effect is to be attributed to the properties in which they agree, and not to those in which they differ. 2. Not to account for the effect of a natural object from the effect of an artificial object. 3. Not to account for the effect of any natural object from a conclusion of our reason concerning its uses, if a natural cause may be assigned. 4. Not to admit any determinate quantity, or any relation of quantity, as the cause of a certain effect, if the effect is produced by different or opposite measures and relations; or if these measures and relations may exist, and yet the effect may not be produced. These are the rules which I have chiefly followed, whilst I examined into the power of proportion considered as a natural cause; and these, if he thinks them just, I request the reader to carry with him throughout the following discussion; whilst we enquire〉 in the first place,[w] in what things we find this quality of beauty; next, to see whether in these, we can find any assignable proportions, in such a manner as ought to convince us, that our idea of beauty results from them. We shall consider this pleasing power, as it appears in vegetables, in the inferior animals, and in man. Turning our eyes to the vegetable creation, we find nothing there so beautiful as flowers; but flowers are almost of every sort of shape, and of every sort of disposition; they are turned and fashioned into an infinite variety of forms; and from these forms, botanists have given them their names, which are almost as various. What proportion do we discover between the stalks and the leaves of flowers, or between the leaves and the pistils? How does the slender stalk of the rose agree with the bulky head under which it bends? but the rose is a beautiful flower; and can we undertake to say that it does not owe a great deal of its beauty even to that disproportion? the rose is a large flower, yet it grows upon a small shrub; the flower of the apple is very small, and it grows upon a large tree; yet the rose and the apple blossom are both beautiful, and the plants that bear them are most engagingly attired notwithstanding this disproportion. What by general consent is allowed to be a more beautiful object than an orange tree, flourishing at once with its leaves, its blossoms,

[w] *in the first place,*] *first,*

and its fruit? but it is in vain that we search here for any proportion between the height, the breadth, or any thing else concerning the dimensions of the whole, or concerning the relation of the particular parts to each other. I grant that we may observe in many flowers, something of a regular figure, and of a methodical disposition of the leaves. The rose has such a figure and such a disposition of its petals; but in an oblique view, when this figure is in a good measure lost, and the order of the leaves confounded, it yet retains its beauty; the rose is even more beautiful before it is full blown; in the bud; before this exact figure is formed; and this is not the only instance wherein method and exactness, the soul of proportion, are found rather prejudicial than serviceable to the cause of beauty.

SECTION III

Proportion not the cause of BEAUTY in ANIMALS

That proportion has but a small share in the formation of beauty, is full as evident among animals. Here the greatest variety of shapes, and dispositions of parts are well fitted, to excite this idea. The swan, confessedly a beautiful bird, has a neck longer than the rest of his body, and but a very short tail; is this a beautiful proportion? we must allow that it is. But then what shall we say to the peacock, who has comparatively but a short neck, with a tail longer than the neck and the rest of the body taken together? How many birds are there that vary infinitely from each of these standards, and from every other which you can fix, with proportions different, and often directly opposite to each other! and yet many of these birds are extremely beautiful; when upon considering them we find nothing in any one part that might determine us, *a priori*, to say what the others ought to be, nor indeed to guess any thing about them, but what experience might shew to be full of disappointment and mistake. And with regard to the colours either of birds or flowers, for there is something similar in the colouring of both, whether they are considered in their extension or gradation, there is nothing of proportion to be observed. Some are of but one single colour; others have all the colours of the rainbow; some are of the primary colours, others are of the mixt; in short, an attentive observer may soon conclude, that there is as little of proportion in the colouring as in the shapes of these objects. Turn next to beasts; examine the head of a beautiful horse; find what proportion that bears to his body, and to his limbs, and what relation these have to each other; and when you have settled these proportions as a standard of beauty, then take a dog or cat, or any other animal, and examine how far the same proportions between their heads and their necks, between those and the body, and so on, are found to hold; I think we may safely say, that they differ in every species, yet that there are individuals found in a great many species so differing, that have a very striking beauty. [3]⟨Now if it be allowed that very different, and even contrary forms and dispositions are consistent with beauty, it amounts I believe to a concession, that no certain measures operating from a natural principle, are necessary to produce it, at least so far as the brute species is concerned.⟩

SECTION IV

Proportion not the cause of BEAUTY in the human species

There are some parts of the human body, that are observed to hold certain proportions to each other; but before it can be proved, that the efficient cause of beauty lies in these, it must be shewn, that wherever these are found exact, the person to whom they belong is beautiful. I mean in the effect produced on the view, either of any member distinctly considered, or of the whole body together. It must be likewise shewn, that these parts stand in such a relation to each other, that the comparison between them may be easily made, and that the affection of the mind may naturally result from it. For my part, I have at several times very carefully examined many of those propor-

[3] See p. 92 n.: *Critical Review*, III, 366–7. Cf. *ibid.*, p. 367: ". . . we may observe that there are degrees of beauty in different kinds of symmetry."

tions, and found them hold very nearly, or altogether alike in many subjects, which were not only very different from one another, but where one has been very beautiful, and the other very remote from beauty. With regard to the parts which are found so proportioned, they are often so remote from each other, in situation, nature, and office, that I cannot see how they admit of any comparison, nor consequently how any effect owing to proportion can result from them. The neck, say they, in beautiful bodies should measure with the calf of the leg; it should likewise be twice the circumference of the wrist. And an infinity of observations of this kind are to be found in the writings, and conversations of many.[4] ⟨But what relation has the calf of the leg to the neck; or either of these parts to the wrist?⟩ These proportions are certainly to be found in handsome bodies. They are as certainly in ugly ones, as any who will take the pains to try, may find. Nay, I do not know but they may be least perfect in some of the most beautiful. [5]⟨You may assign any proportions you please to every part of the human body; and I undertake, that a painter shall religiously observe them all, and notwithstanding produce if he pleases, a very ugly figure. The same painter shall considerably deviate from these proportions, and produce a very beautiful one. And indeed it may be observed in the masterpieces of the ancient and modern statuary, that several of them differ very widely from the proportions of others, in parts very conspicuous, and of great consideration; and that they differ no less from the proportions we find in living men, of forms extremely striking and agreeable. And after all,⟩ how are the partizans of proportional beauty agreed amongst themselves about[x] the proportions of the human body? some hold it to be seven heads;

[x] *agreed amongst . . . about*] *agreed about*

[4] E.g. Leonardo da Vinci. (See J. P. Richter, *The Literary Works of Leonardo da Vinci*, 1883, I, 167–201.) Burke may have had some first-hand knowledge of Leonardo; item no. 221 in the Catalogue of the sale of his library reads: "Da Vinci, Della Pittura, con la Vita da Du Fresne, *Par.*, 1651."

[5] *Critical Review*, III, 367: "Proportion alone will not constitute beauty in every object; but it must always be an ingredient in the beauty of certain objects, particularly in statuary, painting, architecture and music."

some make it eight; whilst others extend it even to ten;[6] a vast[y] difference in such a small number of divisions! Others take other methods of estimating the proportions, and all with equal success. But are these proportions exactly the same in all handsome men? or are they at all the proportions found in beautiful women? nobody will say that they are; yet both sexes are undoubtedly capable of beauty, and the[z] female of the greatest; which advantage I[a] believe will hardly be attributed to the superior exactness of proportion in the fair sex. [7]⟨Let us rest a moment on this point; and consider how much difference there is between the measures that prevail in many similar parts of the body, in the two sexes of this single species only. If you assign any determinate proportions to the limbs of a man, and if you limit human beauty to these proportions, when you find a woman who differs in the make and measures of almost every part, you must conclude her not to be beautiful in spite of the suggestions of your imagination; or in obedience to your imagination you must renounce your rules; you must lay by the scale and compass, and look out for some other cause of beauty. For if beauty be attached to certain measures which operate from a *principle in nature*, why should similar parts with different measures of proportion be found to have beauty, and this too in the very same species? But to open our view a little, it is worth observing, that almost all animals have parts of very much the same nature, and destined nearly to the same purposes; an head, neck, body, feet, eyes, ears, nose and mouth; yet Providence to provide in the best manner for their several wants, and to display the riches of his wisdom and goodness in his creation, has worked out of these few and similar organs,

[y] *heads; some . . . vast*] *heads; others make it eight; a vast*
[z] *are undoubtedly . . . the*] *are capable of beauty, but the*
[a] *which advantage I*] *which I*

[6] Vitruvius (*De Architectura*, III, i, 2) gives 8 heads as the norm and he is followed in this by Leonardo (see J. P. Richter, *op. cit.*, I, 172). Dürer, in his *Four Books of Proportion* (Nürnberg, 1528), gives drawings of bodies ranging from 7 to 10 heads (see W. M. Conway, *Literary Remains of Albrecht Dürer*, Cambridge, 1889, pp. 232–9).

[7] *Critical Review*, III, 367: "... contrary to our author's opinion, we insist upon it, that the well proportioned parts of the human body are constantly found beautiful."

and members, a diversity hardly short of infinite in their disposition, measures, and relation. But, as we have before observed, amidst this infinite diversity, one particular is common to many species; several of the individuals which compose them, are capable of affecting us with a sense of loveliness; and whilst they agree in producing this effect, they differ extremely in the relative measures of those parts which have produced it. These considerations were sufficient to induce me to reject the notion of any particular proportions that operated by nature to produce a pleasing effect; but those who will agree with me with regard to a particular proportion, are strongly pre-possessed in favour of one more indefinite. They imagine, that although beauty in general is annexed to no certain measures common to the several kinds of pleasing plants and animals; yet that there is a certain proportion in each species absolutely essential to the beauty of that particular kind. If we consider the animal world in general, we find beauty confined to no certain measures; but as some peculiar measure and relation of parts, is what distinguishes each peculiar class of animals, it must of necessity be, that the beautiful in each kind will be found in the measures and proportions of that kind; for otherwise it would deviate from its proper species, and become in some sort monstrous: however, no species is so strictly confined to any certain proportions, that there is not a considerable variation amongst the individuals; and as it has been shewn of the human, so it may be shewn of the brute kinds, that beauty is found indifferently in all the proportions which each kind can admit, without quitting its common form; and it is this idea of a common form that makes the proportion of parts at all regarded, and not the operation of any natural cause; indeed a little consideration will make it appear that it is not measure, but manner, that creates all the beauty which belongs to shape. What lights do we borrow from these boasted proportions, when we study ornamental design? It seems amazing to me, that artists, if they were as well convinced as they pretend to be, that proportion is a principal cause of beauty, have not by them at all times accurate measurements of all sorts of beautiful animals to help them to proper proportions when they would contrive any thing elegant, especially as they frequently assert, that it is from an observation of the beautiful in nature they direct their practice. I know that it has been said long since, and echoed backward and forward from one writer to another a thousand times, that the proportions of building have been taken from those of the human body. To make this forced analogy complete, they represent a man with his arms raised and extended at full length, and then describe a sort of square, as it is formed by passing lines along the extremities of this strange figure.[8] But it appears very clearly to me, that the human figure never supplied the architect with any of his ideas. For in the first place, men are very rarely seen in this strained posture; it is not natural to them; neither is it at all becoming. Secondly, the view of the human figure so disposed, does not naturally suggest the idea of a square, but rather of a cross; as that large space between the arms and the ground, must be filled with something before it can make any body think of a square. Thirdly, several buildings are by no means of the form of that particular square, which are notwithstanding planned by the best architects, and produce an effect altogether as good, and perhaps a better. And certainly nothing could be more unaccountably whimsical, than for an architect to model his performance by the human figure, since no two things can have less resemblance or analogy, than a man, and an house or temple; do we need to observe, that their purposes are entirely different? What I am apt to suspect is this: that these analogies were devised to give a credit to the works of art, by shewing a conformity between them and the noblest works in nature, not that the latter served at all to supply hints for the perfection of the former. And I am the more fully convinced, that the patrons of proportion have transferred their artificial ideas to nature, and not borrowed from thence the proportions they use in works of art; because in any discussion of this subject, they always quit as soon as possible the open field of natural beauties, the animal and vegetable kingdoms, and fortify themselves within the artificial lines and angles of architecture. For there is in mankind an

[8] The "analogy" is found in Vitruvius, *De Architectura*, III, i, 3. For the drawing by Leonardo illustrating Vitruvius's idea, see J. P. Richter, *op. cit.*, Plate XVIII.

unfortunate propensity to make themselves, their views, and their works, the measure of excellence in every thing whatsoever. Therefore having observed, that their dwellings were most commodious and firm when they were thrown into regular figures, with parts answerable to each other; they transferred these ideas to their gardens; they turned their trees into pillars, pyramids, and obelisks; they formed their hedges into so many green walls, and fashioned the walks into squares, triangles, and other mathematical figures, with exactness and symmetry; and they thought if they were not imitating, they were at least improving nature, and teaching her to know her business.[9] But nature has at last escaped from their discipline and their fetters; and our gardens, if nothing else, declare, we begin to feel that mathematical ideas are not the true measures of beauty. And surely they are full as little so in the animal, as the vegetable world. For it is not extraordinary, that in these fine descriptive pieces, these innumerable odes and elegies, which are in the mouths of all the world, and many of which have been the entertainment of ages, that in these pieces which describe love with such a passionate energy, and represent its object in such an infinite variety of lights, not one word is said of proportion, if it be what some insist it is, the principal component of beauty; whilst at the same time, several other qualities are very frequently and warmly mentioned? But if proportion has not this power, it may appear odd how men came originally to be so prepossessed in its favour. It arose, I imagine, from the fondness I have just mentioned, which men bear so remarkably to their own works and notions; it arose from false reasonings on the effects of the customary figure of animals; it arose from the Platonic theory of fitness and aptitude.[10] For which reason in the next section, I shall consider the effects of custom in the figure of animals; and afterwards the idea of fitness; since if proportion does not operate by a natural power attending some measures, it must be either by custom, or the idea of utility; there is no other way.

[9] Ridicule of the formal garden was old-fashioned by 1759. Cf. Addison, *Spectator* No. 414 (25 June 1712); Pope, *Guardian* No. 173 (29 Sept. 1713) and *Moral Essay* No. IV (1731), ll. 113–20.

[10] Cf. *Gorgias*, 474–5.

SECTION V

Proportion further considered

If I am not mistaken, a great deal of the prejudice in favour of proportion has arisen, not so much from the observation of any certain measures found in beautiful bodies, as from a wrong idea of the relation which deformity bears to beauty, to which it has been considered as the opposite; on this principle it was concluded, that where the causes of deformity were removed, beauty must naturally and necessarily be introduced.〉 This[b] I believe is a mistake. For *deformity* is opposed, not to beauty, but to the *compleat, common form.* If one of the legs of a man be found shorter than the other, the man is deformed; because there is something wanting to complete the whole idea we form of a man; and this has the same effect in natural faults, as maiming and mutilation produce from accidents. So if the back be humped, the man is deformed; because his back has an unusual figure, and what carries with it the idea of some disease or misfortune; so if a man's neck be considerably longer or shorter than usual, we say he is deformed in that part, because men are not commonly made in that manner. But surely every hour's experience may convince us, that a man may have his legs of an equal length, and resembling each

[b] *sex. Let* . . . (p. 98, l. 9—p. 102, l. 7) . . . *This*] *sex. In fine, take the head as the measure of proportion in any species of animals, as in men; and having found what relation that bears to the other parts, examine the beautiful animals of the winged and four-footed kinds by this rule; and it will shew evidently what a fallacious standard we have chosen; the same will happen if you take any other part of any other animal whatsoever, as your rule to measure by. The proportions of animals are relative to the* usual form *in which we see them; if this is changed, we are shocked in the same manner that we are when any thing happens contrary to expectation. It must not be denied, that if the parts of any animal are so formed that they do not well support each other, the effect is disagreeable; but to have them simply otherwise, that is, not burthensome to one another, does not by any means produce beauty.*

SECTION V. Proportion further considered.

Now if it be allowed, that almost every sort of form, and every manner of arrangement is consistent with beauty, I imagine it amounts to a concession that no particular proportions are necessary to it. But if I am not mistaken, a great deal of the opinions concerning proportion have arisen from this; that deformity *has been considered as the opposite to* beauty*; and that the removal of the former of these qualities gave birth to the latter. This*

other in all respects, and his neck of a just size, and his back quite strait, without having at the same time the least perceivable beauty. ⟨Indeed beauty is so far from belonging to the idea of custom, that in reality what affects us in that manner is extremely rare and uncommon. The beautiful strikes us as much by its novelty as the deformed itself. It is thus in those species of animals with which we are acquainted; and if one of a new species were presented, we should by no means wait until custom had settled an idea of proportion before we decided concerning its beauty or ugliness. Which shews that the general idea of beauty, can be no more owing to customary than to natural proportion.⟩ Deformity arises from the want of the common proportions; but the necessary result of their existence in any object is not beauty. If we suppose proportion in natural things to be relative[c] to custom and use, the nature of use and custom will shew, that beauty, which is a *positive*[d] and powerful quality, cannot result from it. We are so wonderfully formed, that whilst we[e] are creatures vehemently desirous of novelty, we are as strongly attached to habit and custom. But it is the nature of things which hold us by custom to affect us very little whilst we are in possession of them, but strongly when they are absent. I remember to have frequented a certain place, every day for a long time together; and I may truly say, that so far from finding pleasure in it, I[f] was affected with a sort of weariness and disgust; I came, I went, I returned without pleasure; yet if by any means I passed by the usual time of my going thither, I was remarkably uneasy, and was not quiet till I had got into my old track.[11] They who use snuff take it almost without being sensible that they take it, and the acute

[c] *beauty. If . . . relative*] *beauty. I say the common proportions in each species of animals, because these proportions vary in all of them; there can be no absolute proportion assigned which constitutes an universal beauty; and a proportion which cannot be assigned, is, in other words, no proportion at all. But if proportion in natural things be relative*

[d] *positive*] positive [e] *that whilst we*] *that at the same time that we*

[f] *it, I*] *it, that I*

[11] Dixon Wecter suggests that this may be an allusion to the Grecian Coffee-house near Temple Bar, "a haunt of dramatists, critics, and actors rather than of dignified barristers". ("The Missing Years in Burke's Biography", *P.M.L.A.*, LIII, 1119, n 48.)

sense of smell is deadened, so as to feel hardly any thing from so sharp a stimulus; yet deprive the snuff-taker of his box, and he is the most uneasy mortal in the world. ⟨Indeed so far are use and habit from being causes of pleasure, merely as such; that the effect of constant use is to make all things of whatever kind entirely unaffecting. For as use at last takes off the painful effect of many things, it reduces the pleasurable effect of others in the same manner, and brings both to a sort of mediocrity and indifference. Very justly is use called a second nature; and our natural and common state is one of absolute indifference, equally prepared for pain or pleasure. But when we are thrown out of this state, or deprived of any thing requisite to maintain us in it; when this chance does not happen by pleasure from some mechanical cause, we are always hurt. It is so with the second nature, custom, in all things which relate to it.⟩ Thus[g] the want of the usual proportions[h] in men and other animals is sure to disgust, though their presence is by no means any cause of real pleasure. It is true, that the proportions laid down as causes of beauty in the human body are frequently found in beautiful ones, because they are generally found in all mankind; but if it can be shewn too that they are found without beauty, and that beauty frequently exists without them, and that this beauty, where it exists, always can be assigned to other less equivocal causes, it will naturally lead us to conclude, that proportion and beauty are not ideas of the same nature. The true opposite to beauty is not disproportion or deformity, but *ugliness*; and as it proceeds from causes opposite to those of positive beauty, we cannot consider it until we come to treat of that. Between beauty and ugliness there is a sort of mediocrity, in which the assigned proportions are most commonly found, but this has no effect upon the passions.

SECTION VI

FITNESS not the cause of BEAUTY

It is said that the idea of utility, or of a part's being well adapted to answer its end, is the cause of beauty, or indeed

[g] *Thus*] *So*　　[h] *proportions*] *proportion*

beauty itself.[12] ⟨If it were not for this opinion, it had been impossible for the doctrine of proportion to have held its ground very long; the world would be soon weary of hearing of measures which related to nothing, either of a natural principle, or of a fitness to answer some end; the idea which mankind most commonly conceive of proportion, is the suitableness of means to certain ends, and where this is not the question, very seldom trouble themselves about the effect of different measures of things. Therefore it was necessary for this theory to insist, that not only artificial, but natural objects took their beauty from the fitness of the parts for their several purposes. But in framing this theory, I am apprehensive that experience was not sufficiently consulted. For on that principle,⟩ the wedge-like[i] snout of a swine, with its tough cartilage at the end, the[j] little sunk eyes, and the whole make of the head, so[k] well adapted to its offices of digging, and rooting, would be extremely beautiful. The great bag hanging to the bill of a pelican, a thing highly useful to this animal, would be likewise as beautiful in our eyes. The hedgehog, so well secured against all assaults by his prickly hide, and[l] the porcupine with his missile quills, would be then considered as creatures of no small elegance.[m] There are few animals, whose parts are better contrived than those of a monkey;[13] he has the hands of a man, joined to the springy limbs of a beast; he[n] is admirably calculated for running, leaping, grappling, and climbing: and yet there are few animals which seem to have less beauty in the eyes of all mankind.[o] ⟨I need say little on the trunk of the elephant, of such various usefulness, and which is so far from contributing to his beauty. How well fitted is the wolf for

[i] *itself. If* . . . (p. 105, ll. 1–13) . . . *wedge-like*] *itself. This notion is closely allied to the former one of proportion, but surely never arose from experience. For at that rate, the wedge-like*

[j] *the*] *its* [k] *make of* . . . *so*] *make so* [l] *and*] *or* [m] *elegance.*] *beauty.*

[n] *he*] *and*

[o] *animals which* . . . *mankind.*] *animals seem to us to have less beauty.*

[12] See Introduction, pp. lxii–lxiii.

[13] The comment on the monkey which follows is somewhat reminiscent of Aristotle, *Historia animalium*, II, 502 a–b. (For the tradition to which it is linked see William C. McDermott, *The Ape in Antiquity*, Baltimore, 1938.)

running and leaping? how admirably is the lion armed for battle? But will any one therefore call the elephant, the wolf, and the lion, beautiful animals? I believe nobody will think the form of a man's legs so well adapted to running, as those of an horse, a dog, a deer, and several other creatures; at least they have not that appearance: yet I believe a well-fashioned human leg will be allowed far to exceed all these in beauty. If the fitness of parts was what constituted the loveliness of their form, the actual employment of them would undoubtedly much augment it; but this, though it is sometimes so upon another principle, is far from being always the case. A bird on the wing is not so beautiful as when it is perched; nay, there are several of the domestic fowls which are seldom seen to fly, and which are nothing the less beautiful on that account; yet birds are so extremely different in their form from the beast and human kinds, that you cannot on the principle of fitness allow them any thing agreeable, but in consideration of their parts being designed for quite other purposes. I never in my life chanced to see a peacock fly; and yet before, very long before I considered any aptitude in his form for the aerial life, I was struck with the extreme beauty which raises that bird above many of the best flying fowls in the world; though for any thing I saw, his way of living was much like that of the swine, which fed in the farm-yard along with him. The same may be said of cocks, hens, and the like; they are of the flying kind in figure; in their manner of moving not very different from men and beasts. To leave these foreign examples; if beauty in our own species was annexed to use, men would be much more lovely than women; and strength and agility would be considered as the only beauties. But to call strength by the name of beauty, to have but one denomination for the qualities of a Venus and Hercules, so totally different in almost all respects, is surely a strange confusion of ideas, or abuse of words. The cause of this confusion, I imagine, proceeds from our frequently perceiving the parts of the human and other animal bodies to be at once very beautiful, and very well adapted to their purposes; and we are deceived by a sophism, which makes us take that for a cause which is only a concomitant; this is the sophism of the fly; who imagined he raised a great dust, because he stood upon the chariot that really raised it.[14] The stomach, the lungs, the liver, as well as other parts, are incomparably well adapted to their purposes; yet they are far from having any beauty. Again, many things are very beautiful, in which it is impossible to discern any idea of use. And I appeal to the first and most natural feelings of mankind, whether on beholding a beautiful eye, or a well-fashioned mouth, or a well-turned leg, any ideas of their being well fitted for seeing, eating, or running, ever present themselves. What idea of use is it that flowers excite, the most beautiful part of the vegetable world? It is true, that the infinitely wise and good Creator has, of his bounty, frequently joined beauty to those things which he has made useful to us; but this does not prove that an idea of use and beauty are the same thing, or that they are any way dependent on each other.

SECTION VII

The real effects of FITNESS

When I excluded proportion and fitness from any share in beauty, I did not by any means intend to say that they were of no value, or that they ought to be disregarded in works of art. Works of art are the proper sphere of their power; and here it is that they have their full effect. Whenever the wisdom of our Creator intended that we should be affected with any thing, he did not confide the execution of his design to the languid and precarious operation of our reason; but he endued it with powers and properties that prevent the understanding, and even the will, which seizing upon the senses and imagination, captivate the soul before the understanding is ready either to join with them or to oppose them. It is by a long deduction and much study that we discover the adorable wisdom of God

[14] The "sophism" is attributed by Bacon (Essay LIV, "Of Vain Glory") to Aesop, but it is in fact no. 16 of the fables of Laurentius Abstemius (Lorenzo Bevilaqua, *fl. c.* 1500): "De musca quae quadrigis insidens pulverem se excitasse dicebat." If Burke read Abstemius (and not merely Bacon) his source may have been either a very common schoolbook, *Aesopi phrygis fabulae . . . una cum nonnullis variorum autorum fabulis* (edn. Cambridge, 1670, p. 62), or Roger L'Estrange, *Fables of Aesop and other eminent mythologists with moral reflections* (8th edn., 1738, no. 270).

in his works: when we discover it, the effect is very different, not only in the manner of acquiring it, but in its own nature, from that which strikes us without any preparation from the sublime or the beautiful. How different is the satisfaction of an anatomist, who discovers the use of the muscles and of the skin, the excellent contrivance of the one for the various movements of the body, and the wonderful texture of the other, at once a general covering, and at once a general outlet as well as inlet; how different is this from the affection which possesses an ordinary man at the sight of a delicate smooth skin, and all the other parts of beauty which require no investigation to be perceived? In the former case, whilst we look up to the Maker with admiration and praise, the object which causes it may be odious and distasteful; the latter very often so touches us by its power on the imagination, that we examine but little into the artifice of its contrivance; and we have need of a strong effort of our reason to disentangle our minds from the allurements of the object to a consideration of that wisdom which invented so powerful a machine. The effect of proportion and fitness, at least so far as they proceed from a mere consideration of the work itself, produce approbation, the acquiescence of the understanding, but not love, nor any passion of that species. When we examine the structure of a watch, when we come to know thoroughly the use of every part of it, satisfied as we are with the fitness of the whole, we are far enough from perceiving any thing like beauty in the watch-work itself; but let us look on the case, the labour of some curious artist in engraving, with little or no idea of use, we shall have a much livelier idea of beauty than we ever could have had from the watch itself, though the master-piece of Graham.[15] In beauty, as I said, the effect is previous to any knowledge of the use; but to judge of proportion, we must know the end for which any work is designed. According to the end the proportion varies. Thus there is one proportion of a tower, another of an house; one proportion of a gallery, another of an hall, another of a

[15] George Graham (1673–1751), one of a succession of great English clock and watch makers. Invented the mercurial pendulum and the dead-beat escapement. (See F. J. Britten, *Old Clocks and Watches and their Makers*, 1911.)

chamber. To judge of the proportions of these, you must be first acquainted with the purposes for which they were designed. Good sense and experience acting together, find out what is fit to be done in every work of art. We are rational creatures, and in all our works we ought to regard their end ánd purpose; the gratification of any passion, how innocent soever, ought only to be of secondary consideration. Herein is placed the real power of fitness and proportion; they operate on the understanding considering them, which *approves* the work and acquiesces in it. The passions, and the imagination which principally raises them, have here very little to do. When a room appears in its original nakedness, bare walls and a plain ceiling; let its proportion be ever so excellent, it pleases very little; a cold approbation is the utmost we can reach; a much worse proportioned room, with elegant mouldings and fine festoons, glasses, and other merely ornamental furniture, will make the imagination revolt against the reason; it will please much more than the naked proportion of the first room which the understanding has so much approved, as admirably fitted for its purposes. What I have here said and before concerning proportion, is by no means to persuade people absurdly to neglect the idea of use in the works of art. It is only to shew that these excellent things, beauty and proportion, are not the same; not that they should either of them be disregarded.

SECTION VIII

The RECAPITULATION

On the whole; if such parts in human bodies as are found proportioned, were likewise constantly found beautiful, as they certainly are not; or if they were so situated, as that a pleasure might flow from the comparison, which they seldom are; or if any assignable proportions were found, either in plants or animals, which were always attended with beauty, which never was the case; or if, where parts were well adapted to their purposes, they were constantly beautiful, and when no use appeared, there was no beauty, which is contrary to all experience; we might conclude, that beauty consisted in proportion or utility. But since, in all respects, the case is quite otherwise; we may be satisfied, that beauty does not depend on these, let it owe its origin to what else it will.

SECTION IX

Perfection not the cause of BEAUTY

There is another notion current, pretty closely allied to the former; that *Perfection* is the constituent cause of beauty.[16] This opinion has been made to extend much further than to sensible objects. But in these, so far is perfection, considered as such, from being the cause of beauty; that this quality, where it is highest in the female sex, almost always carries with it an idea of weakness and imperfection. Women are very sensible of this; for which reason, they learn to lisp, to totter in their walk, to counterfeit weakness, and even sickness. In all this, they are guided by nature. Beauty in distress is much the most affecting beauty. Blushing has little less power; and modesty in general, which is a tacit allowance of imperfection, is itself considered as an amiable quality, and certainly heightens every other that is so. I know, it is in every body's mouth, that we ought to love perfection. This is to me a sufficient proof, that it is not the proper object of love. Who ever said, we *ought* to love a fine woman, or even any of these beautiful animals, which please us? Here to be affected, there is no need of the concurrence of our will.

SECTION X

How far the idea of BEAUTY may be applied to the qualities of the MIND

Nor is this remark in general less applicable to the qualities of the mind. Those virtues which cause admiration, and are of the sublimer kind, produce terror rather than love. Such as fortitude, justice, wisdom, and the like. Never was any man amiable by force of these qualities. Those which engage our

[16] See Introduction, p. lxiii. See also M. Akenside, *The Pleasures of Imagination* (7th edn., 1765), I, 360–76.

hearts, which impress us with a sense of loveliness, are the softer virtues; easiness of temper, compassion, kindness and liberality; though certainly those latter are of less immediate and momentous concern to society, and of less dignity. But it is for that reason that they are so amiable. The great virtues turn principally on dangers, punishments, and troubles, and are exercised rather in preventing the worst mischiefs, than in dispensing favours; and are therefore not lovely, though highly venerable. The subordinate turn on reliefs, gratifications, and indulgences; and are therefore more lovely, though inferior in dignity. Those persons who creep into the hearts of most people, who are chosen as the companions of their softer hours, and their reliefs from care and anxiety, are never persons of shining qualities, nor strong virtues. It is rather the soft green of the soul on which we rest our eyes, that are fatigued with beholding more glaring objects. It is worth observing, how we feel ourselves affected in reading the characters of Cæsar, and Cato, as they are so finely drawn and contrasted in Sallust. In one, the *ignoscendo*, *largiundo*; in the other, *nil largiundo*. In one, the *miseris perfugium*; in the other, *malis perniciem*.[17] In the latter we have much to admire, much to reverence, and perhaps something to fear; we respect him, but we respect him at a distance. The former makes us familiar with him; we love him, and he leads us whither he pleases. To draw things closer to our first and most natural feelings, I will add a remark made upon reading this section by an ingenious friend. The authority of a father, so useful to our well-being, and so justly venerable upon all accounts, hinders us from having that entire love for him that we have for our mothers, where the parental authority is almost melted down into the mother's fondness and indulgence. But we generally have a great love for our grandfathers, in whom this authority is removed a degree from us, and where the weakness of age mellows it into something of a feminine partiality.

[17] *Bellum Catilinae*, LIV (misquoted). For another reference to Burke's admiration for Sallust as an historian and for "his beautiful painting of characters", see the letter to Shackleton, 21 Mar. 1747 (Samuels, *Early Life*, p. 129). The contrast between Caesar and Cato occurs elsewhere in eighteenth-century writings, e.g. Hume, *A Treatise of Human Nature* (ed. Green and Grose, 1898), II, 362–3.

SECTION XI

How far the idea of BEAUTY may be applied to VIRTUE

From what has been said in the foregoing section, we may easily see, how far the application of beauty to virtue may be made with propriety. The general application of this quality[p] to virtue, has a strong tendency to confound our ideas of things; and it has given rise to an infinite deal of whimsical theory; as the affixing the name of beauty to proportion, congruity and perfection, as well as to qualities of things yet more remote from our natural ideas of it, and from one another, has tended to confound our ideas of beauty, and left us no standard or rule to judge by, that was not even more uncertain and fallacious than our own fancies. ⟨This loose and inaccurate manner of speaking, has therefore misled us both in the theory of taste and of morals; and induced us to remove the science of our duties from their proper basis, (our reason, our relations, and our necessities,) to rest it upon foundations altogether visionary and unsubstantial.⟩

SECTION XII

The real cause of BEAUTY

Having endeavoured to shew what beauty is not, it remains that we should examine, at least with equal attention, in what it really consists. Beauty[q] is a thing much too affecting not to depend upon some positive qualities. And, since[r] it is no creature of our reason, since it strikes us without any reference to use, and even where no use at all can be discerned, since the order and method of nature is generally very different from our measures and proportions, we must conclude that beauty is, for the greater part, some quality in bodies, acting[s] mechanically upon the human mind by the intervention of the senses. We[t]

[p] *this quality*] *this metaphorical quality*

[q] *consists. Beauty*] *consists; for beauty*

[r] *qualities. And, since*] *qualities. Now certainly, since*

[s] *some quality . . . acting*] *some merely sensible quality, acting*

[t] *We*] *And we*

ought therefore to consider attentively in[u] what manner those sensible qualities are disposed, in such things as by experience we find beautiful, or which excite in us the passion of love, or some correspondent affection.

SECTION XIII

Beautiful objects small

The most obvious point that presents itself to us in examining any object, is its extent or quantity. And what degree of extent prevails in bodies, that are held beautiful, may be gathered from the usual manner of expression concerning it. I am told that in most languages, the objects of love are spoken of under diminutive epithets. It is so in all the languages of which I have any knowledge. In Greek the *ιον*, and other diminutive terms, are almost always the terms of affection and tenderness. These diminutives were commonly added by the Greeks[v] to the names of persons with whom they conversed on terms of friendship and familiarity. Though the Romans were a people of less quick and delicate feelings, yet they naturally slid into the lessening termination upon the same occasions. Anciently in the English language the diminishing *ling* was added to the names of persons and things that were the objects of love. Some we retain still, as darling, (or little dear) and a few others. But to this day in ordinary conversation, it is usual to add the endearing name of *little* to every thing we love; the French and Italians make use of these affectionate diminutives even more than we. In the animal creation, out of our own species, it is the small we are inclined to be fond of; little[w] birds, and some of the smaller kinds of beasts. A great beautiful thing, is a manner of expression scarcely ever used; but that of a great ugly thing, is very common. There is a wide difference between admiration and love. The sublime, which is the cause of the former, always dwells on great objects, and terrible; the latter on small ones, and pleasing; we submit to what we admire, but we love what submits to us; in one case we are forced, in the other we are flattered into compliance. In short, the ideas

[u] *consider attentively in*] *consider in*

[v] *the Greeks*] *the same people*

[w] *of; little*] *of. Little*

of the sublime and the beautiful stand on foundations so different, that it is hard, I had almost said impossible, to think of reconciling them in the same subject, without considerably lessening the effect of the one or the other upon the passions. So that attending to their quantity, beautiful objects are comparatively small.

SECTION XIV
SMOOTHNESS

The next property constantly observable in such objects is* *Smoothness*. A quality so essential to beauty, that I do not now recollect any thing beautiful that is not smooth. In trees and flowers, smooth leaves are beautiful; smooth slopes of earth in gardens; smooth streams in the landscape; smooth coats of birds and beasts in animal beauties; in fine women, smooth skins; and in several sorts of ornamental furniture, smooth and polished surfaces. A very considerable part of the effect of beauty is owing to this quality; indeed the most considerable. For take any beautiful object, and give it a broken and rugged surface, and however well formed it may be in other respects, it pleases no longer. Whereas let it want ever so many of the other constituents, if it wants not this, it becomes more pleasing than almost all the others without it. This seems to me so evident, that I am a good deal surprised, that none who have handled the subject have made any mention of the quality of smoothness in the enumeration of those that go to the forming of beauty. For indeed any ruggedness, any sudden projection, any sharp angle, is in the highest degree contrary to that idea.

SECTION XV
Gradual VARIATION

But as perfectly beautiful bodies are not composed of angular parts, so their parts never continue long in the same right line. †They vary their direction every moment, and they change

* Part 4, section 21.

† Part 5, section 23.[18]

[18] This note should read: "Part 4, section 23".

under the eye by a deviation continually carrying on, but for whose beginning or end you will find it difficult to ascertain a point. The view of a beautiful bird will illustrate this observation. Here we see the head increasing insensibly to the middle, from whence it lessens gradually until it mixes with the neck; the neck loses itself in a larger swell, which continues to the middle of the body, when the whole decreases again to the tail; the tail takes a new direction; but it soon varies its new course; it blends again with the other parts; and the line is perpetually changing, above, below, upon every side. In this description I have before me the idea of a dove; it agrees very well with most of the conditions of beauty. It is smooth and downy; its parts are (to use that expression) melted into one another; you are presented with no sudden protuberance through the whole, and yet the whole is continually changing. Observe that part of a beautiful woman where she is perhaps the most beautiful, about the neck and breasts; the smoothness; the softness; the easy and insensible swell; the variety of the surface, which is never for the smallest space the same; the deceitful maze, through which the unsteady eye slides giddily, without knowing where to fix, or whither it is carried. Is not this a demonstration of that change of surface continual and yet hardly perceptible at any point which forms one of the great constituents of beauty? ⟨It gives me no small pleasure to find that I can strengthen my theory in this point, by the opinion of the very ingenious Mr. Hogarth; whose idea of the line of beauty I take in general to be extremely just. But the idea of variation, without attending so accurately to the *manner* of the variation, has led him to consider angular figures as beautiful;[19] these figures, it is true, vary greatly; yet they vary in a sudden and broken manner; and I do not find any natural object which is angular, and at the same time beautiful. Indeed few natural objects are entirely angular. But I think those which approach the most nearly to it, are the ugliest. I must add too, that, so far as I could observe of nature, though the varied line is that alone in which complete beauty is found, yet there is no

[19] *Analysis of Beauty* (1753). For "line of beauty", see chapters IX-X; "variation", *passim*; "angular figures", chapter IV. Cf. Introduction, pp. lxx–lxxii.

particular line which is always found in the most completely beautiful; and which is therefore beautiful in preference to all other lines. At least I never could observe it.〉

SECTION XVI
DELICACY

An air of robustness and strength is very prejudicial to beauty. An appearance of *delicacy*, and even of fragility, is almost essential to it. Whoever examines the vegetable or animal creation, will find this observation to be founded in nature. It is not the oak, the ash, or the elm, or any of the robust trees of the forest, which we consider as beautiful; they are awful and majestic; they inspire a sort of reverence. It is the delicate myrtle, it is the orange, it is the almond, it is the jessamine, it is the vine, which we look on as vegetable beauties. It is the flowery species, so remarkable for its weakness and momentary duration, that gives us the liveliest idea of beauty, and elegance. Among animals; the greyhound is more beautiful than the mastiff; and the delicacy of a gennet, a barb, or an Arabian horse, is much more amiable than the strength and stability of some horses of war or carriage. I need here say little of the fair sex, where I believe the point will be easily allowed me. The beauty of women is considerably owing to their weakness, or delicacy, and is even enhanced by their timidity, a quality of mind analogous to it. I would not here be understood to say, that weakness betraying very bad health has any share in beauty; but the ill effect of this is not because it is weakness, but because the ill state of health which produces such weakness alters the other conditions of beauty; the parts in such a case collapse; the bright colour, the *lumen purpureum juventæ* is gone; and the fine variation is lost in wrinkles, sudden breaks, and right lines.

SECTION XVII
Beauty in COLOUR

As to the colours usually found in beautiful bodies; it may be somewhat difficult to ascertain them, because in the several parts of nature, there is an infinite variety. However, even in this variety, we may mark out something on which to settle. First, the colours of beautiful bodies must not be dusky or muddy, but clean and fair. Secondly, they must not be of the strongest kind. Those which seem most appropriated to beauty, are the milder of every sort; light greens; soft blues; weak whites; pink reds; and violets. Thirdly, if the colours be strong and vivid, they are always diversified, and the object is never of one strong colour; there are almost always such a number of them (as in variegated flowers) that the strength and glare of each is considerably abated. In a fine complexion, there is not only some variety in the colouring, but the colours, neither the red nor the white are strong and glaring. Besides, they are mixed in such a manner, and with such gradations, that it is impossible to fix the bounds. On the same principle it is, that the dubious colour in the necks and tails of peacocks, and about the heads of drakes, is so very agreeable. In reality, the beauty both of shape and colouring are as nearly related, as we can well suppose it possible for things of such different natures to be.

SECTION XVIII
RECAPITULATION

On the whole, the qualities of beauty, as they are merely sensible qualities, are the following. First, to be comparatively small. Secondly, to be smooth. Thirdly, to have a variety in the direction of the parts; but fourthly, to have those parts not angular, but melted as it were into each other. Fifthly, to be of a delicate frame, without any remarkable appearance of strength. Sixthly, to have its colours clear and bright; but not very strong and glaring. Seventhly, or if it should have any glaring colour, to have it diversified with others. These are, I believe, the properties on which beauty depends; properties that operate by nature, and are less liable to be altered by caprice, or confounded by a diversity of tastes, than any others.

SECTION XIX

The PHYSIOGNOMY

The *Physiognomy* has a considerable share in beauty, especially in that of our own species. The manners give a certain determination to the countenance, which being observed to correspond pretty regularly with them, is capable of joining the effect of certain agreeable qualities of the mind to those of the body. So that to form a finished human beauty, and to give it its full influence, the face must be expressive of such gentle and amiable qualities, as correspond with the softness, smoothness, and delicacy of the outward form.

SECTION XX

The EYE

I have hitherto purposely omitted to speak of the *Eye*, which has so great a share in the beauty of the animal creation, as it did not fall so easily under the foregoing heads, though in fact it is reducible to the same principles. I think then, that the beauty of the eye consists, first, in its *clearness*; what *coloured* eye shall please most, depends a good deal on particular fancies; but none are pleased with an eye, whose water (to use that term) is dull and muddy.* We are pleased with the eye in this view, on the principle upon which we like diamonds, clear water, glass, and such like transparent substances. Secondly, the motion of the eye contributes to its beauty, by continually shifting its direction; but a slow and languid motion is more beautiful than a brisk one; the latter is enlivening; the former lovely. Thirdly, with regard to the union of the eye with[x] the neighbouring parts, it is to hold the same rule that is given of other beautiful ones; it is not to make a strong deviation from the line of the neighbouring parts; nor to verge into any exact geometrical figure. Besides all this, the eye affects, as it is expressive of some qualities of the mind, and its principal

* Part 4, section 25.

[x] *regard to . . . with*] *regard to its union with*

power generally arises from this; so that what we have just said of the physiognomy is applicable here.

SECTION XXI

UGLINESS

It may perhaps appear like a sort of repetition of what we have before said, to insist here upon the nature of *Ugliness*. As I imagine it to be in all respects the opposite to those qualities which we have laid down for the constituents of beauty. But though ugliness be the opposite to beauty, it is not the opposite to proportion and fitness. For it is possible that a thing may be very ugly with any proportions, and with a perfect fitness to any uses. Ugliness I imagine likewise to be consistent enough with an idea of the sublime. But I would by no means insinuate that ugliness of itself is a sublime idea, unless united with such qualities as excite a strong terror.

SECTION XXII

GRACE

Gracefulness is an idea not very different from beauty; it consists in much the same things. Gracefulness is an idea belonging to *posture* and *motion*. In both these, to be graceful, it is requisite that there be no appearance of difficulty; there is required a small inflexion of the body; and a composure of the parts, in such a manner, as not to incumber each other, nor to appear divided by sharp and sudden angles. In this ease, this roundness, this delicacy of attitude and motion, it is that all the magic of grace consists, and what is called its *je ne sais quoi*;[20] as will be obvious to any observer who[y] considers attentively the Venus de Medicis, the Antinous, or any statue generally allowed to be graceful in an high degree.

[y] *be obvious . . . who*] *be more obvious to any body who*

[20] The use of this phrase is discussed by J. E. Spingarn, *Critical Essays of the 17th Century*, I, c.

SECTION XXIII

ELEGANCE and SPECIOUSNESS

When any body is composed of parts smooth and polished, without pressing upon each other, without shewing any ruggedness or confusion, and at the same time affecting some *regular shape*, I call it *elegant*. It is closely allied to the beautiful, differing from it only in this *regularity*; which however, as it makes a very material difference, in the affection produced, may very well constitute another species. Under this head I rank those delicate and regular works of art, that imitate no determinate object in nature, as elegant buildings, and pieces of furniture. When any object partakes of the abovementioned qualities, or of those of beautiful bodies, and is withal of great dimensions; it is full as remote from the idea of mere beauty. I call it *fine* or *specious*.

SECTION XXIV

The beautiful in FEELING

The foregoing description of beauty, so far as is taken in by the eye, may be greatly illustrated by describing the nature of objects, which produce a similar effect through the touch. This I call the beautiful in *Feeling*. It corresponds wonderfully with what causes the same species of pleasure to the sight. There is a chain in all our sensations; they are all but different sorts of feeling, calculated to be affected by various sorts of objects, but all to be affected after the same manner. All bodies that are pleasant to the touch, are so by the slightness of the resistance they make. Resistance is either to motion along the surface, or to the pressure of the parts on one another; if the former be slight, we call the body, smooth; if the latter, soft. The chief pleasure we receive by feeling, is in the one or the other of these qualities; and if there be a combination of both, our pleasure is greatly increased. This is so plain, that it is rather more fit to illustrate other things, than to be illustrated itself by any example. The next source of pleasure in this sense, as in every other, is the continually presenting somewhat new; and we find that bodies which continually vary their surface, are much the most pleasant, or beautiful, to the feeling, as any one that pleases may experience. The third property in such objects is, that though the surface continually varies its direction, it never varies it suddenly. The application of any thing sudden, even though the impression itself have little or nothing of violence, is disagreeable. The quick application of a finger a little warmer or colder than usual, without notice, makes us start; a slight tap on the shoulder, not expected, has the same effect. Hence it is that angular bodies, bodies that suddenly vary the direction of the outline, afford so little pleasure to the feeling. Every such change is a sort of climbing or falling in miniature; so that squares, triangles, and other angular figures, are neither beautiful to the sight nor feeling. Whoever compares his state of mind, on feeling soft, smooth, variated, unangular bodies, with that in which he finds himself, on the view of a beautiful object, will perceive a very striking analogy in the effects of both; and which may go a good way towards discovering their common cause. Feeling and sight in this respect, differ in but a few points. The touch takes in the pleasure of softness, which is not primarily an object of sight; the sight on the other hand comprehends colour, which can hardly be made perceptible to the touch; the touch again has the advantage in a new idea of pleasure resulting from a moderate degree of warmth; but the eye triumphs in the infinite extent and multiplicity of its objects. But there is such a similitude in the pleasures of these senses, that I am apt to fancy, if it were possible that one might discern colour by feeling, (as it is said some blind men have done) that the same colours, and the same disposition of colouring, which are found beautiful to the sight, would be found likewise most grateful to the touch. But setting aside conjectures, let us pass to the other sense; of hearing.

SECTION XXV

The beautiful in SOUNDS

In this sense we find an equal aptitude to be affected in a soft and delicate manner; and how far sweet or beautiful sounds agree with our descriptions of beauty in other senses, the experience of every one must decide. Milton has described this species of music in one of his juvenile poems.* I need not say that Milton was perfectly well versed in that art; and that no man had a finer ear, with a happier manner[z] of expressing the affections of one sense by metaphors taken from another. The[a] description is as follows.

> ——*And ever against eating cares,*
> *Lap me in* soft *Lydian airs;*
> *In notes with many a* winding *bout*
> *Of* linked sweetness long drawn *out;*
> *With wanton heed, and giddy cunning,*
> *The* melting *voice through* mazes *running;*
> Untwisting *all the chains that tye*
> *The hidden soul of harmony.*[21]

Let us parallel this with the softness, the winding surface, the unbroken continuance, the easy gradation of the beautiful in other things; and all the diversities of the several senses, with all their several affections, will rather help to throw lights from one another to finish one clear, consistent idea of the whole, than to obscure it by their intricacy and variety.

To[b] the abovementioned description I shall add one or two remarks. The first is; that the beautiful in music will not bear that loudness and strength of sounds, which[c] may be used to raise other passions; nor notes, which are shrill, or harsh, or deep; it agrees best with such as are clear, even, smooth, and weak. The second is; that great variety, and quick transitions from one measure or tone to another, are contrary to the genius of the beautiful in music. Such† transitions often excite

* Il allegro.

† I ne'er am merry, when I hear sweet music.
SHAKESPEARE.[22]

[z] *and that . . . manner*] *and had as fine an ear, with as happy a manner*
[a] *another. The*] *another, as any man that ever was. The*
[b] *variety. To*] *variety. SECTION XXVI. Continued. To*
[c] *which*] *that*

[21] *L'Allegro*, ll. 135–42 (misquoted).
[22] *The Merchant of Venice*, V, i, 69 (misquoted).

mirth, or other sudden and tumultuous passions; but not that sinking, that melting, that languor, which is the characteristical effect of the beautiful, as it regards every sense. The passion excited by beauty is in fact nearer to a species of melancholy, than to jollity and mirth. I do not here mean to confine music to any one species of notes, or tones, neither is it an art in which I can say I have any great skill. My sole design in this remark is, to settle a consistent idea of beauty. The infinite variety of the affections of the soul will suggest to a good head, and skilful ear, a variety of such sounds, as are fitted to raise them. It can be no prejudice to this, to clear and distinguish some few particulars, that belong to the same class, and are consistent with each other, from the immense croud of different, and sometimes contradictory ideas, that rank vulgarly under the standard of beauty. And of these it is my intention to mark such only of the leading points as shew the conformity of the sense of hearing, with all the other senses in the article of their pleasures.

SECTION XXVI[d]

TASTE and SMELL

This general agreement of the senses is yet more evident on minutely considering those of taste and smell. We metaphorically apply the idea of sweetness to sights, and sounds; but as the qualities of bodies by which they are fitted to excite either pleasure or pain in these senses, are not so obvious as they are in the others, we shall refer an explanation of their analogy, which is a very close one, to that part, wherein we come to consider the common efficient cause of beauty as it regards all the senses. I do not think any thing better fitted to establish a clear and settled idea of visual beauty, than this way of examining the similar pleasures of other senses; for one part is sometimes clear in one of these senses, that is more obscure in another; and where there is a clear concurrence of all, we may with more certainty speak of any one of them. By this means, they bear witness to each other; nature is, as it were, scrutinized;

[d] *SECTION XXVI.*] *SECTION XXVII.*

and we report nothing of her, but what we receive from her own information.

SECTION XXVII[e]

The Sublime and Beautiful compared

On closing this general view of beauty, it naturally occurs, that we should compare it with the sublime; and in this comparison there appears a remarkable contrast. For sublime objects are vast in their dimensions, beautiful ones comparatively small; beauty should be smooth, and polished; the great, rugged and negligent; beauty should shun the right line, yet deviate from it insensibly; the great in many cases loves the right line, and when it deviates, it often makes a strong deviation; beauty should not be obscure; the great ought to be dark and gloomy; beauty should be light and delicate; the great ought to be solid, and even massive. They are indeed ideas of a very different nature, one being founded on pain, the other on pleasure; and however they may vary afterwards from the direct nature of their causes, yet these causes keep up an eternal distinction between them, a distinction never to be forgotten by any whose business it is to affect the passions. 〈In the infinite variety of natural combinations we must expect to find the qualities of things the most remote imaginable from each other united in the same object. We must expect also to find combinations of the same kind in the works of art. But when we consider the power of an object upon our passions, we must know that when any thing is intended to affect the mind by the force of some predominant property, the affection produced is like to be the more uniform and perfect, if all the other properties or qualities of the object be of the same nature, and tending to the same design as the principal;

> *If black, and white blend, soften, and unite,*
> *A thousand ways, are there no black and white?*[23]

If the qualities of the sublime and beautiful are sometimes found united, does this prove, that they are the same, does it prove,

[e] *SECTION XXVII.*] *SECTION XXVIII.*

[23] Pope, *Essay on Man*, II, 213–4 (misquoted).

that they are any way allied, does it prove even that they are not opposite and contradictory? Black and white may soften, may blend, but they are not therefore the same. Nor when they are so softened and blended with each other, or with different colours, is the power of black as black, or of white as white, so strong as when each stands uniform and distinguished.〉

The end of the Third Part.

A PHILOSOPHICAL ENQUIRY INTO THE ORIGIN OF OUR IDEAS OF THE SUBLIME AND BEAUTIFUL

Part Four

SECTION I

Of the efficient cause of the SUBLIME and BEAUTIFUL

WHEN I say, I intend to enquire into the efficient cause of sublimity and beauty, I would not be understood to say, that I can come to the ultimate cause. I do not pretend that I shall ever be able to explain, why certain affections of the body produce such a distinct emotion of mind, and no other; or why the body is at all affected by the mind, or the mind by the body. A little thought will shew this to be impossible. But I conceive, if we can discover what affections of the mind produce certain emotions of the body; and what distinct feelings and qualities of body shall produce certain determinate passions in the mind, and no others, I fancy a great deal will be done; something not unuseful towards a distinct knowledge of our passions, so far at least as we have them at present under our consideration. This is all, I believe, we can do. If we could advance a step farther, difficulties would still remain, as we should be still equally distant from the first cause. When Newton first discovered the property of attraction, and settled its laws, he found it served very well to explain several of the most remarkable phænomena in nature; but yet with reference to the general system of things, he could consider attraction but as an effect, whose cause at that time he did not attempt to trace. But when he afterwards began to account for it by a subtle elastic æther,[1] this great man (if in so great a man it be not impious to discover any thing like a blemish) seemed to have quitted his usual cautious manner of philosophising; since, perhaps, allowing all that has been advanced on this subject to be sufficiently proved, I think it leaves us with as many difficulties as it found us. That great chain of causes, which linking one to another even to the throne of God himself, can never be unravelled by any industry of ours. When we

[1] *Philosophiae Naturalis Principia Mathematica* (English transl., 1729), II, 393.

go but one step beyond the immediately sensible qualities of things, we go out of our depth. All we do after, is but a faint struggle, that shews we are in an element which[f] does not belong to us. So that when I speak of cause, and efficient cause, I only mean, certain affections of the mind, that cause certain changes in the body; or certain powers and properties in bodies, that work a change in the mind. As if I were to explain the motion of a body falling to the ground, I would say it was caused by gravity, and I would endeavour to shew after what manner this power operated, without attempting to shew why it operated in this manner; or if I were to explain the effects of bodies striking one another by the common laws of percussion, I should not endeavour to explain how motion itself is communicated.

SECTION II

ASSOCIATION

It is no small bar in the way of our enquiry into the cause of our passions,[g] that the occasion of many of them are given, and that their governing motions are communicated[h] at a time when we have not capacity to reflect on them; at a time of which all sort[i] of memory is worn out of our minds. For besides such things as affect us in various manners according to their natural powers, there are associations made at that early season, which we find it very hard afterwards to distinguish from natural effects. Not to mention the unaccountable antipathies which we find in many persons, we all find it impossible to remember when a steep became more terrible than a plain; or fire or water more dreadful than a clod of earth; though all these are very probably either conclusions from experience, or arising from the premonitions of others; and some of them impressed, in all likelihood, pretty late. But as it must be allowed that many things affect us after a certain manner, not by any natural powers they have for that purpose, but by association; so it would be absurd on the other hand, to say

[f] *which*] *that*
[g] *our enquiry . . . passions,*] *our enquiries into the cause of the passions,*
[h] *communicated*] *impressed*
[i] *sort*] *sorts*

that all things affect us by association only; since[j] some things must have been originally and naturally agreeable or disagreeable, from which the others derive their associated powers; and it would be, I fancy, to little purpose to look for the cause[k] of our passions in association, until we fail of it[l] in the natural properties of things.

SECTION III

Cause of PAIN and FEAR

I have before observed,* that whatever is qualified to cause terror, is a foundation capable of the sublime; to which I add, that not only these, but many things from which we cannot probably apprehend any danger have a similar effect, because they operate in a similar manner. I observed too, that† whatever produces pleasure, positive and original pleasure, is fit to have beauty engrafted on it. Therefore, to clear up the nature of these qualities, it may be necessary to explain the nature of pain and pleasure on which they depend.[2] A man who suffers under violent bodily pain; (I suppose the most violent, because the effect may be the more obvious.) I say a man in great pain[m] has his teeth set, his eye-brows are violently contracted, his forehead is wrinkled, his eyes are dragged inwards, and rolled with great vehemence, his hair stands on end, the voice is forced out in short shrieks and groans, and the whole fabric totters. Fear or terror, which is an apprehension of pain or death, exhibits exactly the same effects, approaching in violence to those just mentioned in proportion to the nearness of the cause, and the weakness of the subject. This is not only so in the human species, but I have more than once observed in dogs, under an apprehension of punishment, that they have writhed their bodies, and yelped, and howled, as if they had actually felt the blows. From hence I conclude that

* Part I, section 8.[3] † Part I, section 10.

[j] *that all . . . since*] *that nothing affects us otherwise; since*
[k] *cause*] *causes* [l] *it*] *them* [m] *in great pain*] *in pain*

[2] In the passage which follows Burke perhaps draws on Lucretius, *De Rerum Natura*, III, 152–60.

[3] This note should presumably read: "Part I, section 7."

pain, and fear, act upon the same parts of the body, and in the same manner, though somewhat differing in degree. That pain and fear consist in an unnatural tension of the nerves; that this is sometimes accompanied with an unnatural strength, which sometimes suddenly changes into an extraordinary weakness; that these effects often come on alternately, and are sometimes[n] mixed with each other. This is the nature of all convulsive agitations, especially in weaker subjects, which are the most liable to the severest impressions of pain and fear. The only difference between pain and terror, is, that things which cause pain operate on the mind, by the intervention of the body; whereas things that cause terror generally affect the bodily organs by the operation of the mind suggesting the danger; but both agreeing, either primarily, or secondarily, in producing a tension, contraction, or violent emotion of the nerves*, they [o] agree likewise in every thing else. For[p] it appears very clearly to me, from this, as well as from many other examples, that when the body is disposed, by any means whatsoever, to such emotions as it would acquire by the means of a certain passion; it will of itself excite something very like that passion in the mind.

SECTION IV

Continued

To this purpose Mr. Spon,[4] in his[q] Recherches d'Antiquité, gives us a curious story of the celebrated physiognomist

* I do not here enter into the question debated among physiologists, whether pain be the effect of a contraction, or a tension of the nerves. Either will serve my purpose; for by tension, I mean no more than a violent pulling of the fibres, which compose any muscle or membrane, in whatever way this is done.

[n] *and are sometimes*] *and sometimes*
[o] *nerves*, they*] *nerves†. They*
[p] *else. For*] *else; for*
[q] *his*] *the*

[4] Jacob Spon (1647–85), a physician, chiefly known for his archaeological expedition to Italy, Greece, and the Near East, in 1675–6, with the English botanist and archaeologist, Sir George Wheler (1650–1723), in an age when direct exploration of Greek remains was in its early stages. He brought back numerous Greek and Latin inscriptions. In his *Recherches Curieuses d'Antiquité*

Campanella;[5] this man, it seems, had not only made very accurate observations on human faces, but was very expert in mimicking such, as were any way remarkable. When he had a mind to penetrate into the inclinations of those he had to deal with, he composed his face, his gesture, and his whole body, as nearly as he could into the exact similitude of the person he intended to examine; and then carefully observed what turn of mind he seemed to acquire by this change. So that, says my author, he was able to enter into the dispositions and thoughts of people, as effectually as if he had been changed into the very men. I have often observed, that on mimicking the looks and gestures, of angry, or placid, or frighted, or daring men, I have involuntarily found my mind turned to that passion whose appearance I endeavoured to imitate; nay, I am convinced it is hard to avoid it; though one strove to separate the passion from its correspondent gestures. Our minds and bodies are so closely and intimately connected, that one is incapable of pain or pleasure without the other. Campanella, of whom we have been speaking, could so abstract his attention from any sufferings of his body, that he was able to endure the rack itself without much pain; and in lesser pains, every body must have observed, that when we can employ our attention on any thing else, the pain has been for a time suspended; on the other hand, if by any means the body is indisposed to perform such gestures, or to be stimulated into such emotions as any passion usually produces in it, that passion itself never can arise, though its cause should be never so strongly in action; though it should be merely mental, and immediately affecting none of the senses. As an opiate, or spirituous liquors shall suspend the operation of grief, or fear, or anger, in spite of all our efforts to the contrary; and this by inducing in the body a disposition contrary to that which it receives from these passions.

(Lyon, 1683) he considers the value of medals as an historical guide to the personal appearance of the monarchs represented. In this connection he mentions physiognomy and relates the story of Campanella (*op. cit.*, p. 358).

[5] Tomasso Campanella (1568–1639), a Dominican. A philosopher and follower of Nicholas of Cusa and Telesio, he rejected scholastic Aristotelianism and advocated the direct study of man and nature. He was imprisoned at Naples for his alleged connection with a revolt against the Spaniards, and there tortured.

SECTION V

How the Sublime is produced

Having considered terror as producing an unnatural tension and certain violent emotions of the nerves; it easily follows, from what we have just said, that whatever is fitted to produce such a tension, must be productive of a passion similar to terror*, and consequently must be a source of the sublime, though it should have no idea of danger connected with it. So that little remains towards shewing the cause of the sublime, but to shew that the instances we have given of it in the second part, relate to such[r] things, as are fitted by nature to produce this sort of tension, either by the primary operation of the mind or the body. With regard to such things as affect by the associated idea of danger, there can be no doubt but that they produce terror, and act by some modification of that passion; and that terror, when sufficiently violent, raises the emotions of the body just mentioned, can as little be doubted. But if the sublime is built on terror, or some passion like it, which has pain for its object; it is previously proper to enquire how any species of delight can be derived from a cause so apparently contrary to it. I say, *delight*, because, as I have often remarked, it is very evidently different in its cause, and in its own nature, from actual and positive pleasure.

SECTION VI

How pain can be a cause of delight

Providence has so ordered it, that a state of rest and inaction, however it may flatter our indolence, should[s] be productive of many inconveniencies; that it should generate such disorders, as may force us to have recourse to some labour, as a thing

* Part 2, section 2.

[r] *we have . . . such*] *we gave of it, in the second part, are of such*
[s] *flatter our . . . should*] *flatter some principle of indolence in us, should*

absolutely requisite to make us pass our lives with tolerable satisfaction; for the nature of rest is to suffer all the parts of our bodies to fall into a relaxation, that not[t] only disables the members from performing their functions, but takes away the vigorous tone of fibre which is requisite for carrying on the[u] natural and necessary secretions. At the same time, that in this languid inactive state, the nerves are more liable to the most horrid convulsions, than when they are sufficiently braced and strengthened. Melancholy, dejection, despair, and often self-murder, is the consequence of the gloomy view we take of things in this relaxed state of body. The best remedy for all these evils is exercise or *labour*; and labour is a surmounting of *difficulties*, an exertion of the contracting power of the muscles; and as such resembles pain, which consists in tension or contraction, in every thing but degree. Labour is not only requisite to preserve the coarser organs in a state fit for their functions, but it is equally necessary to these finer and more delicate organs, on which, and by which, the imagination, and perhaps the other mental powers act. Since it is probable, that not only the inferior parts of the soul, as the passions are called, but the understanding itself makes use of some fine corporeal instruments in its operation; though what they are, and where they are, may be somewhat hard to settle: but that it does make use of such, appears from hence; that a long exercise of the mental powers induces a remarkable lassitude of the whole body; and on the other hand, that great bodily labour, or pain, weakens, and sometimes actually destroys the mental faculties. Now, as a due exercise is essential to the coarse muscular parts of the constitution, and that without this rousing they would become languid, and diseased, the very same rule holds with regard to those finer parts we have mentioned; to[v] have them in proper order, they must be shaken and worked to a proper degree.

[t] *into a . . . not*] *into such a relaxation, as not*

[u] *away the . . . the*] *away that vigour which is requisite towards the performing the*

[v] *diseased, the . . . to*] *diseased, and clogged with heterogeneous and hurtful matter; the very same rule holds with regard to the former; to*

SECTION VII

EXERCISE necessary for the finer organs

As common labour, which is a mode of pain, is the exercise of the grosser, a mode of terror is the exercise of the finer parts of the system; and if a certain mode of pain be of such a nature as to act upon the eye or the ear, as they are the most delicate organs, the affection[w] approaches more nearly to that which has a mental cause. In all these cases, if the pain and terror are so modified as not to be actually noxious; if the pain is not carried to violence, and the terror is not conversant about the present destruction of the person, as these emotions clear the parts, whether fine, or gross, of a dangerous and troublesome incumbrance, they are capable of producing delight; not pleasure, but a sort of delightful horror, a sort of tranquillity tinged with terror; which as it belongs to self-preservation is one of the strongest of all the passions. Its object is the sublime*. Its highest degree I call *astonishment*; the subordinate degrees are awe, reverence, and respect, which by the very etymology of the words shew from what source they are derived, and how they stand distinguished from positive pleasure.

SECTION VIII

Why things not dangerous produce a passion[x] like TERROR

†A mode of terror, or of pain, is always the cause of the sublime. For terror, or associated danger, the foregoing explication is, I believe, sufficient. It will require something more trouble to shew, that such examples, as I have given of the sublime in the second part, are capable of producing a mode of pain, and of being thus allied to terror, and to be accounted for on the same principles. And first of such objects as are great in their dimensions. I speak of visual objects.

* Part 2, section 2.

† Part 1, section 7. Part 2, section 2.

[w] *the affection*] *it*

[x] *produce a passion*] *produce passion*

SECTION IX[y]

Why visual objects of great dimensions are Sublime

Vision is performed by having a picture formed by the rays of light which are reflected from the object, painted in one piece, instantaneously, on the retina, or last nervous part of the eye. Or, according to others, there is but one point of any object painted on the eye in such a manner as to be perceived at once; but by moving the eye, we gather up with great celerity, the several parts of the object, so as to form one uniform piece. If the former opinion be allowed, it will be considered, that* though[z] all the light reflected from a large body[a] should strike the eye in one instant; yet we must suppose that the body itself is formed[b] of a vast number of distinct points, every one of which, or the ray from every one, makes an impression on the retina. So that, though the image of one point should cause but a small tension of this membrane, another, and another, and another stroke, must in their progress cause a very great one, until it arrives at last to the highest degree; and the whole capacity of the eye, vibrating in all its parts must approach near to the nature of what causes pain, and consequently must produce an idea of the sublime. Again,[c] if we take it, that one point only of an object is distinguishable at once; the matter will amount nearly to the same thing, or rather it will make the origin of the sublime from greatness of dimension yet clearer. For if but one point is observed at once, the eye must traverse the vast space of such bodies with great quickness, and consequently the fine nerves and muscles destined to the motion of that part must be very much strained; and their great sensibility must make them highly affected by this straining. Besides,[d] it

* Part 2, section 7.

[y] *SECTION IX.*] *SECTION XI.*

[z] *considered, that* though*] *considered, that a body of great dimensions,* though*

[a] *a large body*] *it*

[b] *yet we . . . formed*] *yet with regard to its extent we must suppose it formed*

[c] *Again,*] *Or*

[d] *them highly. . . Besides,*] *them the more affected by it. Besides*

signifies just nothing to the effect produced, whether a body has its parts connected and makes its impression at once; or making but one impression of a point at a time, it causes a succession of the same, or others, so quickly, as to make them seem united; as is evident from the common effect of whirling about a lighted torch or piece of wood; which if done with celerity, seems a circle of fire.[6]

SECTION X

UNITY why requisite to vastness

It may be objected to this theory, that the eye generally receives an equal number of rays at all times, and that therefore a great object cannot affect it by the number of rays, more than that variety of objects which the eye must always discern whilst it remains open. But to this I answer, that admitting an equal number of rays, or an equal quantity of luminous particles to strike the eye at all times, yet if these rays frequently vary their nature, now to blue, now to red, and so on, or their manner of termination as to a number of petty squares, triangles, or the like, at every change, whether of colour or shape, the organ has a sort of relaxation or rest; [7]⟨but this relaxation and labour so often interrupted, is by no means productive of ease; neither has it the effect of vigorous and uniform labour. Whoever has remarked the different effects of some strong exercise, and some little piddling action, will understand why a teazing fretful employment, which at once wearies and weakens the body, should have nothing great; these sorts of impulses which are rather teazing than painful, by continually and suddenly altering their tenor and direction,⟩ prevent that full tension,

[6] Newton, using the example of whirling a burning coal, makes the same observation (*Opticks*, 3rd. edn., 1721, p. 123).

[7] *Critical Review*, III, 369: "We . . . conceive he is mistaken in his theory. . . . Such a quick and abrupt succession of contrasted colours and shapes, will demand a quick succession of changes in the conformation of the eye, which, instead of relaxing and refreshing, harrass the organ into the most painful exertions. Not but that in vast objects, the eye demands a repose, as a man finds enjoyment and rest in sitting down at the end of a long excursion; yet he would find it very unpleasant and even fatiguing to sit down and rest at the end of every six yards."

that species of uniform labour which is allied to strong pain,[e] and causes the sublime. The sum[f] total of things of various kinds, though it should equal the number of the uniform parts composing some *one* entire object, is not equal in its effect upon the organs of our bodies. Besides the one already assigned, there is another very[g] strong reason for the difference. The mind in reality hardly ever can attend diligently to more than one thing at a time; if this thing be little, the effect is little, and a number of other little objects cannot engage the attention; the mind is bounded by the bounds of the object; and what is not attended to, and what does not exist, are much the same in the effect; but the eye or the mind (for in this case there is no difference) in great uniform objects does not readily arrive at their bounds; it has no rest, whilst it contemplates them; the image is much the same every where. So that every thing great by its quantity must necessarily be, one, simple and entire.

SECTION XI

The artificial INFINITE

We have observed, that a species of greatness arises from the artificial infinite; and that this infinite consists[h] in an uniform succession of great parts: we observed too, that the same uniform succession had a like power in sounds. But because the effects of many things are clearer in one of the senses than in another, and that all the senses[i] bear an analogy to, and illustrate one another; I shall begin with this power in sounds, as the cause of the sublimity from succession is rather more obvious in the sense of hearing. And I shall here once for all observe, that an investigation of the natural and mechanical causes of our passions, besides the curiosity of the subject, gives,

[e] *prevent that . . . pain,] which prevents that tension, that species of labour which is allied to pain,*

[f] *The sum] For the sum*

[g] *bodies. Besides . . . very] bodies. It is next to rest in all things, to vary our labour; and it is not so only in our labours, but in our studies. Besides this, there is a very*

[h] *this infinite consists] this consists*

[i] *all the senses] they all*

if they are discovered, a double strength and lustre to any rules we deliver on such matters. When the ear receives any simple sound, it is struck by a single pulse of the air, which makes the ear-drum and the other membranous parts vibrate according to the nature and species of the stroke. If the stroke be strong, the organ of hearing suffers a considerable degree of tension. If the stroke be repeated pretty soon after, the repetition causes an expectation of another stroke. And it must be observed, that expectation itself causes a tension. This is apparent in many animals, who, when they prepare for hearing any sound, rouse themselves, and prick up their ears; so that here the effect of the sounds is considerably augmented by a new auxiliary, the expectation. But though after a number of strokes, we expect still more, not being able to ascertain the exact time of their arrival, when they arrive, they produce a sort of surprise, which increases this tension yet further. For, I have observed, that when at any time I have waited very earnestly for some sound, that returned at intervals, (as the successive firing of cannon) though I fully expected the return of the sound, when it came, it always made me start a little; the ear-drum suffered a convulsion, and the whole body consented with it. The tension of the part thus increasing at every blow, by the united forces of the stroke itself, the expectation, and the surprise, it is worked up to such a pitch as to be capable of the sublime; it is brought just to the verge of pain. Even when the cause has ceased; the organs of hearing being often successively struck in a similar manner, continue to vibrate in that manner for some time longer; this is an additional help to the greatness of the effect.

SECTION XII

The vibrations must be similar

But if the vibration be not similar at every impression, it can never be carried beyond the number of actual impressions; for move any body, as a pendulum, in one way, and it will continue to oscillate in an arch of the same circle, until the known causes make it rest; but if after first putting it in motion in one direction, you push it into another, it can never reassume the first direction; because it can never move itself, and consequently it can have but the effect of that last motion; whereas, if in the same direction you act upon it several times, it will describe a greater arch, and move a longer time.

SECTION XIII

The effects of SUCCESSION in visual objects explained

If we can comprehend clearly how things operate upon one of our senses; there can be very little difficulty in conceiving in what manner they affect the rest. To say a great deal therefore upon the corresponding affections of every sense, would tend rather to fatigue us by an useless repetition, than to throw any new light upon the subject, by that ample and diffuse manner of treating it; but as in this discourse we chiefly attach ourselves to the sublime, as it affects the eye, we shall consider particularly why a successive disposition of uniform parts in the same right line should be sublime,* and upon what principle this disposition[j] is enabled to make a comparatively small quantity of matter produce a grander effect, than a much larger quantity disposed in another manner. To avoid the perplexity of general notions; let us set before our eyes a colonnade of uniform pillars planted in a right line; let us take our stand, in such a manner, that the eye may shoot along this colonnade, for it has its best effect in this view. In our present situation it is plain, that the rays from the first round pillar will cause in the eye a vibration of that species; an image of the pillar itself. The pillar immediately succeeding increases it; that which follows renews and enforces the impression; each in its order as it succeeds, repeats impulse after impulse, and stroke after stroke, until the eye long exercised in one particular way cannot lose that object immediately; and being violently roused by this continued agitation, it presents the mind with a grand or sublime conception. But instead of viewing a rank of uniform pillars;

* Part 2, section 10.

[j] *this disposition*] it

let us suppose, that they succeed each other, a round and a square one alternately. In this case the vibration caused by the first round pillar perishes as soon as it is formed; and one of quite another sort (the square) directly occupies its place; which however it resigns as quickly to the round one; and thus the eye proceeds, alternately, taking up one image and laying down another, as long as the building continues. From whence it is obvious, that at the last pillar, the impression is as far from continuing as it was at the very first; because in fact, the sensory can receive no distinct impression but from the last; and it can never of itself resume a dissimilar impression: besides, every variation of the object is a rest and relaxation to the organs of sight; and these reliefs prevent that powerful emotion so necessary to produce the sublime. To produce therefore a perfect grandeur in such things as we have been mentioning, there should be a perfect simplicity, an absolute uniformity in disposition, shape and colouring. Upon this principle of succession and uniformity it may be asked, why a long bare wall should not be a more sublime object than a colonnade; since the succession is no way interrupted; since the eye meets no check; since nothing more uniform can be conceived? A long bare wall is certainly not so grand an object as a colonnade of the same length and height. It is not altogether difficult to account for this difference. When we look at a naked wall, from the evenness of the object, the eye runs along its whole space, and arrives quickly at its termination; the eye meets nothing which may interrupt its progress; but then it meets nothing which may detain it a proper time to produce a very great and lasting effect. The view of a bare wall, if it be of a great height and length, is undoubtedly grand: but this is only *one* idea, and not a *repetition* of *similar* ideas; it is therefore great, not so much upon the principle of *infinity*, as upon that of *vastness*. But we are not so powerfully affected with any one impulse, unless it be one of a prodigious force indeed, as[k] we are with a succession of similar impulses; because the nerves of the sensory do not (if I may use the expression) acquire a habit of repeating the same feeling in such a manner as to continue it longer than its cause is in action; besides, all the effects which I have attributed

[k] *force indeed, as*] *force, as*

to expectation and surprise in section 11. can have no place in a bare wall.

SECTION XIV

Locke's opinion concerning darkness, considered

It is Mr. Locke's opinion, that darkness is not naturally an idea of terror; and that, though an excessive light is painful to the sense, that the greatest excess of darkness is no ways troublesome.[8] He observes indeed in another place, that a nurse or an old woman having once associated the ideas of ghosts and goblins with that of darkness; night ever after becomes painful and horrible to the imagination.[9] The authority of this great man is doubtless as great, as that of any man can be, and it seems to stand in the way of our general principle.* We have considered darkness as a cause of the sublime; and we have all along considered the sublime as depending on some modification of pain or terror; so that, if darkness be no way painful or terrible to any, who have not had their minds early tainted with superstitions, it can be no source of the sublime to them. But with all deference to such an authority; it seems to me, that an association of a more general nature, an association which takes in all mankind may make darkness terrible; for in utter darkness, it is impossible to know in what degree of safety we stand; we are ignorant of the objects that surround us; we may every moment strike against some dangerous obstruction; we may fall down a precipice the first step we take; and if an[1] enemy approach, we know not in what quarter to defend ourselves; in such a case strength is no sure protection; wisdom can only act by guess; the boldest are staggered, and he who would pray for nothing else towards his defence, is forced to pray for light.

> *Ζεῦ πάτερ, ἀλλὰ σὺ ῥῦσαι ὑπ' ἠέρος υἷας 'Αχαιῶν,*
> *ποίησον δ' αἴθρην, δὸς δ' ὀφθαλμοῖσιν ἰδέσθαι·*
> *ἐν δὲ φάει καὶ ὄλεσσον.*[10]

* Part 2, section 3.

[1] *an*] *any*

[8] *Essay*, II, vii, 4. [9] *Ibid.*, II, xxiii, 10.

[10] Homer, *Iliad*, XVII, 645–7. The passage is quoted by Longinus (*On the Sublime*, IX).

As to the association of ghosts and goblins; surely it is more natural to think, that darkness being originally an idea of terror, was chosen as a fit scene for such terrible representations, than that such representations have made darkness terrible. The mind of man very easily slides into an error of the former sort; but it is very hard to imagine, that the effect of an idea[m] so universally terrible in all times, and in all countries, as darkness, could[n] possibly have been owing to a set of idle stories, or to any cause of a nature so trivial, and of an operation so precarious.

SECTION XV

DARKNESS terrible in[o] its own nature

Perhaps it may appear on enquiry, that blackness and darkness are in some degree painful by their natural operation, independent of any associations whatsoever. I must observe, that the ideas of darkness and blackness are much the same; and they differ only in this, that blackness is a more confined idea. Mr. Cheselden has given us a very curious story of a boy, who had been born blind, and continued so until he was thirteen or fourteen years old; he was then couched for a cataract, by which operation he received his sight. Among many remarkable particulars that attended his first perceptions, and judgments on visual objects, Cheselden tells us, that the first time the boy saw a black object, it gave him great uneasiness; and that some time after, upon accidentally seeing a negro woman, he was struck with great horror at the sight.[11] The horror, in this case,

[m] *that the . . . idea*] *that an idea*
[n] *darkness, could*] *darkness has been, could* [o] *in*] *by*

[11] William Cheselden (1688–1752), one of the greatest of English surgeons, was known principally for his lateral operation for the stone. Burke's reference is to Cheselden's lengthy "Account of some Observations made by a young Gentleman, who was born blind, or lost his Sight so early, that he had no Remembrance of ever having seen, and was couch'd between 13 and 14 Years of Age" (*Philosophical Transactions of the Royal Society* (1729), XXXV, 447–50). Burke particularly has in mind the following statement: "Now Scarlet [the boy] thought the most beautiful of all Colours, and of

can scarcely be supposed to arise from any association. The boy appears by the account to have been particularly observing, and sensible for one of his age: and therefore, it is probable, if the great uneasiness he felt at the first sight of black had arisen from its connexion with any other disagreeable ideas, he would have observed and mentioned it. For an idea, disagreeable only by association, has the cause of its ill effect on the passions evident enough at the first impression; in ordinary cases, it is indeed frequently lost; but this is, because the original association was made very early, and the consequent impression repeated often. In our instance, there was no time for such an habit; and there is no reason to think, that the ill effects of black on his imagination were more owing to its connexion with any disagreeable ideas, than that the good effects of more cheerful colours were derived from their connexion with pleasing ones. They had both probably their effects from their natural operation.

SECTION XVI

Why DARKNESS[p] is terrible

It may be worth while to examine, how darkness can operate in such a manner as to cause pain. It is observable, that[q] still as we recede from the light, nature has so contrived it, that the pupil is enlarged by the retiring of the iris, in proportion to our recess. Now instead of declining from it but a little, suppose that we withdraw entirely from the light; it is reasonable to think, that the contraction of the radial fibres of the iris[r] is proportionably greater; and that this part may by great darkness come to be so contracted, as to strain the nerves that

others the most gay were the most pleasing, whereas the first Time he saw Black, it gave him great Uneasiness, yet after a little Time he was reconcil'd to it; but some Months after, seeing by accident a Negroe Woman, he was struck with great Horror at the Sight" (*op. cit.*, p. 448). The conclusions Burke draws from this case were questioned in *The Literary Magazine*, II, 188.

[p] *Why DARKNESS*] *The cause why DARKNESS*

[q] *pain. It . . . that*] *pain; that is, to produce a tension in those nerves, which form the organs of sight. It may be observed, that*

[r] *the contraction . . . iris*] *the expansion of the iris*

compose it beyond[s] their natural tone; and by this means to produce a painful sensation. Such a tension it seems there certainly is, whilst we are involved in darkness; for in such a state whilst the eye remains open, there is a continual nisus to receive light; this is manifest from the flashes,[t] and luminous appearances which often seem in these circumstances to play before it; and which can be nothing but the effect of spasms, produced by its own efforts in pursuit of its object; several[u] other strong impulses will produce the idea of light in the eye, besides the substance of light itself, as we experience on many occasions. [12]⟨Some who allow darkness to be a cause of the sublime, would infer from the dilatation of the pupil, that a relaxation may be productive of the sublime as well as a convulsion; but they do not, I believe, consider, that although the circular ring of the iris be in some sense a sphincter, which may possibly be dilated by a simple relaxation, yet in one respect it differs from most of the other sphincters of the body, that it is furnished with antagonist muscles, which are the radial fibres of the iris; no sooner does the circular muscle begin to relax, than these fibres wanting their counterpoise, are forcibly drawn back, and open the pupil to a considerable wideness. But though we were not apprized of this, I believe any one will find if he opens his eyes and makes an effort to see in a dark place, that a very perceivable pain ensues. And I have heard some ladies remark, that after having worked a long time upon a ground of black, their eyes were so pained and weakened they could hardly see.⟩ It may perhaps be objected to this

[s] *so contracted, . . . beyond*] *so expanded, as to stretch the nerves that compose it far beyond*

[t] *light; this . . . flashes,*] *light, as appears by the flashes,*

[u] *several*] *for many*

[12] *Monthly Review*, XVI, 480 n.: "The muscles of the uvea act in the contraction, but are relaxed in the dilatation of the ciliary circle. Therefore, when the pupil dilates, they are in a state of relaxation, and the relaxed state of a muscle, is its state of rest. In an amaurosis, where these muscles are never employed, the pupil is always dilated. Hence darkness is a state of rest to the visual organ, and consequently the obscurity which he justly remarks to be often a cause of the sublime, can affect the sensory by no painful impression; so that the sublime is often caused by a relaxation of the muscles, as well as by a tension."

theory of the mechanical effect of darkness ,that[v] the ill effects of darkness or blackness seem rather mental than corporeal; and I own it is true, that they do so; and so do all those that depend on the affections of the finer parts of our system. The ill effects of bad weather appear often no otherwise, than in a melancholy and dejection of spirits, though without doubt, in this case, the bodily organs suffer first, and the mind through these organs.

SECTION XVII

The effects of BLACKNESS

Blackness is but a *partial darkness*; and therefore it derives some of its powers from being mixed and surrounded with coloured bodies. In its own nature, it cannot be considered as a colour. Black bodies, reflecting none, or but a few rays, with regard to sight, are but as so many vacant spaces dispersed among the objects we view. When the eye lights on one of these vacuities, after having been kept in some degree of tension by the play of the adjacent colours upon it, it suddenly falls into a relaxation; out of which it as suddenly recovers by a convulsive spring. To illustrate this; let us consider, that when we intend to sit on a chair, and find it much lower than was expected, the shock is very violent; much more violent than could be thought from so slight a fall as the difference between one chair and another can possibly make. If,[w] after descending a flight of stairs, we attempt inadvertently to take another step in the manner of the former ones, the shock is extremely rude and disagreeable; and by no art, can we cause such a shock by the same means, when we expect and prepare for it. When I say, that this is owing to having the change made contrary to expectation; I do not mean solely, when the *mind* expects. I mean likewise, that when any organ of sense is for some time affected in some one manner, if it be suddenly affected otherwise there ensues a convulsive motion; such a convulsion as is caused when any thing happens against the expectance of the mind. And though it may appear strange that such a change as produces a relaxation, should immediately produce a sudden

[v] *objected to . . . that*] *objected, that*

[w] *If,*] *Or if,*

convulsion; it is yet most certainly so, and so in all the senses. Every one knows that sleep is a relaxation; and that silence, where nothing keeps the organs of hearing in action, is in general fittest to bring on this relaxation; yet when a sort of murmuring sounds dispose a man to sleep, let these sounds cease suddenly, and the person immediately awakes; that is, the parts are braced up suddenly, and he awakes. This I have often experienced myself, and I have heard the same from observing persons. In like manner, if a person in broad day light were falling asleep, to introduce a sudden darkness would prevent his sleep for that time, though silence and darkness in themselves, and not suddenly introduced, are very favourable to it. This I knew only by conjecture on the analogy of the senses when I first digested these observations; but I have since experienced it. And I have often experienced, and so have a thousand others; that on the first inclining[x] towards sleep, we have been suddenly awakened[y] with a most violent start; and that this start was generally preceded by a sort of dream of our falling down a precipice: whence does this strange motion arise; but from the too sudden relaxation of the body, which by some mechanism in nature restores itself by as quick and vigorous an exertion of the contracting power of the muscles? the dream itself is caused by this relaxation; and it is of too uniform a nature[z] to be attributed to any other cause. The parts relax too suddenly, which is in the nature of falling; and this accident of the body induces this image in the mind. When we are in a confirmed state of health and vigour, as all changes are then less sudden, and less on the extreme, we[a] can seldom complain of this disagreeable sensation.

SECTION XVIII

The effects of BLACKNESS moderated

Though the effects of black be painful originally, we must not think they always continue so. Custom reconciles us to every thing. After we have been used to the sight of black objects,

[x] *inclining*] *declining* [y] *awakened*] *awaked* [z] *a nature*] *nature*
[a] *less sudden, . . . we*] *less violent with us, we*

the terror abates, and the smoothness and glossiness or some agreeable accident of bodies so coloured, softens in some measure the horror and sternness of their original nature; yet the nature of the original impression still continues. Black will always have something melancholy in it, because the sensory will always find the change to it from other colours too violent; or if it occupy the whole compass of the sight, it will then be darkness; and what was said of darkness, will be applicable here. I do not purpose to go into all that might be said to illustrate this theory of the effects of light and darkness; neither will I examine all the different effects produced by the various modifications and mixtures of these two causes. If the foregoing observations have any foundation in nature, I conceive them very sufficient to account for all the phænomena that can arise from all the combinations of black with other colours. To enter into every particular, or to answer every objection, would be an endless labour. We have only followed the most leading roads, and we shall observe the same conduct in our enquiry into the cause of beauty.

SECTION XIX

The physical cause of LOVE

When we have before us such objects as excite love and complacency, the body is affected, so far as I could observe, much in the following manner. The head reclines something on one side; the eyelids are more closed than usual, and the eyes roll gently with an inclination to the object, the mouth is a little opened, and the breath drawn slowly, with now and then a low sigh: the whole body is composed, and the hands fall idly to the sides. All this is accompanied with an inward sense of melting and languor. These appearances are always proportioned to the degree of beauty in the object, and of sensibility in the observer. And this gradation from the highest pitch of beauty and sensibility, even to the lowest of mediocrity and indifference, and their correspondent effects, ought to be kept in view, else this description will seem exaggerated, which it certainly is not. But from this description it is almost impossible not to conclude, that beauty acts by relaxing the solids of the whole system. There are all the appearances of such a relaxation; and a relaxation somewhat below the natural tone seems to me to be the cause of all positive pleasure. [13]⟨Who is a stranger to that manner of expression so common in all times and in all countries, of being softened, relaxed, enervated, dissolved, melted away by pleasure? The universal voice of mankind, faithful to their feelings, concurs in affirming this uniform and general effect; and although some odd and particular instance may perhaps be found, wherein there appears a considerable degree of positive pleasure, without all the characters of relaxation, we must not therefore reject the conclusion we had drawn from a concurrence of many experiments, but we must still retain it, subjoining the exceptions which may occur according to the judicious rule laid down by Sir Isaac Newton in the third book of his Optics.[14]⟩ Our position will, I conceive, appear confirmed beyond[b] any reasonable doubt, if we can shew that such things as we have already observed to be the genuine constituents of beauty, have each of them separately taken a natural tendency to relax the fibres. And if it must be[c] allowed us, that the appearance of the human body, when all these constituents are united together before the sensory, further favours this opinion, we may ven-

[b] *Our position . . . beyond*] *This will, I conceive, appear beyond*
[c] *it must be*] *it be*

[13] *Critical Review*, III, 369–70: "But how will this theory agree with those tumults and transports that beauty so often excites? . . . to use the words of an English ballad,

—For whilst I gaze, my bosom glows;
My blood in tides impet'ous flows;
Hope, fear and joy alternate roll,
And floods of transport whelm my soul."

[14] *Opticks* (3rd. edn., 1721), p. 380: ". . . although the arguing from Experiments and Observations by Induction be no Demonstration of general Conclusions; yet it is the best way of arguing which the Nature of Things admits of, and may be looked upon as so much the stronger, by how much the Induction is more general. And if no Exception occur from Phænomena, the Conclusion may be pronounced generally. But if at any time afterwards any Exception shall occur from Experiments, it may then begin to be pronounced with such Exceptions as occur."

ture, I believe, to conclude, that the passion called love is produced by this relaxation. By the same method of reasoning, which we have used in the enquiry into the causes of the sublime, we may likewise conclude, that as a beautiful object presented to the sense, by causing a relaxation in the body, produces the passion of love in the mind; so if by any means the passion should first have its origin in the mind, a relaxation of the outward organs will as certainly ensue in a degree proportioned to the cause.

SECTION XX

Why SMOOTHNESS is beautiful

It is to explain the true cause of visual beauty, that I call in the assistance of the other senses. If it appears that *smoothness* is a principal cause of pleasure to the touch, taste, smell, and hearing, it will be easily admitted a constituent of visual beauty; especially as we have before shewn, that this quality is found almost without exception in all bodies that are by general consent held beautiful. There[d] can be no doubt that bodies which are rough and angular, rouse and vellicate the organs of feeling,[e] causing a sense of pain, which consists in the violent tension or contraction of the muscular fibres. On the contrary, the application of smooth bodies relax; gentle stroking with a smooth hand allays violent pains and cramps, and relaxes the suffering parts from their unnatural tension; and it has therefore very often no mean effect in removing swellings and obstructions. The sense of feeling is highly gratified with smooth bodies. A bed smoothly laid, and soft, that is, where the resistance is every way inconsiderable, is a great luxury, disposing to an universal relaxation, and inducing beyond any thing else, that species of it called sleep.

SECTION XXI

SWEETNESS, its nature

Nor is it only in the touch, that smooth bodies cause positive pleasure by relaxation. In the smell and taste, we find all things

[d] *beautiful. There*] *beautiful. Now with respect to the sense of* feeling, *there*
[e] *organs of feeling,*] *parts,*

agreeable to them, and which are commonly called sweet, to be of a smooth nature, and that they all evidently tend to relax their respective sensories. Let us first consider the taste. Since it is most easy to enquire into the property of liquids, and since all things seem to want a fluid vehicle to make them tasted at all, I intend rather to consider the liquid than the solid parts of our food. The vehicles of all tastes are *water* and *oil*. And what determines the taste is some salt, which affects variously according to its nature, or its manner of being combined with other things. Water and oil simply considered are capable of giving some pleasure to the taste. Water, when simple, is insipid, inodorous, colourless, and smooth; it is found when *not cold* to be a great resolver of spasms, and lubricator of the fibres; this power it probably owes to its smoothness. For as fluidity depends, according to the most general opinion, on the roundness, smoothness, and weak cohesion of the component parts of any body; and as water acts merely as a simple fluid; it follows, that the cause of its fluidity is likewise the cause of its relaxing quality; namely, the smoothness and slippery texture of its parts. The other fluid vehicle of tastes is *oil*. This too, when simple, is insipid,[f] inodorous, colourless, and smooth to the touch and taste. It is smoother than water, and in many cases yet more relaxing. Oil is in some degree pleasant to the eye, the touch and the taste, insipid as it is. Water is not so grateful, which I do not know on what principle to account for, other than that water is not so soft and smooth. Suppose that to this oil or water were added a certain quantity of a specific salt, which had a power of putting the nervous papillæ of the tongue into a gentle vibratory motion; as suppose sugar dissolved in it. The smoothness of the oil, and the vibratory power of the salt, cause the sense we call sweetness. In all sweet bodies, sugar, or a substance very little different from sugar, is constantly found; every species of salt examined by the microscope has its own distinct, regular, invariable form. That of nitre is a pointed oblong; that of sea salt an exact cube; that of sugar a perfect globe. If you have tried how smooth globular bodies, as the marbles with which

[f] *is insipid,*] *is somewhat insipid,*

boys amuse themselves, have affected the touch when they are rolled backward and forward and over one another, you will easily conceive how sweetness, which consists in a salt of such nature, affects the taste; for a single globe, (though somewhat pleasant to the feeling) yet by[g] the regularity of its form, and the somewhat too sudden deviation of its parts from a right line, it is nothing near so pleasant to the touch as several globes, where the hand gently rises to one and falls to another; and this pleasure is greatly increased if the globes are in motion, and sliding over one another; for this soft variety prevents that weariness, which the uniform disposition of the several globes would otherwise produce. Thus in sweet liquors, the parts of the fluid vehicle though most probably round, are yet so minute as to conceal the figure of their component parts from the nicest inquisition of the microscope; and consequently being so excessively minute, they have a sort of flat simplicity to the taste, resembling the effects of plain smooth bodies to the touch; for if a body be composed of round parts excessively small, and packed pretty closely together, the surface will be both to the sight and touch as if it were nearly plain and smooth. It is clear from their unveiling their figure to the microscope, that the particles of sugar are considerably larger than those of water or oil, and consequently that their effects from their roundness will be more distinct and palpable to the nervous papillæ of that nice organ the tongue: they will induce that sense called sweetness, which in a weak manner we discover in oil, and in a yet weaker in water; for insipid as they are, water and oil are in some degree sweet; and it may be observed, that insipid things of all kinds approach more nearly to the nature of sweetness than to that of any other taste.

SECTION XXII

SWEETNESS relaxing

In the other senses we have remarked, that smooth things are relaxing. Now it ought to appear that sweet things, which are

[g] *globe, (though . . . feeling) yet by*] *globe, though . . . feeling, by*

the smooth of taste, are relaxing too. [15]⟨It is remarkable, that in some languages soft and sweet have but one name. *Doux* in French signifies soft as well as sweet. The Latin *Dulcis*, and the Italian *Dolce*, have in many cases the same double signification.⟩ That sweet things are generally relaxing[h] is evident; because all such, especially those which are most oily, taken frequently or in a large quantity, very much enfeeble the tone of the stomach. Sweet smells, which bear a great affinity to sweet tastes, relax very remarkably. The smell of flowers disposes people to drowsiness; and this relaxing effect is further apparent from the prejudice which people of weak nerves receive from their use. It were worth while to examine, whether tastes of this kind, sweet ones, tastes that are caused by smooth oils and a relaxing salt are not the originally pleasant tastes. For many which use has rendered such, were not at all agreeable at first. The way to examine this is, to try what nature has originally provided for us, which she has undoubtedly made originally pleasant: and to analyse this provision. *Milk* is the first support of our childhood. The component parts of this are water, oil, and a sort of a very sweet salt called the sugar of milk. All these when blended have a great *smoothness* to the taste, and a relaxing quality to the skin. The next thing children covet is *fruit*, and of fruits, those principally which are sweet; and every one knows that the sweetness of fruit is caused by a subtle oil and such a salt as that mentioned in the last section. Afterwards, custom, habit, the desire of novelty, and a thousand other causes, confound,[i] adulterate, and change our palates, so that[j] we can no longer reason with any satisfaction about them. Before we quit this article we must observe; that as smooth things are, as such, agreeable to the taste, and are found of a relaxing quality; so on the other hand, things which are found by experience to be of a strengthening quality, and fit to brace the fibres, are almost universally rough and pungent to the taste, and in many cases rough even to the touch. We often apply the quality of sweetness, metaphorically, to visual objects.

[h] *generally relaxing*] *generally so* [i] *confound,*] *so mix,* [j] *so that*] *that*

[15] *Critical Review*, III, 370: "We are of a different opinion, and take it for granted, that sweet things act by stimulation, upon the taste as well as upon the smell."

For the better carrying on this remarkable analogy of the senses, we may here call sweetness the beautiful of the taste.

SECTION XXIII

VARIATION, why beautiful

Another principal property of beautiful objects is, that the line of their parts is continually varying its direction; but it varies it by a very insensible deviation, it never varies it so quickly as to surprise, or by the sharpness of its angle to cause any twitching or convulsion of the optic nerve. Nothing long continued in the same manner, nothing very suddenly varied can be beautiful; because both are opposite to that agreeable relaxation, which is the characteristic effect of beauty. It is thus in all the senses. A motion in a right line, is that manner of moving next to a very gentle descent, in which we meet the least resistance; yet it is not that manner of moving, which next to a descent, wearies us the least. Rest certainly tends to relax; yet there is a species of motion which relaxes more than rest; a gentle oscillatory motion, a rising and falling. Rocking sets children to sleep better than absolute rest; there is indeed scarce any thing at that age, which gives more pleasure than to be gently lifted up and down; the manner of playing which their nurses use with children, and the weighing and swinging used afterwards by themselves as a favourite amusement, evince this very sufficiently. Most people must have observed the sort of sense they have had, on being swiftly drawn in an easy coach, on a smooth turf, with gradual ascents and declivities. This will give a better idea of the beautiful, and point out its probable cause better than almost any thing else. On the contrary; when one is hurried over a rough, rocky, broken road, the pain felt by these sudden inequalities shews why similar sights, feelings and sounds, are so contrary to beauty; and with regard to the feeling, it is exactly the same in its effect, or very nearly the same, whether, for instance, I move my hand along the surface of a body of a certain shape, or whether such a body is moved along my hand. But to bring this analogy of the senses home to the eye; if a body presented to that sense has such a waving surface that the rays of light reflected from it are in a continual insensible deviation from the strongest to the weakest, (which is always the case in a surface gradually unequal,) it[k] must be exactly similar in its effect on the eye and touch; upon the one of which it operates directly,[l] on the other indirectly. And this body will be beautiful if the lines which compose its surface are not continued, even so varied, in a manner that may weary or dissipate the attention. The variation itself must be continually varied.

SECTION XXIV

Concerning[m] SMALLNESS

To avoid a sameness which may arise from the too frequent repetition of the same reasonings, and of illustrations of the same nature, I will not enter very minutely into every particular that regards beauty, as it is founded on the disposition of its quantity, or its quantity itself. In speaking of the magnitude of bodies there is great uncertainty, because the ideas of great and small, are terms almost entirely relative to the species of the objects, which are infinite. It is true, that having once fixed the species of any object, and the dimensions common in the individuals of that species, we may observe some that exceed, and some that fall short of the ordinary standard: these which greatly exceed, are by that excess, provided the species itself be not very small, rather great and terrible than beautiful; but as in the animal world, and in a good measure in the vegetable world likewise, the qualities that constitute beauty may possibly be united to things of greater dimensions; when they are so united they constitute a species something different both from the sublime and beautiful, which I have before called *Fine*; but this kind I imagine has not such a power on the passions, either as vast bodies have which are endued with the correspondent qualities of the sublime; or as the qualities of beauty have when united in a small object. The affection

[k] *weakest, (which . . . unequal,) it*] *weakest, which . . . unequal, it*

[l] *touch; upon . . . directly,*] *touch; one of which operates on it directly,*

[m] *attention. The . . . SECTION XXIV. Concerning*] *attention. SECTION XXI. Concerning*

produced by large bodies adorned with the spoils of beauty, is a tension continually relieved; which approaches to[n] the nature of mediocrity. But if I were to say how I find myself affected upon such occasions, I should say, that the sublime suffers less by being united to some of the qualities of beauty, than beauty does by being joined to greatness of quantity, or any other properties of the sublime. There is something so over-ruling in whatever inspires us with awe, in all things which belong ever so remotely to terror, that nothing else can stand in their presence. There lie the qualities of beauty either dead and unoperative; or at most exerted to mollify the rigour and sternness of the terror, which is the natural concomitant of greatness. Besides the extraordinary great in every species, the opposite to this, the dwarfish and diminutive ought to be considered. Littleness, merely as such, has nothing contrary to the idea of beauty. The humming bird both in shape and colouring yields to none of the winged species, of which it is the least; and perhaps his beauty is enhanced by his smallness. But there are animals, which when they are extremely small are rarely (if ever) beautiful. There is a dwarfish size of men and women, which is almost constantly so gross and massive in comparison of their height, that they present us with a very disagreeable image. But should a man be found[o] not above two or three feet high, supposing such a person to have all the parts of his body of a delicacy suitable to such a size, and otherwise endued with the common qualities of other beautiful bodies, I am pretty well convinced that a person of such a stature might be considered as beautiful; might be the object of love; might give us very pleasing ideas on viewing him. The only thing which could possibly interpose to check our[p] pleasure is, that such creatures, however formed, are unusual, and are often therefore considered as something monstrous. The large and gigantic, though very compatible with the sublime, is contrary to the beautiful. It is impossible to suppose a giant the[q] object of love. When we let our imaginations loose in romance, the ideas we naturally[r] annex to that size are those of tyranny, cruelty, injustice, and every

[n] *to*] *nearer to*
[o] *But should . . . found*] *But if a man was found*
[p] *our*] *this*
[q] *giant the*] *giant to be the*
[r] *ideas naturally*] *ideas we naturally* (*See Note on Text*)

thing horrid and abominable. We paint the giant ravaging the country, plundering the innocent traveller, and afterwards gorged with[s] his half-living flesh: such are Polyphemus,[16] Cacus, and others, who make so great[t] a figure in romances and heroic poems. The event we attend to with the greatest satisfaction is their defeat and death. I do not remember in all that multitude of deaths with which the Iliad is filled, that the fall of any man remarkable for his great stature and strength touches us with pity; nor does it appear that the author, so well read in human nature, ever intended it should. It is Simoisius in the soft bloom of youth, torn from his parents, who tremble for a courage so ill suited to his strength;[17] it is another hurried by war from the new embraces of his bride, young, and fair, and a novice to the field, who melts us by his untimely fate.[18] Achilles, in spite of the many qualities of beauty which Homer has bestowed on his outward form, and the many great virtues with which he has adorned his mind, can never make us love him. It may be observed, that Homer has given the Trojans, whose fate he has designed to excite our compassion, infinitely more of the amiable social virtues than he has distributed among his Greeks. With regard to the Trojans, the passion he chuses to raise is pity; pity is a passion[u] founded on love; and these *lesser*, and if I may say, domestic virtues, are certainly[v] the most amiable. But he has made the Greeks far their superiors in the politic and military virtues. The councils of Priam are weak; the arms of Hector comparatively feeble; his courage far below that of Achilles. Yet we love Priam more than Agamemnon, and Hector more than his conqueror Achilles. Admiration is the passion which Homer would excite in favour of the Greeks,

[s] *gorged with*] *gorging himself with* [t] *so great*] *such*
[u] *pity; pity . . . passion*] *pity; a passion* [v] *certainly*] *by far*

[16] Polyphemus, a son of Poseidon, was one of the Cyclopes. He was blinded by Odysseus. (*Odyssey*, IX, 106 ff.) The giant, Cacus, son of Vulcan, lived in a cave on the Aventine Mount. He stole, and hid in his cave, cattle belonging to Hercules who slew him on discovering the hiding-place. (*Aeneid*, VIII, 190 ff.)

[17] Simoisius, the son of Anthemion, was killed by the spear of Telamonian Aias. (*Iliad*, IV, 473 ff.)

[18] Iphidamas, the son of Antenor and husband of Theano, was killed by Agamemnon. (*Iliad*, XI, 221–31.)

and he has done it by bestowing on them the virtues which have but little to do with love. This short digression is perhaps not wholly beside our purpose, where our business is to shew, that objects of great dimensions are incompatible with beauty, the more incompatible as they are greater; whereas the small, if ever they fail of beauty, this failure is not to be attributed to their size.

SECTION XXV[w]

Of COLOUR

With regard to colour, the disquisition is almost infinite; but I conceive the principles laid down in the beginning of this part are sufficient to account for the effects of them all, as well as for the agreeable effects of transparent bodies, whether fluid or solid. Suppose I look at a bottle of muddy liquor, of a blue or red colour: the blue or red rays cannot pass clearly to the eye, but are suddenly and unequally stopped by the intervention of little opaque bodies, which without preparation change the idea, and change it too into one disagreeable in its own nature, conformable to the principles laid down in section 24. But when the ray passes without such opposition through the glass or liquor, when the glass or liquor are quite transparent, the light is something softened in the passage, which makes it more agreeable even as light; and the liquor reflecting all the rays of its proper colour *evenly*, it has such an effect on the eye, as smooth opaque bodies have on the eye and touch.[19] So that the pleasure here is compounded of the softness of the transmitted, and the evenness of the reflected light. This pleasure may be heightened by the common principles in other things, if the shape of the glass which holds the transparent liquor be so judiciously varied, as to present the colour gradually and interchangeably weakened and strengthened with all that variety which judgment in affairs of this nature shall suggest.

[w] *SECTION XXVI.*] *SECTION XXVI.* (*See Note on Text*)

[19] This illustration clearly owes much to Burke's reading of Newton's experiments with light and colour described in the *Opticks*. (A copy of Newton's *Opticks*, 1730, and of his *Theory of Light and Colours*, 1742, appeared in the sale of Burke's library. Catalogue item no. 325.)

On a review of all that has been said of the effects, as well as the causes of both; it will appear, that the sublime and beautiful are built on principles very different, and that their affections are as different: the great has terror for its basis; which, when it is modified, causes that emotion in the mind, which I have called astonishment; the beautiful is founded on mere positive pleasure, and excites in the soul that feeling, which is called love. Their causes have made the subject of this fourth part.

The end of the Fourth Part.

A PHILOSOPHICAL ENQUIRY INTO THE ORIGIN OF OUR IDEAS OF THE SUBLIME AND BEAUTIFUL

Part Five

SECTION I

Of WORDS

NATURAL objects[x] affect us, by the laws of that connexion, which Providence has established between certain motions and configurations of bodies, and certain consequent feelings in our minds. Painting affects in the same manner, but with the superadded pleasure of imitation. Architecture[y] affects by the laws of nature, and the law of reason; from which latter result the rules of proportion, which make a work to be praised or censured, in the whole or in some part, when the end for which it was designed is or is not properly answered. But as to words; they seem to me to affect us in a manner very different from that in which we are affected by natural objects,[z] or by painting or architecture; yet words have as considerable a share in exciting ideas of beauty and of the sublime as any of those,[a] and sometimes a much greater than any of them; therefore an enquiry into the manner by which they excite such emotions is far from being unnecessary in a discourse of this kind.

SECTION II

The common effect of POETRY, not by raising ideas of things

The common notion of the power of poetry and eloquence, as well as that of words in ordinary conversation, is; that they affect the mind by raising in it ideas of those things for which custom has appointed them to stand. To examine the truth of this notion, it may be requisite to observe that words may be divided into three sorts.[1] The[b] first are such as represent many simple ideas *united by nature* to form some one determinate

[x] *objects*] *things* [y] *imitation. Architecture*] *imitation; architecture*
[z] *objects,*] *things,* [a] *those,*] *these,* [b] *sorts. The*] *sorts; the*

[1] Burke's classification of words is reminiscent of Locke's (*Essay*, III, iv–v).

composition, as man, horse, tree, castle, &c. These I call *aggregate words*. The second, are they that stand for one simple idea of such compositions and no more; as red, blue, round, square, and the like. These[c] I call *simple abstract* words. The third, are those, which are formed by an union, an *arbitrary* union of both the others, and of the various relations between them,[d] in greater or lesser degrees of complexity; as virtue, honour, persuasion, magistrate, and the like. These[e] I call *compounded abstract* words. Words, I am sensible, are capable of being classed into more curious distinctions; but these seem to be natural, and enough for our purpose; and they are disposed in that order in which they are commonly taught, and in which the mind gets the ideas they are substituted for. I shall begin with the third sort of words; compound abstracts, such as virtue, honour, persuasion, docility. Of[f] these I am convinced, that whatever power they may have on the passions, they do not derive it from any representation raised in the mind of the things for which they stand. As compositions, they are not real essences, and hardly cause, I think, any real ideas. No body, I believe, immediately on hearing the sounds, virtue, liberty, or honour, conceives any precise notion of the particular modes of action and thinking, together with the mixt and simple ideas, and the several relations of them for which these words are substituted; neither has he any general idea, compounded of them; for if he had, then some of those particular ones, though indistinct perhaps, and confused, might come soon to be perceived. But this, I take it, is hardly ever the case. For put yourself upon analysing one of these words, and you must reduce it from one set of general words to another, and then into the simple abstracts and aggregates, in a much longer series than may be at first imagined, before any real idea emerges to light, before[g] you come to discover any thing like the first principles of such compositions; and when you have made such a discovery of the original ideas, the effect of the composition is utterly lost. A train of thinking of this sort, is

[c] *like. These*] *like; these*
[d] *of the . . . them,*] *of various relations concerning them,*
[e] *complexity; as . . . like. These*] *complexity, as . . . like; these*
[f] *docility. Of*] *docility; of*
[g] *light, before*] *light, and before*

much too long to be pursued in the ordinary ways of conversation, nor is it at all necessary that it should. Such words are in reality but mere sounds; but they are sounds, which being used on particular occasions, wherein we receive some good, or suffer some evil, or see others affected with good or evil; or which[h] we hear applied to other interesting things or events; and being[i] applied in such a variety of cases that we know readily by habit to what things they belong, they produce in the mind, whenever they are afterwards mentioned, effects similar to those of their occasions. The sounds being often used without reference to any particular occasion, and carrying still their first impressions, they at last utterly lose their connection with the particular occasions that gave rise to them; yet the sound without any annexed notion continues to operate as before.

SECTION III

General words before IDEAS

Mr Locke has somewhere observed with his usual sagacity, that most general words, those belonging to virtue and vice, good and evil, especially, are taught before the particular modes of action to which they belong are presented to the mind; and with them, the love of the one, and the abhorrence of the other; for the minds of children are so ductile, that a nurse, or any person about a child, by seeming pleased or displeased with any thing, or even any word, may give the disposition of the child a similar turn.[2] When afterwards, the several occurrences in life come to be applied to these words; and that which is pleasant often appears under the name of evil; and what is disagreeable to nature is called good and virtuous; a strange confusion of ideas and affections arises in the minds of many; and an appearance of no small contradiction between their notions and their actions. There are many, who love virtue, and who detest vice, and this not from hypocrisy or affectation, who notwithstanding very[j] frequently act ill and wickedly in

[h] *evil; or which*] *evil, or that*

[i] *events; and being*] *events, and which being*

[j] *notwithstanding very*] *notwithstanding this very*

[2] *Essay*, III, v, 15; III, ix, 9.

particulars without the least remorse; because these particular occasions never came into view, when the passions on the side of virtue were so warmly affected by certain words heated originally by the breath of others; and for this reason, it is hard to repeat certain sets of words, though owned by themselves unoperative, without being in some degree affected, especially if a warm and affecting tone of voice accompanies them, as suppose,

Wise, valiant, generous, good and great.

These words, by having no application, ought to be unoperative; but when words commonly sacred to great occasions are used, we are affected by them even without the occasions. When words which have been generally so applied are put together without any rational view, or in such a manner that they do not rightly agree with each other, the stile is called bombast. And it requires in several cases much good sense and experience to be guarded against the force of such language; for when propriety is neglected, a greater[k] number of these affecting words may be taken into the service, and a greater[l] variety may be indulged in combining them.

SECTION IV

The effect of WORDS

If words have all their possible extent of power, three effects arise in the mind of the hearer. The first is, the *sound*; the second, the *picture*, or representation of the thing signified by the sound; the third is, the *affection* of the soul produced by one or by both of the foregoing. *Compounded abstract* words, of which we have been speaking, (honour, justice, liberty, and the like,) produce the first and the last of these effects, but not the second. *Simple abstracts*, are used to signify some one simple idea without much adverting to others which may chance to attend it, as blue, green, hot, cold, and the like; these are capable of affecting all

[k] *language; for . . . greater*] *language; because the more that propriety is neglected, the greater*

[l] *a greater*] *the greater*

three of the purposes of words; as the *aggregate* words, man, castle, horse, &c. are in a yet higher degree. But I am of opinion, that the most general effect even of these words, does not arise from their forming pictures of the several things they would represent in the imagination; because on a very diligent examination of my own mind, and getting others to consider theirs, I do not find that once in twenty times any such picture is formed, and when it is, there is most commonly a particular effort of the imagination for that purpose. But the aggregate words operate as I said of the compound abstracts, not by presenting any image to the mind, but by having from use the same effect on being mentioned, that their original has when it is seen. Suppose we were to read a passage to this effect. "The river Danube rises in a moist and mountainous soil in the heart of Germany, where winding to and fro it waters several principalities, until turning into Austria and leaving the walls of Vienna it passes into Hungary; there with a vast flood augmented by the Saave and the Drave it quits Christendom, and rolling through the barbarous countries which border on Tartary, it enters by many mouths into the Black sea." In this description many things are mentioned, as mountains, rivers, cities, the sea, &c. But let anybody examine himself, and see whether he has had impressed on his imagination any pictures of a river, mountain, watery soil, Germany, &c. Indeed it is impossible, in the rapidity and quick succession of words in conversation, to have ideas both of the sound of the word, and of the thing represented; besides, some words expressing real essences, are so mixed with others of a general and nominal import, that it is impracticable to jump from sense to thought, from particulars to generals, from things to words, in such a manner as to answer the purposes of life; nor is it necessary that we should.

SECTION V

Examples that WORDS may affect without raising IMAGES

I find it very hard to persuade several that their passions are affected by words from whence they have no ideas; and yet harder to convince them, that in the ordinary course of conversation we are sufficiently understood without raising any images of the things concerning which we speak. It seems to be an odd subject of dispute with any man, whether he has ideas in his mind or not. Of this at first view, every man, in his own forum, ought to judge without appeal. But strange as it may appear, we are often at a loss to know what ideas we have of things, or whether we have any ideas at all upon some subjects. It even requires a good deal of[m] attention to be thoroughly satisfied on this head. Since I wrote these papers I found two very striking instances of the possibility there is, that a man may hear words without having any idea of the things which they represent, and yet afterwards be capable of returning them to others, combined in a new way, and with great propriety, energy and instruction. The first instance, is that of Mr. Blacklock, a poet blind from his birth. Few men blessed with the most perfect sight can describe visual objects with more spirit and justness than this blind man; which cannot possibly be attributed to his having a clearer conception of the things he describes than is common to other persons. Mr. Spence, in an elegant preface which he has written to the works of this poet, reasons very ingeniously, and I imagine for the most part very rightly upon the cause of this extraordinary phenomenon; but I cannot altogether agree with him, that some improprieties in language and thought which occur in these poems have arisen from the blind poet's imperfect conception of visual objects, since such improprieties, and much greater, may be found in writers even of an higher class than Mr. Blacklock, and who, notwithstanding, possessed the faculty of seeing in its full perfection.[3] Here is a poet doubtless as much affected by his

[m] *a good deal of*] *some*

[3] Thomas Blacklock (1721–91), a native of Annan, Dumfriesshire, lost his sight at six months through small-pox. He was educated at Edinburgh University and his *Poems* were first published in 1746. Hume, who helped Blacklock in other ways, circulated his poems and brought them to the notice of Joseph Spence, former Oxford Professor of Poetry. In 1754 Spence published his *Account of the Life, Character, and Poems of Mr. Blacklock* which became the prefatory matter to the 2nd edn. of the *Poems* in 1756. Burke's strictures on Spence refer to the original *Account*. There (pp. 59–61) Spence

own descriptions as any that reads them can be; and yet he is affected with this strong enthusiasm by things of which he neither has, nor can possibly have any idea further than that of a bare sound; and why may not those who read his works be affected in the same manner that he was, with as little of any real ideas of the things described? The second instance is of Mr. Saunderson, professor of mathematics in the university of Cambridge. This learned man had acquired great knowledge in natural philosophy, in astronomy, and whatever sciences depend upon mathematical skill. What was the most extraordinary, and the most to my purpose, he gave excellent lectures upon light and colours; and this man taught others the theory of those ideas which they had, and which he himself undoubtedly had not.[4] But it is probable, that[n] the words red, blue, green, answered to him as well as the ideas of the colours themselves; for the ideas of greater or lesser degrees of refrangibility being applied to these words, and the blind man being instructed in what other respects they were found to agree or to disagree, it was as easy for him to reason upon the words as if he had been fully master of the ideas. Indeed it must be owned he could make no new discoveries in the way of experiment. He did nothing but what we do every day in common discourse. When I wrote this last sentence, and used the words *every day*

[n] *But it . . . that*] *But the truth is, that*

comments on some "improprieties" e.g. the use of "Blaze" as "a Characteristic of Beauty"; the "Application of the Epithet of Rayless to Silence." These criticisms were omitted in 1756. It should be noted that Johnson was sceptical about Spence ("that foolish fellow") and his theory as to how Blacklock obtained his ideas of visible objects (Boswell, *Life of Johnson*, ed. Hill and Powell, I, 466). For interesting data about Blacklock's ideas of colour see Hume's letter to Spence, 15 Oct. 1754 (*Letters of Hume*, ed. J. Y. T. Grieg, Oxford, 1932, I, 201).

[4] Dr. Nicholas Saunderson (1682–1739) lost his sight at an early age through small-pox. He showed great natural ability in mathematics and, through the assistance of friends, went to Cambridge in 1707. As a lecturer and, from 1711, Lucasian Professor of Mathematics, he became well-known for his lucid exposition of mathematical principles. (For an account of his life see his *Elements of Algebra*, Cambridge, 1740, Vol. I, Introduction.) On "the blind man" in eighteenth-century literature and Saunderson as the illustrative example, see K. MacLean, *John Locke and English Literature of the 18th Century* (Yale, 1936), p. 106.

and *common discourse*, I had no images in my mind of any succession of time; nor of men in conference with each other; nor do I imagine that the reader will have any such ideas on reading it. Neither when I spoke of red, blue, and green, as well as of refrangibility; had I these several colours, or the rays of light passing into a different medium, and there diverted from their course, painted before me in the way of images. I know very well that the mind possesses a faculty of raising such images at pleasure; but then an act of the will is necessary to this; and in ordinary conversation or reading it is very rarely that any image at all is excited in the mind. If I say, "I shall go to Italy next summer," I am well understood. Yet I believe no body has by this painted in his imagination the exact figure of the speaker passing by land or by water, or both; sometimes on horseback, sometimes in a carriage; with all the particulars of the journey. Still less has he any idea of Italy, the country to which I proposed to go; or of the greenness of the fields, the ripening of the fruits, and the warmth of the air, with the change to this from a different season, which are the ideas for which the word *summer* is substituted; but least of all has he any image from the word *next*; for this word stands for the idea of many summers, with the exclusion of all but one: and surely the man who says *next summer*, has no images of such a succession, and such an exclusion. In short, it is not only of those ideas which are commonly called abstract, and of which no image at all *can* be formed, but even of particular real beings, that we converse without having any idea of them excited in the imagination; as will certainly appear on a diligent examination of our own minds. [5]〈Indeed so little does poetry depend for its effect on the power of raising sensible images, that I am convinced it would lose a very considerable part of its energy, if this were the necessary result of all description. Because that union of affecting words which is the most powerful of all poetical instruments, would frequently lose its force along with its propriety and consistency, if the sensible images were always excited. There is not perhaps in the whole Eneid a more

[5] *Literary Magazine*, II, 188: "He who is most picturesque and clearest in his imagery, is ever stiled the best poet, because from such a one we see things clearer, and of course we feel more intensely."

grand and laboured passage, than the description of Vulcan's cavern in Etna, and the works that are there carried on. Virgil dwells particularly on the formation of the thunder which he describes unfinished under the hammers of the Cyclops. But what are the principles of this extraordinary composition?

Tres imbris torti radios, tres nubis aquosæ
Addiderant; rutili tres ignis et alitis austri;
Fulgores nunc terrificos, sonitumque, metumque
Miscebant operi, flammisque sequacibus iras.[6]

This seems to me admirably sublime; yet if we attend coolly to the kind of sensible image which a combination of ideas of this sort must form, the chimeras of madmen cannot appear more wild and absurd than such a picture. "*Three rays of* "*twisted showers, three of watery clouds, three of fire, and three of the* "*winged south wind*; *then mixed they in the work terrific lightnings, and* "*sound, and fear, and anger, with pursuing flames.*" This strange composition is formed into a gross body; it is hammered by the Cyclops, it is in part polished, and partly continues rough. The truth is, if poetry gives us a noble assemblage of words, corresponding to many noble ideas, which are connected by circumstances of time or place, or related to each other as cause and effect, or associated in any natural way, they may be moulded together in any form, and perfectly answer their end. The picturesque connection is not demanded; because no real picture is formed; nor is the effect of the description at all the less upon this account. What is said of Helen by Priam and the old men of his council, is generally thought to give us the highest possible idea of that fatal beauty.

" οὐ νέμεσις Τρῶας καὶ ἐϋκνήμιδας Ἀχαιοὺς
τοιῇδ' ἀμφὶ γυναικὶ πολὺν χρόνον ἄλγεα πάσχειν·
αἰνῶς ἀθανάτῃσι θεῇς εἰς ὦπα ἔοικεν.[7]

They cry'd, no wonder such celestial charms
For nine long years have set the world in arms;
What winning graces! what majestic mien!
She moves a goddess, and she looks a queen. POPE.[8]

[6] *Aeneid*, VIII, 429–32. (For another view of this passage see R. Payne Knight. *Analytical Inquiry*, III, i, 82.)

[7] *Iliad*, III, 156–8.

[8] *Iliad*, III, 205–8.

Here is not one word said of the particulars of her beauty; nothing which can in the least help us to any precise idea of her person; but yet we are much more touched by this manner of mentioning her than by these long and laboured descriptions of Helen, whether handed down by tradition, or formed by fancy, which are to be met with in some authors. I am sure it affects me much more than the minute description which Spenser has given of Belphebe;[9] though I own that there are parts in that description, as there are in all the descriptions of that excellent writer, extremely fine and poetical. The terrible picture which Lucretius has drawn of religion, in order to display the magnanimity of his philosophical hero in opposing her, is thought to be designed with great boldness and spirit.

Humana ante oculos fœdè cum vita jaceret,
In terris, oppressa gravi sub religione,
Quæ caput e cæli regionibus ostendebat
Horribili desuper visu mortalibus instans;
Primus Graius homo mortales tollere contra
Est oculos ausus.——[10]

What idea do you derive from so excellent a picture? none at all most certainly; neither has the poet said a single word which might in the least serve to mark a single limb or feature of the phantom, which he intended to represent in all the horrors imagination can conceive. In reality poetry and rhetoric do not succeed in exact description so well as painting does; their business is to affect rather by sympathy than imitation; to display rather the effect of things on the mind of the speaker, or of others, than to present a clear idea of the things themselves. This is their most extensive province, and that in which they succeed the best.〉

SECTION VI[o]

POETRY not strictly an imitative art

Hence we may observe that poetry, taken in its most general sense, cannot with strict propriety be called an art of imitation.

[o] *SECTION VI.*] *SECTION IV.*; *SECTION VI.* B.M.

[9] *Faerie Queene*, II, iii, 21–31.

[10] *De Rerum Natura*, I, 62–7 (misquoted).

It is indeed an imitation so far as it describes the manners and passions of men which their words can express; where *animi motus effert interprete lingua.*[11] There it is strictly imitation; and all merely *dramatic* poetry is of this sort. But *descriptive* poetry operates chiefly by *substitution*; by the means of sounds, which by custom have the effect of realities. Nothing is an imitation further than as it resembles some other thing; and words undoubtedly have no sort of resemblance to the ideas for which they stand.

SECTION VII[p]

How WORDS influence the passions

Now, as words affect, not by any original power, but by representation, it might be supposed, that their influence over the passions should be but light; yet it is quite otherwise; for we find by experience that eloquence and poetry are as capable, nay indeed much more capable of making deep and lively impressions than any other arts, and even than nature itself in very many cases. And this arises chiefly from these three causes. First, that we take an extraordinary part in the passions of others, and that we are easily affected and brought into sympathy by any tokens which are shewn of them; and there are no tokens which can express all the circumstances of most passions so fully as words; so that if a person speaks upon any subject, he can not only convey the subject to you, but likewise the manner in which he is himself affected by it. Certain it is, that the influence of most things on our passions is not so much from the things themselves, as from our opinions concerning them; and these again depend very much on the opinions of other men, conveyable for the most part by words only. Secondly; there are many things of a very affecting nature, which can seldom occur in the reality, but the words which represent them often do; and thus they have an opportunity of making a deep impression and taking root in the mind, whilst the idea of the reality was transient; and to some perhaps never

[p] *SECTION VII.*] *SECTION VI.* B.M.

[11] Horace, *De Arte Poetica*, l. 111.

really occurred in any shape, to whom it is notwithstanding very affecting, as war, death, famine, &c. Besides, many ideas have never been at all presented to the senses of any men but by words, as God, angels, devils, heaven and hell, all of which have however a great influence over the passions. Thirdly; by words we have it in our power to make such *combinations* as we cannot possibly do otherwise. By this power of combining we are able, by the addition of well-chosen circumstances, to give[q] a new life and force to the simple object. In painting we may represent any fine figure we please; but we never can give it those enlivening touches which it may receive from words. To represent an angel in a picture, you can only draw a beautiful young man winged; but what painting can furnish out any thing so grand as the addition of one word, "the "angel of the *Lord?*" It is true, I have here no clear idea, but these words affect the mind more than the sensible image did, which is all I contend for. A picture of Priam dragged to the altar's foot, and there murdered, if it were well executed would undoubtedly be very moving; but there are very aggravating circumstances which it could never represent.

Sanguine fœdantem quos ipse sacraverat *ignes.*[12]

As a further instance, let us consider those lines of Milton, where he describes the travels of the fallen angels through their dismal habitation,

———O'er many a dark and dreary vale
They pass'd, and many a region dolorous;
O'er many a frozen, many a fiery Alp;
Rock, caves, lakes, fens, bogs, dens and shades of death,
A universe of death.[13]

Here is displayed the force of union in

Rocks, caves, lakes, dens, bogs, fens and shades;

which yet would lose the greatest part of their effect, if they were not the

Rocks, caves, lakes, dens, bogs, fens and shades———
———of Death.

[q] *are able . . . to give*] *can . . . give*

[12] Virgil, *Aeneid*, II, 502.

[13] *Paradise Lost*, II, 618–22.

This idea or this affection caused by a word, which nothing but a word could annex to the others, raises a very great degree of the sublime; and this sublime is raised yet higher by what follows, a "*universe of Death.*" Here are again two ideas not presentable but by language; and an union of them great and amazing beyond conception; [14]⟨if they may properly be called ideas which present no distinct image to the mind;— but still it will be difficult to conceive how words can move the passions which belong to real objects, without representing these objects clearly. This is difficult to us, because we do not sufficiently distinguish, in our observations upon language, between a clear expression, and a strong expression. These are frequently confounded with each other, though they are in reality extremely different. The former regards the understanding; the latter belongs to the passions. The one describes a thing as it is; the other describes it as it is felt. Now, as there is a moving tone of voice, an impassioned countenance, an agitated gesture, which affect independently of the things about which they are exerted, so there are words, and certain dispositions of words, which being peculiarly devoted to passionate subjects, and always used by those who are under the influence of any passion; they touch and move us more than those which far more clearly and distinctly express the subject matter. We yield to sympathy, what we refuse to description. The truth is, all verbal description, merely as naked description, though never so exact, conveys so poor and insufficient an idea of the thing described, that it could scarcely have the smallest effect, if the speaker did not call in to his aid those modes of speech that mark a strong and lively feeling in himself. Then, by the contagion of our passions, we catch a fire already kindled in another, which probably might never have been struck out by

[14] *Literary Magazine*, II, 189: "In his last chapter he has made some just observations concerning the power of words, but recurs again to his theory of their not exciting ideas; than which nothing can be more false. No man perhaps has settled with precision, the determinate meaning of every word that signifies a complex idea; but if he has some of the leading ideas, that make up the compounded one, . . . it is sufficient for the writer's purpose, and words will ever excite ideas according to the understandings and imaginations of mankind."

the object described. Words, by strongly conveying the passions, by those means which we have already mentioned, fully compensate for their weakness in other respects. It may be observed that very polished languages, and such as are praised for their superior clearness and perspicuity, are generally deficient in strength. The French language has that perfection, and that defect. Whereas the oriental tongues, and in general the languages of most unpolished people, have a great force and energy of expression; and this is but natural. Uncultivated people are but ordinary observers of things, and not critical in distinguishing them; but, for that reason, they admire more, and are more affected with what they see, and therefore express themselves in a warmer and more passionate manner. If the affection be well conveyed, it will work its effect without any clear idea; often without any idea at all of the thing which has originally given rise to it.〉

It[r] might be expected from the fertility of the subject, that I should consider poetry as it regards the sublime and beautiful more at large; but it must be observed that in this light it has been often and well handled already. It[s] was not my design to enter into the criticism of the sublime and beautiful in any art, but to attempt to lay down such principles as may tend to ascertain, to distinguish, and to form a sort of standard for them; which purposes I thought might be best effected by an enquiry into the properties of such things in nature as raise love and astonishment in us; and by shewing in[t] what manner they operated to produce these passions. Words were only so far to be considered, as to shew upon what principle they were

[r] *conception; if* . . . (p. 175, l. 6—p. 176, l. 17) . . . *It*] *conception. Whoever attentively considers this passage of Milton, and indeed all of the best and most affecting descriptions of poetry, will find, that it does not in general produce its end by raising the images of things, but by exciting a passion similar to that which real objects excite by other instruments. And in proportion as words of a sublime effect, or words which are used to express the objects of love and tenderness, are joined in a manner found by experience the best for these purposes; in that proportion the most perfect kinds of the sublime and beautiful are formed in poetry. It compasses all its other ends in a manner analogous. It*

[s] *that in* . . . *It*] *that this matter has been handled by many authors before. It*

[t] *and by* . . . *in*] *and in*

capable of being the representatives of these natural things, and by what powers they were able to affect us often as strongly as the things they represent, and[u] sometimes much more strongly.

[u] *as the . . . and*] *as things in nature do, and*

The END.

APPENDIX

A LIST OF EDITIONS OF THE *ENQUIRY* PUBLISHED DURING BURKE'S LIFETIME[1]

1. *T.P.*: A | Philosophical Enquiry | INTO THE | ORIGIN of our IDEAS | OF THE | SUBLIME | AND | BEAUTIFUL. | [Publisher's monogram] | LONDON: | Printed for R. and J. DODSLEY, in Pall-mall. | [Rule] | MDCCLVII.
H.T.: ON THE | SUBLIME | AND | BEAUTIFUL. | [Price Bound Three Shillings.]
Collation: 8°. (7″ × 4¼″) A–M⁸ N⁴; pp. [i–iv], v–viii, [8], 1–184.
Contents: p.[i], *H.T.*; p. [ii], blank; p. [iii], *T.P.*; p. [iv], blank; pp. v–viii, THE PREFACE; A5ʳ–A8ᵛ, THE CONTENTS; pp. 1–39, PART I; p. 40, blank; pp. 41–72, PART II; pp. 73–115, PART III; p. 116, blank; pp. 117–166, PART IV; pp. 167–184, PART V.
Running-titles: pp. vi–viii, The PREFACE.; A5ᵛ–A8ᵛ, CONTENTS.; pp. 2–184, On the SUBLIME | and BEAUTIFUL.
Note: pp. 104–5, 136–7: On the SUBLIME. | and BEAUTIFUL.
pp. 126–7: On the SUBLIME | and BEAUTIFUL
CW] p. 4 its [it's] p. 48 mists [mists,] p. 71 lustrat [lustrate] p. 72 PART [A Philo] p. 83 prtion [portion] p. 135 cannon [cannon)] p. 145 light [lights] p. 153 putting [ting]
Signing and numbering: D4 and I2 unsigned.
Error in pagination: p. 12 misnumbered "82".
Press numbers: p. 14: 2 p. 47: 2 p. 90: 2 p. 107: 1 p. 138: 2 p. 158: 2 p. 175: 2
Copies: British Museum; Bodleian Library.

[1] A full description is given for the 1st and 2nd edns. only, since they alone have been treated as authoritative in the preparation of this edition. Moreover, a complete bibliography of Burke's works is being undertaken by Professor Todd, of Harvard University. I am indebted to Professor Todd for item No. 5 and to the Philadelphia Free Library for No. 11. The list is arranged chronologically in the following groups: London edns.; other British edns.; foreign edns.

2. *T.P.*: A | Philosophical Enquiry | INTO THE | ORIGIN of our IDEAS | OF THE | SUBLIME | AND | BEAUTIFUL. | The SECOND EDITION. | With an introductory DISCOURSE concerning | TASTE, and several other Additions. | [Publisher's monogram] | LONDON: | Printed for R. and J. DODSLEY, in Pall-mall. | [Rule] | MDCCLIX.
Collation: 8°. ($8\frac{5}{32}'' \times 5''$) A–Y8 Z4; pp. [i–ii], iii–ix, [7], 1–342, [2].
Contents: p. [i], *T.P.*; p. [ii], blank; pp. iii–ix, THE PREFACE.; A5v–A8v, THE CONTENTS.; pp. 1–40, INTRODUCTION. ON TASTE.; pp. 41–93, PART I; p. 94, blank; pp. 95–160, PART II; pp. 161–239, PART III; p. 240, blank; pp. 241–310, PART IV; pp. 311–42, PART V; 1 blank leaf.
Running-titles: pp. iv–ix, The PREFACE.; A6r–A8v, CONTENTS.; pp. 2–40, INTRODUCTION. | ON TASTE.; pp. 42–342, On the SUBLIME | and BEAUTIFUL.
Note: pp. 340–1: On the SUBLIME | and BEAUTIFUL *CW*] p. 132 cial [ficial] p. 156 taste. [taste,] p. 160 PART [A Philo] p. 305 we [naturally] p. 310 PART [A Philo] pp. 49, 69, 330 no *CW*.
Signing and numbering: F3 unsigned.
Press numbers: p. 212: 1 p. 244: 1 p. 296: 1
Copies: British Museum; Bodleian Library; King's College Library, Newcastle-upon-Tyne. (British Museum copy inscribed: To | Mrs Mountague | from | The Author.)

3.[2] *T.P.*: A | Philosophical Enquiry | [&c. as in 2] | The THIRD EDITION. | [&c. as in 2] | MDCCLXI.

4. *T.P.*: A | Philosophical Enquiry | [&c. as in 2] | The FOURTH EDITION. | [&c. as in 2] | Printed for R. and J. DODSLEY in Pall-mall. | [Rule] | MDCCLXIV.

5. *T.P.*: A | Philosophical Enquiry | [&c. as in 2] | THE FIFTH EDITION. | [&c. as in 2] | Printed for R. and J. Dodsley in Pall-mall. | [Rule] | MDCCLXVII.

6. *T.P.*: A | Philosophical Enquiry | [&c. as in 2] | The SIXTH EDITION. | [&c. as in 2] | Printed for J. Dodsley in Pall-mall. | [Rule] | M.DCC.LXX.

7. *T.P.*: A | Philosophical Enquiry | [&c. as in 2] | The SEVENTH

[2] Unless stated to the contrary, the collation (except for the size of leaf which varies) of all succeeding editions repeats that of the 2nd.

EDITION. | [&c. as in 2] | LONDON, | Printed for J. Dodsley, in Pall-mall. | MDCCLXXIII.[3]

8. *T.P.*: A | Philosophical Enquiry | [&c. as in 2] | The EIGHTH EDITION. | With an Introductory DISCOURSE concerning | TASTE, and several other Additions. | [Device] | LONDON, | Printed for J. DODSLEY, in Pall-mall. | MDCCLXXVI.

9. *T.P.*: A | Philosophical Enquiry | [&c. as in 2] | The NINTH EDITION. | [&c. as in 8] | LONDON: | [&c. as in 8] | MDCCLXXXII.

10. *T.P.*: A | Philosophical Enquiry | [&c. as in 2] | BEAUTIFUL. | With an Introductory DISCOURSE concerning | TASTE, and several other Additions. | [Rule] | A NEW EDITION. | [Rule] | LONDON: | Printed for J. DODSLEY, in Pall-mall. | [Rule] | MDCCLXXXVII.

11. *T.P.*: A | Philosophical Enquiry | INTO THE | ORIGIN OF OUR IDEAS | OF THE | SUBLIME and BEAUTIFUL. | WITH | AN INTRODUCTORY DISCOURSE CONCERNING | TASTE; | AND SEVERAL OTHER ADDITIONS. | [Rule] | A NEW EDITION. | [Double rule] | LONDON: | Printed for J. DODSLEY, in Pall-mall. | [Rule] | M.DCC.XCIII.

12. *T.P.*: A | Philosophical Enquiry | [&c. as in 2] | THE FOURTH EDITION. | [&c. as in 8] Additions. | To which is added, | A VINDICATION of NATURAL SOCIETY, af- | ter the Manner of a late Noble Writer, by | the same Author. | DUBLIN: | Printed by and for SARAH COTTER, under Dick's | Coffee-house in Skinner-Row. M,DCC,LXVI.
Collation: 12°. A^{8}B–M^{12}N^{8} 2A–2D^{12} E^{6}; pp. [i–ii], iii–viii, [8], 1–280, [i–ii], iii–x, 1–94, [4].

13. *T.P.*: A | Philosophical Enquiry | INTO THE | ORIGIN OF OUR IDEAS | OF THE | SUBLIME | AND | BEAUTIFUL. | THE FIFTH EDITION. | WITH AN | INTRODUCTORY DISCOURSE concerning | TASTE, and several other Additions. | To which is added, | A VINDICATION of NATURAL SOCIETY, | after the Manner of a late Noble Writer, | by the same Author. | BERWICK: | Printed for R. and J. TAYLOR. | M,DCC,LXXII.
Collation: 12°. A^{6}B–M^{12}; pp. [i–ii], iii–vii, [5], 1–194, [i–ii], iii–viii, 1–62.

[3] According to William Bowyer's paper stock ledger (Bodleian MS Don. b. 4), fol. 47, there were 756 copies of this edition printed. Bowyer, who printed either some sheets or the whole book, delivered 50 copies to Dodsley on 23 Feb. 1773, and 706 copies on 1 March.

14. *T.P.*: THE | SUBLIME | AND | BEAUTIFUL. | [Double rule] | BY *EDMUND BURKE*, Esq. | [Double rule] | WITH AN | INTRODUCTORY DISCOURSE | *CONCERNING TASTE*, | AND OTHER ADDITIONS. | [Rule] | Of all Books whatever read BURKE on the Sublime. | *Shenstone's Letters*, | [Rule] | OXFORD: | PRINTED and Sold at the Universities of Oxford, | Cambridge, Edinburgh, Glasgow, St. Andrews, | Aberdeen, and Dublin. | 1796.
Collation: 12°. π^1 A^5 C–S^6; pp. [2], [i–ii], iii–vi, [4], 1–194.

15. Two volumes in one.
Vol. I. *T.P.*: RECHERCHES | *PHILOSOPHIQUES* | Sur l'origine des idées que nous avons | du Beau & du Sublime, | PRÉCÉDÉES D'UNE DISSERTATION | *SUR LE GOUT*, | Traduites de l'Anglois de M. BURKE, | *Par l'Abbé D . . . F. . . .* | TOME I. | [Device] | *A LONDRES*, | *Et se vend à Paris*, | Chez HOCHEREAU, Quai de Conti, vis-à-vis | les Marches du Pont-neuf, au Phénix. | [Double rule] | M.DCC.LXV.
Vol. II. *T.P.*: RECHERCHES | *PHILOSOPHIQUES* | [&c. as in Vol. I] TOME II. | [&c. as in Vol. I.]
Vol. I. *H.T.*: RECHERCHES | *PHILOSOPHIQUES* | Sur l'origine des idées que nous avons | du Beau & du Sublime.
Collation: 8°. Vol. I: a^{10} A–M^8 N^6; pp. [4], [i–ii], iii–iv, [4], v–xii, 1–204. Vol. II: a^4 A–N^8 O^4; pp. [8], 1–216.
Note: The translator was the Abbé L.-A. DesFrançois. (See *A Checklist of the Correspondence of Edmund Burke*, ed. Copeland & Smith, Cambridge, 1955, p. 176.)

16. *T.P.*: **Burkes, | Philosophische Untersuchungen | über den | Ursprung unsrer Begriffe | vom | Erhabnen | und | Schönen.** | [Device] | [Rule] | **Nach der fünften Englischen Ausgabe.** | [Rule] | **Riga, | bey Johann Friedrich Hartknock, 1773.**
Colophon, **T7**^{v}: **Leipzig, | gedruckt bey Bernhard Christoph Breitkopf | und Sohn**
Collation: 8°. x^8 **A–S**^{8} **T**^{7}; pp. [16], 1–302.

17. *T.P.*: A | PHILOSOPHICAL INQUIRY | INTO THE | ORIGIN OF OUR IDEAS | OF THE | SUBLIME | AND | BEAUTIFUL. | WITH AN INTRODUCTORY DISCOURSE CONCERNING TASTE, | AND SEVERAL OTHER ADDITIONS. | A NEW EDITION. | [Rule] | BASIL: | Printed and sold by J. J. TOURNEISEN. | MDCCXCII.
Collation: 8°. A–T^8 V^2; pp. [i–ii], iii–x, [6], 1–291 [1].

INDEX

Note. The contents of footnotes are included but they are not separately identified. With a few necessary exceptions only those works to which Burke directly refers or alludes in the *Enquiry* are separately listed.